CW00832690

Savages, Romans, and Despots

Thinking about Others from Montaigne to Herder

ROBERT LAUNAY

The University of Chicago Press
Chicago and London

The University of Chicago Press, Chicago 60637
The University of Chicago Press, Ltd., London
© 2018 by The University of Chicago
All rights reserved. No part of this book may be used or reproduced in any
manner whatsoever without written permission, except in the case of brief
quotations in critical articles and reviews. For more information, contact the
University of Chicago Press, 1427 E. 60th St., Chicago, IL 60637.
Published 2018
Printed in the United States of America

27 26 25 24 23 22 21 20 19 18   1 2 3 4 5

ISBN-13: 978-0-226-57525-4 (cloth)
ISBN-13: 978-0-226-57539-1 (paper)
ISBN-13: 978-0-226-57542-1 (e-book)
DOI: https://doi.org/10.7208/chicago/9780226575421.001.0001

Library of Congress Cataloging-in-Publication Data

Names: Launay, Robert, 1949– author.
Title: Savages, Romans, and despots : thinking about others from Montaigne to
   Herder / Robert Launay.
Description: Chicago ; London : The University of Chicago Press, 2018. |
   Includes bibliographical references and index.
Identifiers: LCCN 2018006356 | ISBN 9780226575254 (cloth : alk. paper) |
   ISBN 9780226575391 (pbk. : alk. paper) | ISBN 9780226575421 (e-book)
Subjects: LCSH: Other (Philosophy) | Other minds (Theory of knowledge) |
   Anthropology—Philosophy.
Classification: LCC BD460.O74 L38 2018 | DDC 909—dc23
LC record available at https://lccn.loc.gov/2018006356

♾ This paper meets the requirements of ANSI/NISO Z39.48-1992
(Permanence of Paper).

"Je suis comme cet antiquaire qui partit de son pays, arriva en Egypte, jeta un coup d'oeil sur les pyramides, et s'en retourna." (I am like that antiquarian who left his country, arrived in Egypt, took one look at the pyramids, and went back home.)

MONTESQUIEU, *The Spirit of Laws*

CONTENTS

ONE

Maps of Mankind

In 1777, in a letter to the Scottish historian William Robertson, Edmund Burke wrote: ". . . Now the Great Map of Mankind is unrolld at once; and there is no state or Gradation of barbarism, and no mode of refinement which we have not at the same instant under our View. The very different Civility of Europe and of China; the barbarism of Persia and of Abyssinia. The erratick manners[1] of Tartary, and of arabia. The Savage State of North America, and of New Zealand (Burke 1984:102)." The inclusion of New Zealand was a novelty. Captain James Cook had circumnavigated the islands less than a decade earlier. His account, as well as that of Bougainville before him, were responsible for the identification of Pacific islanders as "savages" on a par with North American Indians. Burke's inclusion of an African realm, Abyssinia, comparatively high up on the scale of civility demonstrates that Africa was not yet irredeemably relegated to the realm of savagery.[2] The mention of Abyssinia was a nod to Samuel Johnson, who had begun his literary career with a translation (actually a translation of the French translation from the original Portuguese) of the travels of the Jesuit Jerome Lobo (1984). Most surprising of all, China still shared pride of place with Europe, a distinction that it was already in the process of losing.

Exactly one hundred years later, in 1877, Lewis Henry Morgan (1985) published *Ancient Society*, in which he traced the progress of humankind from lower, middle, and upper savagery through lower, middle, and upper barbarism to civilization. As with Burke, but in far greater detail, each stage was identified by examples from various societies, past or present, from around the globe. Each stage was marked by the adoption of different technologies: the use of fire; the bow and arrow; pottery; the domestication of animals and plants; the smelting of iron; and, finally, alphabetic writing. Such material progress was accompanied by different modes of government, different forms of the family, and different ideas of property. Even more than Burke, Morgan identified Oceania as the locus classicus of savagery. His book enshrined the notion that Native Australians represented the most primitive surviving human society. Thanks, if indirectly, to Morgan, some of the most prominent thinkers of the turn of the twentieth century—Émile Durkheim (1995) and Sigmund Freud (1950)—would focus their critical attention on Native Australians as "primitive" exemplars of universal human characteristics. Morgan's depiction of Native Americans was considerably less derogatory. A denizen of Rochester in upstate New York, Morgan was not only personally acquainted with Iroquois but studied and wrote about their society extensively. This is hardly to suggest that he was invariably open-minded. He specifically selected a phonetic alphabet as the distinguishing mark of civilization in order to exclude the Chinese and other Asian ideographic alphabets.

Morgan's book achieved canonical status in the discipline of anthropology, but its influence extended far more broadly. Karl Marx, for one, was an enthusiastic reader—so much so that, after Marx's death, Friedrich Engels went on to write *The Origin of the Family, Private Property, and the State* (1986), very explicitly basing his account on Morgan's text.

It would be tempting to treat Morgan's text as a long (550-page!) elaboration of Burke's short passage, a fully developed treatment of ideas Burke had only sketched out embryonically. There are, of course, obvious resemblances. Both texts classify all the world's peoples in a graded hierarchy, with modern Europe (and, for Morgan, North America) at the summit. Burke's text is literally panoptic, evoking a metaphor of Europeans on a summit perusing the spectacle of inferior gradations of humanity "at the same instant under our View." Morgan's guiding metaphor, on the other hand, is organic. Savagery contains the "germs" of institutions and ideas that progressively grow to maturity through the stages of human development. Iroquois councils, for example, embody the "germ" of modern parliamentary democracy.

These metaphors are hardly incidental. Rather, they are concrete conceptualizations of different ideas of history, illustrated by the radically different ways in which Greeks and Romans enter into their schemas. Burke's panoptic vision literally replaces history: "We need no longer go to History to trace [human Nature] in all its stages and periods" (Burke 1984:102). History, the recent invention of the Greeks, was also a token of their limits. The Greeks and Romans had no access to the sweeping vision of the world's peoples in the various "gradations" we moderns can enjoy from our heights. The Greeks and Romans are even more important to Morgan, but in a very different way. He devotes six long chapters to a demonstration of how the

Greeks and Romans, before they existed in history as we are familiar with them, were for all intents and purposes identical to the Iroquois. For Burke, the contemplation of North American "savages" obviates history; for Morgan, it allows us to write history more completely. Burke's gradations of human nature bear more than superficial resemblance to the Great Chain of Being (Lovejoy 1936), the hierarchical classification of all forms of life from the lowliest up to humankind (excelled only by the angels and by God). For Morgan, the forms were not so much "gradations" as "stages" that told a story: our story, of how we came to be who we are. Burke's spectacle is static; Morgan's unfolds.

The idea that non-Europeans embodied the distant past of modern Europe was hardly an original idea by Morgan's time. To pick but one example, Hegel's lectures on world history, delivered in 1830 and 1831, also situate the origins of history outside of Europe: "World history travels from east to west; for Europe is the absolute end of history, just as Asia is the beginning (Hegel 1975:197)." For Hegel, world history was embodied by different peoples in different, succeeding epochs: Oriental, Greek, Roman, and finally German (Hegel 1956). "Savages" were outside the pale of history, and consequently uninteresting to Hegel. Native Americans were "like unenlightened children, living from one day to the next, and untouched by higher thoughts or aspirations (1975:165)." In any case, most of them had been exterminated by European settlers. Africa was no better: "Life there consists of a succession of contingent happenings and surprises. No aim or state exists whose development could be followed; and there is no subjectivity, but merely a series of subjects who destroy one another" (Hegel 1975).

Ultimately, Hegel's conception of history was not very different from that of Morgan and his peers: a sequence that extended from savages to Orientals to ancient Greeks and Romans and finally to modern Europeans. Simply, Hegel was radically dismissive of the "savages" at the center of the pre-occupations of thinkers who, in the second half of the nineteenth century, came to think of themselves as "anthropologists" or "ethnologists."[3] The difference was largely due to radical shifts in understandings of time in the course of the nineteenth century. Hegel's chronology was still broadly Biblical, a time frame he shared with most of his contemporaries. By the time Morgan wrote *Ancient Society*, the anthropologists had already incorporated geological time into their understanding of world history.[4] For them, history as Hegel understood it represented a relatively recent phase of human life on earth. For the bulk of human history—or, more specifically, prehistory[5]— "savagery" was the embodiment of the human condition.

Such formulations of universal history were standard fare in the nineteenth century. By then, the categories of "modern" and "Europe" were taken for granted, at least by those who defined themselves in these terms. Upon reflection, neither term is self-evident. Continents, like nations, are "imagined communities" (Anderson 1991). In the Middle Ages, Europe admittedly existed in maps, but no one thought of themselves as "European" until, at the earliest, the fifteenth century (Hay 1957; Pagden 2002). The emergence of the concept of "modern" was roughly contemporary. Well before the emergence of any notion of "modernity," "modern" was opposed to "ancient," and thus depended on the imagined time of "classical antiquity" (Weiss 1969). Needless to say, medieval thinkers were quite cognizant of ancient Greeks and Romans, whom they simply did not consider as qualitatively different from their own contemporaries. Medieval illustrators routinely depicted Greek and Roman rulers as idealized medieval kings, distinguished by their heraldry rather than by their apparel. While the opposition between the past and the present is relatively straightforward, the contrast between "ancient" and "modern" involves a hiatus, the imagination of a prestigious distant past as distinct from the recent and distinctly unglorious past.

For modern Europeans to be convinced of their superiority, they had first to think of themselves as "modern" and "European." The emergence of such notions was implicitly comparative, opposing "moderns" to "ancients," "Europeans" to non-Europeans. By the nineteenth century, such notions were conflated. Non-Europeans were, in a radical sense, not "modern."[6] However, it would be a grave mistake to assume that this was always the case. As these notions were formulated in the course of what we now call "early modern Europe"—roughly from the sixteenth to the eighteenth centuries— the relationship of "savages," "Orientals," and "ancients" to contemporary Europeans and to one another was not fixed by any means, and was not embedded in an imaginary time line that asserted European superiority.

In short, early modern Europeans defined their identity in contrast to "others." I prefer to refer to "others" rather than the more fashionable, but problematic, notion of "the Other." "Others" almost invariably exist in various shapes and sizes. I shall argue in this book that "savages," "Orientals," and "ancients" were all "others" of modern Europeans, but that they were hardly equivalent, and that the very differences between them were a constant focus of reflection for early modern European thinkers. I must insist that I fully realize how deeply offensive terms such as "savages" and "Orientals" are to many readers, with good reason. (By definition, there are no longer any "ancients," or that, too, might be a controversial term.) However, to the extent that Europeans (and not only early moderns) thought and, in some cases, continue to think in terms of these categories, I want to use them as (imaginary) points of reference. Of course, using "others" as a foil to define one's own identity is, if not a human universal, so widely prevalent that it hardly serves to distinguish early modern Europeans. The point is, rather, that Morgan and his intellectual heirs were and continue to be engaged in a theoretical elaboration of such differences and their implications, an extensive comparative discourse about how and why such differences matter.

Such theoretical discourses were hardly restricted to Europe. Ibn Khaldun's *Muqaddimah* (1958), written in 1377, is a prominent example. Herodotus's *Histories* and Tacitus's *Germania* are examples from the ancient world, all the more important in that they constituted explicit and essential models and points of reference for early modern European thinkers. Herodotus's account of the Persian Wars centered on the opposition between Greeks and "barbarians" (i.e., speakers of "foreign" languages) in order to account for the improbable victory of the Greeks over the overwhelming might of the Persian Empire, against which neither Mesopotamia nor Egypt had been able to resist.[7] Herodotus was not only fascinated by the range of differences between Greeks and different varieties of "barbarians," but crucially concerned with identifying which of these differences were morally salient. For Herodotus, the realm of "custom"—modes of worship, burial practices, food preparation, sexual mores, and marriage, to name only some examples—was morally neutral. Political behavior, on the other hand, was intrinsically linked to morality; in a world governed (at least in the long term) by moral forces, it could determine the ability of a people like the Greeks to resist repeated Persian invasions. Tacitus, writing in the early days of the Roman Empire, used his description of "barbarian" Germanic tribes to the opposite effect. As a member of the senatorial class whose power, if not prestige, had been radically curtailed, he offered a depiction of Rome in his other historical works that was one of corruption and moral decay. The Germans, by contrast, whatever their failings, came closer to incarnating the legendary virtues of the Roman Republic (courage, loyalty, honesty, marital fidelity) so sorely lacking in the empire.

What distinguished these classical authors from their early modern counterparts was, most flagrantly, the absence of a category of "antiquity" per se. Of course, Tacitus contrasted (at least implicitly) the vices of the empire with the past virtues of the early republic, but such a contrast was qualitatively different from the division of time into "ancient" and "modern." Herodotus's extensive descriptions of Egyptians and Scythians were not framed in terms of the categories of "Orientals" and "savages," as they very definitely would be in early modern Europe. Early modern thinkers were characterized not simply by their deployment of the categories "savage," "Oriental" and "ancient," but more importantly by the fact that these categories were in continual dialogue with one another, though not necessarily all at the same time. For example, Montaigne's account of the Tupinamba "cannibals" of Brazil (chapter 3) was interlaced with references to classical antiquity; in one passage, he compared their way of life to Plato's *Republic*. Montesquieu's *Spirit of Laws* (chapter 8) systematically contrasted Asian "despotism" with ancient republics as archetypes of different modes of government. From the sixteenth to the eighteenth centuries, "savages," "Orientals" and "Ancients" were systematically compared not only to contemporary Europeans but to one another. However, these four terms were not arranged as a single sequence until the very end of the eighteenth century, when European hegemony over all the rest of the globe was firmly established.

The question remains: How can we understand the relationship between early modern European understandings of others and more recent, if not contemporary, approaches, between—for example—Burke's text and Morgan's? One obvious solution is to treat early modern (and sometimes earlier) approaches as precursors of modern ones. This is typical of disciplinary histories—for example, surveys of the history of anthropology, where early modern (especially Enlightenment) descriptions and discussions of non-Europeans routinely figure in the opening chapter.[8] Histories of other disciplines[9] often adopt a similar perspective, even citing the same thinkers, while omitting the focus on non-Europeans. The problem with such histories is that they read history backwards. Modern disciplines are the inevitable endpoint. Earlier thinkers are relevant to the extent that they contribute to their emergence. Of course, the authors in question did not—could not—have any awareness that they were doing any such thing. To read Burke's text as a prefiguration of Morgan's is a recipe for misunderstanding, if not miscategorizing, his own preoccupations.

The quest for roots or origins suffers from similar defects. Such an enterprise can be couched in disciplinary terms—for example, *The Philosophical Roots of Anthropology* (Adams 1998). Unfortunately, some of the themes Adams identifies—"progressivism" and "primitivism," for example—are far too general to be of much analytical utility. Such considerations are not limited to quests for the origins or roots of particular disciplines. Intellectual historians have also written genealogies of "primitivism" (e.g., Lovejoy and Boas 1935) or "progress" (e.g., Nisbet 1969). Such accounts project modern conceptions of "progress" and "primitivity" anachronistically, ignoring the contexts in which specific ideas were formulated or their place in the overall scheme of particular arguments. If the search for predecessors has the merit of extending the scope of inquiry beyond the institutional origins of modern academic disciplines in the nineteenth century, it is ultimately at the expense of stressing continuity and overlooking equally fundamental discontinuities.

However, disciplinary histories and quests for the origins of ideas are hardly the only ways of writing anachronistically. Accounts of the failings of early modern thinkers can be just as problematic as narratives of their successes. Hodgen's (1971) extremely detailed and informative account of early modern "anthropology" deplores its unreliability, its superficiality, and its lack of critical thinking in ways that bear little if any relation to the preoccupations or aims of the writers in question. Modern liberal biases are particularly apparent in discussions of the open-mindedness or intolerance of earlier thinkers, most of all in cases where the same thinker appears simultaneously to display both attitudes at the same time. Sir John Mandeville (chapter 2), for instance, wrote favorably about Muslims, eastern Christians, and even "pagans" while simultaneously demonizing Jews. To label Jews as "the most significant exception to the tolerance that is so impressively articulated elsewhere in Mandeville's travels" (Greenblatt 1991:50) is to beg the question, not least by framing it in the anachronistic terms of "tolerance." Some two centuries later, Jean Bodin would pen a long dialogue in which seven sages—including a Roman Catholic, a Lutheran, a Calvinist, a Jew, and a Muslim, among others—amicably discussed theological issues, but also a treatise insisting that witches constituted a real menace and needed to be exterminated. It is only if we assume that open-mindedness, much less tolerance, is a generalized disposition that attitudes such as Mandeville's or Bodin's appear as problematic if not contradictory.

Paradoxically, the depictions of early moderns as either precursors or failed anthropologists suffer from precisely the lack of insight that Hodgen attributes to early modern authors: the inability to take "others" (in this case, individuals who are historically rather than culturally different) on their own terms. To think of early modern authors, not to mention ancient or medieval ones, as "anthropologists" or even "ethnographers" is radically anachronistic, the historical equivalent of "ethnocentrism," a refusal to acknowledge that they were engaged, for better or for worse, in very different projects with different aims and different stakes. In this book I have approached these authors by attempting to understand their thought in their own terms rather than in ours. I have been inspired by Michel Foucault's (1971, 1976) project of an "archaeology of knowledge," though not necessarily by his specific analyses. Knowledge, for Foucault, does not consist of a series of answers that progressively come to approach (or at least prefigure) our own vision of reality. Rather, knowledge is embedded in different *epistemes*, grids of metatheoretical presuppositions that determine which questions "make sense" and which ones are, implicitly if not explicitly, ruled out. While I have neither the ambition nor the ability to propose such a scheme, I am concerned with understanding early modern authors in terms of the kinds of questions they are asking, and not simply their answers.

For the most part I have avoided detailed consideration of the voluminous travel literature written between the sixteenth and eighteenth centuries. Such a deliberate omission may seem surprising. Travel writers have often been depicted as "ethnographers" avant la lettre.[10] Indeed, some of them (but hardly all!) were perspicacious and thorough observers of exotic peoples. Of course, there were significant differences. Particularly beginning in early modern Europe, one central feature of travel writing was the construction of the author's persona (Launay 2003) whereas, at least until the vogue of postmodernism, ethnographic writing has even more assiduously attempted to efface that persona. In any case, discussions of travel writing generally revolve around questions of "representation." Most obviously, and least interestingly, such representations are not infrequently ethnocentric. Positivist histories of the discipline—admittedly no longer in fashion— were concerned with distinguishing between "good" and comparatively less ethnocentric representations, harbingers of the discipline to come, as opposed to "bad" pejorative representations of others, a testament to how far we have progressed.

More recently, postcolonial criticism has taken a somewhat different approach to the analysis of European representations of others, especially in the wake of Edward Said's *Orientalism* (1978).[11] Said, as a literary critic, furnishes a close and critical reading of various works of nineteenth-century travel literature: Edward Lane's (1908) scholarly treatise, *The Manners and Customs of the Modern Egyptians*, as well as the narratives of tours by French literati to the Middle East: Lamartine, Chateaubriand, Nerval, and Flaubert. All of these works convey similar tropes of what Said characterizes pejoratively as "Orientalism," whether they are the product of sophisticated tourism, as in the French examples, or of multiyear sojourns involving the study of the Arabic language, as was the case for Lane. In other words, the narrators' experience is filtered through a preexisting interpretive lens that produces a specific sort of narrative.[12] Seen in this light, representations are never innocent, but are always formulated in terms of certain presuppositions and enunciated in the pursuit of particular agendas. The agenda that Said identifies is the European and later North American domination of the

Middle East in particular and the rest of the world in general. The contention that representations inevitably reveal—or, worse, conceal—agendas is irreproachable; unmotivated representations do not exist, after all. This does not imply that such agendas are necessarily sinister, even if they must at some level be self-interested.

Similar analyses (e.g., Todorov 1982) have been applied to other parts of the globe, notably the Spanish conquest of the New World. The argument, to oversimplify it drastically, is that the misrepresentation of others is a fundamental element of a discursive formation (in Foucault's 1972 sense of the word) which underpins the ideology of imperialism in its multifaceted forms. In many respects, this remains a powerful and compelling critique. There can be no doubt that representations of others can be and have been deployed, unintentionally as well as intentionally, for the purposes of dominating them. However, it is a grievous oversimplification to suggest that this is inevitably the case. Until the end of the eighteenth century, European hegemony in other parts of the globe, particularly Asia, was hardly a foregone conclusion. European control was generally limited to coastal enclaves, with the aim of achieving commercial rather than political supremacy. The situation in much of the Americas was admittedly very different. It is easy to read concerns with domination retroactively and anachronistically. Even so, representations of others were unsurprisingly put to a variety of uses, and cannot be reduced to a single dimension, however important. Ultimately, postcolonial critics, like the earlier generation of positivist historians in search of predecessors, tend to interpret the past in terms of the preoccupations of the present, if far more pessimistically.

Not surprisingly, intellectual historians have been far more sensitive to placing such representations within specific historical contexts, and my work has been indebted to their contributions, especially those of Michèle Duchet (1971, 1984), Frank Lestringant (1990, 1993, 1994, 1997), George Huppert (1970, 1999), P. J.Marshall and Glyndwr Williams (1982), Anthony Pagden (1986, 1993), John Pocock (1999. 2005), John Zammito (2002), and Han Vermuelen (2015), to name only a few. However, the aims of this book, not to mention the methods, are different. Intellectual history is primarily concerned with situating ideas, texts, and authors as precisely as possible in terms of intellectual and sociopolitical currents. Such background has been indispensable to my own attempt to delineate the contours not of a specific idea or set of ideas per se, but rather of a much broader comparative project to define "modern Europeans" in contrast to others who were either not "modern" or not European. This is a project which only began to take shape in sixteenth-century Europe. It cannot be reduced to comparisons of "us" to "them," of ourselves (whoever that might be) to others. Such comparisons can be found well before the sixteenth century, and certainly (I should say obviously) outside Europe.[13] For the early modern European thinkers who are the subject of this book, the comparison revolved around several specific poles: "ancient" Greeks and Romans; Asian "despots"; and North American (and later Oceanian) "savages." In the nineteenth century, the premise of this comparative approach was radically transformed: "modernity" was intrinsically equated with Europeanness. Non-Europeans, increasingly racialized as nonwhites, were categorically denied the status of "modern." This transformation underlies the hiatus between Burke's schema and Morgan's. The aim of this volume is to situate contemporary, post-Victorian understandings of others in terms of a project that is both older and broader, but where the relationship between the constituent terms was by no means fixed.

The book begins with a fourteenth-century work, the *Travels* of Sir John Mandeville (chapter 2), which substantially precedes the early modern period. I have included it precisely as a useful point of comparison. Although composed in the form of a travel narrative, the book has recently been characterized as a sort of encyclopedia (Castro Hernandez 2013), a catalog of contemporary knowledge about the world as a whole. Mandeville is thoroughly comparative, constantly evaluating his own society in terms of a panoply of "others," real and imaginary. Yet Mandeville is anything but "modern" and "European." Christendom, not Europe, is Mandeville's imaginary community. His terms of comparison are not "ancients," "savages" or "Orientals," though Aristotle, Alexander the Great, cannibals, Brahmins, and the court of Cathay all figure in his cast of characters. The Greeks and Romans he mentions are not "ancients," but figures from a broader, more generalized past. Mandeville is concerned with contrasting his world, situated on one edge of the earth, with the center (Jerusalem) and with the antipodes, literally and figuratively its opposite. His terms of comparison are religious: Christians, Muslims, Jews, pagans.

Aside from Mandeville, this book really begins in the Renaissance, and specifically in late-sixteenth-century France, with the work of Montaigne (chapter 3) and Bodin (chapter 4). The wars of religion in France from 1562 to 1598 pitted not only Catholics against Protestants but also the hard-line Catholic League against the monarchy. The crisis led French thinkers to reevaluate the domains not only of religion, but of morality, law, and politics, in order to formulate a radically original comparative study of social institutions, and in order to determine what kinds of legal and political systems were appropriate in different times and places (Huppert 1970). Arguably, the intellectual bases for a comparative framework that pitted "savages," Asians, ancient Greeks and Romans, and contemporary Europeans were initially and most thoroughly laid out in Renaissance France.

By and large, these theoretical attempts at comparison were not continued in the seventeenth century, even as the demand for travel literature expanded at a remarkable rate. On one hand, absolute monarchies were understandably averse to any relativist theories that might all too easily be applied to subversive ends. Yet even theoretical formulations that called absolute monarchies into question, most obviously the various versions of social contract theory, were framed on a priori rather than comparative grounds. As it turned out, the Jesuits (chapters 5, 6) were the paradoxical heirs of the comparative approach, deployed to radically different ends:[14] to convert them, different kinds of societies required different strategies. More than rival orders, the Jesuits capitalized on the expanding demand for travel literature by publishing accounts of their missions, which included detailed descriptions of the peoples they were attempting to convert. In particular, the Jesuits managed in different ways to establish exclusive though certainly not uncontested footholds in China and in New France (modern Quebec). Their descriptions provided paradigms for Asian empires as well as "savage" government that underpinned the comparative schemes of Enlightenment thinkers.

A poem read at the Académie française in 1687 suggesting that the achievements of France under Louis XIV had actually outdone the accomplishments of the ancients sparked the Quarrel of the Ancients and the Moderns (chapter 7), spreading from France to England, marking the resurrection of the comparative agenda among secular thinkers. These efforts at comparison remained relatively unsystematic until Montesquieu's *Spirit of Laws* (chapter 8), which resuscitated the sixteenth-century project to determine what kind of regime was appropriate in specific times and places. Like Hegel a century later, Montesquieu was remarkably unconcerned with "savages." At the same time, however, a discourse on "savagery" was deployed in the service of a radical critique of European institutions, for example in fictional dialogues by Lahontan and Diderot (chapter 9) pitting clever savages against their rather dimwitted European interlocutors. While French thinkers laid the intellectual groundwork for the comparison between "savages," "Orientals," "ancients" and "modern Europeans," British and especially Scottish authors such as Adam Ferguson, John Millar, and Edward Gibbon were responsible for elaborating a synthesis (chapter 10), a global narrative of history encompassing "savages," "Orientals," "ancients" and "Modern Europeans," though not yet proclaiming the smug triumphalism characteristic of comparable nineteenth-century schemes. At the same time, in Germany, Johann Gottfried Herder (chapter 11) was elaborating a very different synthesis—*Another Philosophy of History*, as he explicitly labeled it—in deliberate opposition to both the French and the Scottish elaborations of philosophical history.

It has occurred to me in retrospect that the majority of the authors I have discussed are French, even including many of the Jesuits. This is arguably the result of my own biases and shortsightedness. But I would argue that the British and German authors with whom I conclude were themselves thoroughly cognizant of and often openly indebted to their French predecessors and contemporaries. Ferguson cited Montesquieu and Rousseau, and relied on French Jesuits for his descriptions of American "savages." As for Gibbon, he was a frequent visitor to France, fully integrated into the intellectual circles of the French Enlightenment. Herder's very attempt to provide an alternative to French theory demonstrates, in a different vein, its importance in the formation of his ideas.

I want to suggest that from the late sixteenth through most of the eighteenth century, the French were the principal (though hardly the exclusive) proponents of comparative theoretical speculation. In the late sixteenth century, the politico-religious conflict in France opened the door to institutional critique framed in comparative terms, a critique that was effectively squelched, at least in the short term, by the centralizing monarchy in the seventeenth century. Britain was plagued by similar conflict, especially in the seventeenth century, although the kinds of critique generated by Cromwell or even by the Glorious Revolution later in the century were of a very different order, and formulated in deductive rather than in comparative and empirical terms. Certainly, in the eighteenth century the British, not to mention the Germans, were as avid consumers of travel literature as the French. Frequently, books written in one language were promptly translated into the other. But French authors during the Enlightenment had to be cagier about avoiding the ire of the French monarchy and/or the Church. Diderot, for example, was subjected to a brief involuntary sojourn in the Chateau of Vincennes, comparable to if less infamous than the Bastille, in the wake of a publication deemed irreligious by the authorities. "Savages," "Orientals," and "ancients" were convenient rhetorical vehicles for (putatively indirectly) discussing politics and religion in contemporary France. Anglo-Saxon anthropology owes an unacknowledged debt to French censorship in the eighteenth century, which obliged French thinkers to resort to the "view from afar" (to borrow Lévi-Strauss's [1985] characterization of the anthropological perspective) in order to write critically about affairs at home. Be this as it may, the deployment of "savages," "Orientals" and "ancients" as utopian models or as dystopian antimodels opened a space for critical reflection. At its worst, such a space could convey a smug sense of "modern European" superiority over the rest of the world; at its best, it could attempt to make modern Europeans conscious of the value of other ways of being in the world.

TWO

The World Turned Upside Down: Mandeville

"... it behoves a man who wants to see wonders sometimes to go out of his way."

—Sir John Mandeville

It was definitely not the best of times. Fourteenth-century writers were harshly critical of the age. For example, Eustache Deschamps, courtly poet and moralist, characterized the period in ballad form:

> Temps de doleur et de temptacion,
> Ages de plour, d'envie et de tourment;
> Temps de langour et de dampnacion,
> Aages meneur près du definement;
> Temps plains d'orreur, qui tout fait faussement;
> Aages menteur plain d'orgueil et d'envie,
> Temps sanz honeur et sanz vray jugement,
> Aage en tristour qui abrége la vie." (Deschamps 1832:5)

> [Time of sorrow and of temptation,
> Age of tears, desire and torment;
> Time of languor and of damnation,
> Age leading up to the end of the world;
> Time full of horror, which does everything falsely;
> Age of lies full of pride and envy,
> Time without honor and without true judgment,
> Age of sadness that cuts life short.]

Deschamps and many others were convinced not only that the times were disastrous, but that they had taken a sharp turn for the worse: "Le temps passé fut vertu et haultesse / Mais aujourdui ne voy régner que vice." (Deschamps 1832:97) [The past was a time of virtue and nobility / But today I see nothing reign but vice.] For those who attempt to understand an age in more prosaic terms, in terms of the production, distribution, and exchange of ordinary "commodities" and not just the productions of literary and artistic elites, the fourteenth century was equally a turning point.[1] From the eleventh to the thirteenth centuries, western Europe had experienced a continuous period of expansion. New lands once on the margins of settled society were brought into cultivation. New towns sprang up alongside them, and the population continued to expand. This long period of growth and prosperity came to a catastrophic halt in the fourteenth century. In the first place, agricultural expansion had reached its limits. Simultaneously, there was a significant change in climate, involving heavier rainfalls that damaged cereal agriculture. Food shortages, always a problem in preindustrial economies, became chronic, leading to devastating famines, particularly in urban areas. Last and certainly not least came the bubonic plague, whose first wave hit western Europe in the middle of the century. The trends of the preceding centuries were reversed: population declined sharply, and the total extent of arable land under cultivation diminished.

Not surprisingly, the fourteenth century saw its share of political and religious crises alongside these economic and demographic catastrophes. The Hundred Years' War broke out in 1337; the French nobility suffered a crushing and humiliating defeat at Crécy in 1346. It was "the age *par excellence* of 'popular revolutions'" (Mollat and Wolff 1973:11): the Jacquerie in France, the Ciompi in Florence, and Wat Tyler's uprising in England among others. Throughout most of the fourteenth century, from 1309 to 1377, the seat of the Papacy was Avignon, not Rome. The legitimacy of the Church was under constant attack from within and, by the end of the century, from dissident movements such as the Lollards, though admittedly challenges to the authority of the Church were hardly new in the fourteenth century.

One might expect that these various crises would have led western Europe to turn inward upon itself. In one sense, this was indeed the case. The economic and demographic expansion of western Europe throughout the eleventh to thirteenth centuries corresponded precisely to the era of the Crusades: the first launched in 1095 by Pope Urban II at Clermont; the last led by St. Louis in 1270, culminating in the unsuccessful siege of Tunis. Acre, the last Christian stronghold in the Holy Land, fell in 1291. The closest equivalent to the Crusades in the fourteenth century was the disastrous French expedition against the Turks, routed at Nicopolis in 1396.

Yet paradoxically, the fourteenth century saw the rise of a new genre, the secular travel book, written in the vernacular rather than in Latin. The first such work to appear is the one with which modern readers are by far the most familiar, the account of Marco Polo's travels, the *Divisament dou Monde*, as recorded by Rustichello of Pisa in 1298 when they were fellow prisoners of the Genoese. Rustichello was a writer of romances—that is to say, of entertainment for a secular elite literate specifically in French.[2] The book is indeed addressed to "emperors and kings, dukes and marquises, counts, knights, and townsfolk, and all people who wish to know the various races of men and the peculiarities of the various regions of the world . . ." (Polo 1958:33). The list underscores its presumed appeal to a courtly audience; townsfolk come last (and least) and the clergy are conspicuous by their absence. Of equal significance, the reasons given for Polo's narrative are "wishing to occupy his [enforced!] leisure as well as to afford entertainment to readers . . ." (ibid.). This account of distant and exotic peoples and places is doubly a literature of *escape*: for Polo, from the boredom of captivity; for the reader, as a courtly divertissement.

Polo's book was not received without skepticism, and he earned the nickname "Marco milione" ("Marco millions") for what was perceived, rightly or wrongly, as his penchant for exaggeration. Admittedly, Polo's contemporaries found it hard to accept the existence of a secular realm as large, populous, and prosperous as China. Certain details which we now know to be quite accurate seemed totally incredible—for example, that the Chinese accepted paper money in lieu of "hard" currency, gold or silver. Over the centuries, however, Polo's reputation for veracity has increased, especially as compared to the other great fourteenth-century narrative of travel to the East, *The Book of John de Mandeville*, written some sixty years later.[3] Mandeville draws extensively on other sources in both Latin and French, most notably the itineraries of Friar Odoric of Pordenone and of William of Boldensele, and the encyclopaedic compendia of Vincent of Beauvais, the *Speculum naturale* and *Speculum historiale*. (The itineraries were originally written in Latin, but were translated into French by Jean Le Long of Ypres in 1351, as part of a compendium that Mandeville may well have used.) Indeed, so much of the book can be traced to other sources that many contemporary scholars assume that "Sir John Mandeville" is an entirely fictional persona. Even the nationality of the anonymous author or authors of the book is open to question. Paradoxically, in comparison to Marco Polo, Mandeville might be characterized as more scholarly, drawing on his knowledge of the library rather than his direct experience of the world. (Tellingly, Mandeville, in his description of Cathay, makes little if any use whatsoever of Polo's account.)[4] Yet the fact remains that Mandeville's book apparently enjoyed a popularity even greater than Polo's, not only in the fourteenth century but well into the sixteenth. More than 250 manuscripts have survived, in French, English, Latin, German, Dutch, Danish, Czech, Italian, Spanish and Irish. At least thirty-five editions were printed by 1500.[5] Its readers, some two centuries after its composition, ranged from Leonardo da Vinci, who owned a copy of the book, to Domenico Scandella, alias Menocchio, an obscure Italian miller whose heretical views—some of which he specifically attributed to his reading of Mandeville—attracted the unwelcome and ultimately fatal attention of Church authorities (Ginzburg 1982:41–49).

Marco Polo has enjoyed a reputation as a perceptive and reliable first-hand observer, Mandeville as a plagiarist and a fanciful liar. For instance, Hodgen (1964:103) contrasts "the relatively truthful account written by Marco Polo" to "the mendacious romance which appeared under the name of Sir John Mandeville." This view is echoed by Helms (1988:239), who interprets the fact that "the fables associated with the *Book of Sir John de Mandeville* began to outweigh in general popularity the direct observations recorded in legitimate travel accounts such as the *Travels of Marco Polo*" as a sign of a temporary European "reversion" to earlier cosmological schemas. Such comparisons are embedded in positivist narratives of the advance of knowledge and rational thought. With the erosion of faith in the inexorable march of intellectual progress, the contrast between Polo and Mandeville has seemed less straightforward.[6] Both Polo and Mandeville readily employ the rhetoric of wonder, of marvels,[7] although Polo, unlike Mandeville, alternatively furnishes remarkably deadpan descriptions. Wood (1996) has even suggested that Marco Polo never actually traveled to China—he never, for example, mentions the Great Wall—although few other scholars are quite so skeptical. At the same time, Mandeville has enjoyed a surprising revival.[8] Contemporary scholars have accepted the narrator as a fictional persona rather than as a fraud, seeing the composition of the book not as an egregious instance of plagiarism, but rather as the skillful reworking and interweaving of other narratives into a highly original synthesis.[9] Indeed, the narrative is compelling, building up a single vision of the world and not just a patchwork of facts and fancies. Much of the book is, in a literal sense, fantastic, peopled with imagined and imaginary characters:

> There are many different kinds of people in these isles. In one, there is a race of great stature, like giants, foul and horrible to look at; they have one eye only, in the middle of their foreheads. They eat raw flesh and raw fish. In another part, there are ugly folk without heads, who have eyes in each shoulder; their mouths are round, like a horseshoe, in the middle of their chest. In yet

another part there are headless men whose eyes and mouths are on their backs. And there are in another place folk with flat faces, without noses or eyes; but they have two small holes instead of eyes, and a flat lipless mouth . . . (p. 137).[10]

It would be a grave mistake to dismiss Mandeville's enduring appeal as a token of medieval (or, for that matter, of Renaissance) ignorance, gullibility, or taste for the sensational. For a medieval audience, Mandeville's account had all the merits of Polo's, and more. The purpose of Polo's book, as we have seen, was primarily to entertain the reader and to satisfy his curiosity about "all the great wonders and curiosities of Greater Armenia and Persia, of the Tartars and of India, and of many other territories." (Polo 1958:33). It also provided various practical tips to travelers; but such tips, after all, were then, as now, prone to go out of date in light of changing political and economic circumstances. Mandeville, too, apparently wrote in French, the language of romances and other forms of courtly literature. He, too, entertained while providing pertinent information about other, generally eastern parts of the known world. Additionally, he furnished a host of travel tips, less for the merchant who wished to do business in Cathay than for the pious pilgrim who wanted to visit the Holy Land. Like Polo, he repeatedly asserted the veracity of his account on the grounds that he was there and saw it with his own eyes, or else heard it from reliable witnesses. But, over and above all this, Mandeville infused his narrative with meaning. Polo's description is centered around his admittedly extensive travels; Mandeville is concerned to describe nothing less than the world. For Mandeville, everything in the world has a meaning, a purpose, or a moral. Take, for example, this passage about the kingdom of Calanok:[11]

In that land, too, there is a marvel that is not in other lands. For all kinds of fish in the sea come at a certain time of the year, each kind in turn, and gather close to the shore—some on the shore. They lie there three days, and the men of that country come there and take what they want. And then that kind of fish goes away, and another kind comes ashore for another three days; and people take of them . . . No man knows the cause of this. But the folk of that land say that God shows them that grace to do honour to their King, as the most worthy earthly monarch, because he has so many wives and begets so many children on them, filling the world, as God commanded Adam and Eve, when He said . . . "Increase and multiply and fill the earth, and be lords of the fishes in the sea." This seems to me one of the greatest marvels I saw in any land, that fish who have the whole sea to swim in at their pleasures should voluntarily come and offer themselves to be killed without any compulsion by any creature. And indeed I am sure it does not happen without some great cause and meaning. (p.133)

Indeed, the rather improbable "folk" explanation is typical of one of the principal interpretive strategies Mandeville and his contemporaries employ, turning what might seem to be the most unlikely and recalcitrant phenomena into allegory, and most particularly into an allegory of scripture. Admittedly, in this particular passage, Mandeville seems to shrink from the implications of this particular "reading" of the marvel in question. Yet his conclusion underscores not only the possibility but the necessity of precisely this kind of hermeneutics. Mandeville's text consistently conveys a sense not so much of the meaning of the world as of its intrinsic meaningfulness. Admittedly, such significance emerges much more sharply in some parts of the narrative than in others. Mandeville does not moralize on every page, nor does he necessarily provide even a tentative or a "folk" exegesis of the cosmic significance of everything he reports. Had he done so, one suspects that the book would have been deadly dull, and would never had enjoyed such lasting popularity.

This conviction of the intrinsic significance of other peoples in the world, no matter how distant or different from "us" (however defined) in their ways of life or physical appearance, links Mandeville to modern concerns. For Mandeville, such "exotic" peoples take on significance in terms of a cosmology in which everything has its place, its meaning, its moral.[12] What, then, was the place of these peoples in Mandeville's world?

Mandeville's World

Commentators have often treated Mandeville's book as if it were divided into two parts: a comparatively straightforward description of the Holy Land and of various routes by which it can be reached from western Europe, followed by what strikes modern readers as a highly fanciful account of lands and "isles" to the east. But this bipartite division is an anachronism, an imposition of contemporary criteria of "realism" and "imagination" and indeed of modern sensibilities, which tend to find the first portion of the book relatively humdrum compared to the fanciful description of the East. An emphasis on the apparent differences between these supposed halves obscures an understanding of the overall structure of the book. The narrative flows continually and more or less consistently from west to east, from the western isles of western Europe to the Indies of Prester John. Unlike Marco

Polo, whose narrative takes us out to Cathay and back, Mandeville never tells us about the return journey. The reader (and the narrator?) are simply whisked back in the last few paragraphs.

The structure of the book reflects, in a very literal sense, Mandeville's notions about the structure of the world. Simply put, the earth is a sphere with Jerusalem at the center and the apex (Mandeville 1983:127–31). The firmament revolves "like a wheel on an axle-tree" around an axis delineated by the Pole Star and its southern equivalent, the Pole Antarctic. Mandeville insists not only on the world's roundness, but also its circumnavigability:

> I have often thought of a story I have heard, when I was young, of a worthy man of our country who went once upon a time to see the world. He passed India and many isles beyond India, where there are more than 5,000 isles, and travelled so far by land and sea, girdling the globe, that he found an isle where he heard his own language being spoken. For he heard one who was driving a plough team say such words to them as he had heard men say to oxen in his own land when they were working the plough. He marveled greatly, for he did not understand how this could be . . . But after he heard that marvel, he could not get transport any further, so he turned back the way he had come; so he had a long journey! (p. 129)

From this conception of a spherical globe, Mandeville derives the notion of antipodes, which is to say that every place on the globe has its polar opposite on the other side.

> Each part of the earth and sea has its opposite, which always balances it. And understand that to my way of thinking the land of Prester John, Emperor of India, is exactly below us. For if a man were to go from Scotland or England to Jerusalem, he would be going upwards all the way. For our land is in the lowest part of the West, and the land of Prester John is the lowest part of the East. They have day when we have night, and night when we have day. And however much a man climbs when he goes from our country to Jerusalem, he must descend as much to the land of Prester John. The cause is that the earth and the sea is [sic] round. For it is a commonplace that Jerusalem is in the middle of the earth . . . (p. 129)

What is so striking about this particular passage about cosmology is that it replicates exactly the course of Mandeville's presumed journey and the entire structure of the book: upwards from England—the Western extremity and the lowest part of the world—to Jerusalem, and back down from Jerusalem to the empire of Prester John, situated precisely at the antipodes of England. Seen in the light of this passage, the two "halves" of the book are precisely and deliberately symmetrical. (Incidentally, this symmetry would explain why Mandeville as a fictional persona should be an English voyager, although it is by no means certain that the "author"—to the extent that modern conceptions of "authority" are at all relevant in this case—was English.) The journey itself, of course, takes on a moral as well as a cosmological significance, and not only because it is literally a pilgrimage. The subject of the entire book is the relationship of Christendom to both the center of the world and the antipodes.

Journey to the Center of the World

The very first sentence of Mandeville's narrative emphasizes the special nature of the Holy Land, "among all other lands . . the most worthy land and mistress over all others, and . . . blessed and hallowed and consecrated by the precious blood of Our Lord Jesus Christ; in which land it pleased Him to take life and blood by Our Lady Saint Mary and to travel round that land with His blessed feet." The Holy Land is best because it is where Christ chose to be incarnated; but also, suggests Mandeville, "that land He chose before all other lands as the best and most honourable in the world, for, as the philosopher [Aristotle] says . . . 'The excellence of things is in the middle.'" Specifically, "He that was King of all the world wanted to suffer death at Jerusalem which is in the middle of the world so that it might be known to men of all parts of the world how dearly He bought man, whom He had made in His own likeness, because of the great love He had towards him." (p. 43)

Not only is Jerusalem the central place of the world, but the incarnation is the central time. Spatial and temporal distance is metaphorically equated with spiritual distance. The metaphor is not always applied consistently, but there can be no doubt that Mandeville, by emphasizing western Europe's place at the outer and lowest extremity, wants to convey a sense of its profound spiritual alienation from "central" Christian values. Moreover, the pilgrimage to the Holy Land is both geographically and spiritually an ascent; conversely, Christ's message radiates outward from the center in both space and time.

The capacity for the message to radiate outwards includes, one must insist, movement backwards in time. The most powerful image of such backward radiation is found in the following "marvel" of Mandeville:

... in the church of Saint Sophia [in Constantinople] once upon a time an
emperor wanted to lay to rest the body of his father, when he was dead; and
as they dug the grave, they found a body in the earth, and on that body lay
a great plate of gold; and thereon was written in Hebrew, in Greek and in
Latin . . . 'Jesus Christ shall be born of the Virgin Mary, and I believe in Him.'
And the date when this was written and laid in the earth was two thousand
years before the Incarnation of Christ. (p. 50)

Mandeville is deeply concerned about the ways in which the spiritual
link between Christendom in the fourteenth century and the Holy Land
at the time of the Incarnation can be maintained and indeed reinforced.
Relics, of course, constitute one such tangible link, especially insofar as they
can travel. On various occasions, Mandeville mentions the exhumation and
reburial of the bodies of saints. But he is particularly interested in the instruments of the Passion, which constitute the most intense material links
between Christ and Christian worshipers. Much of Mandeville's (pp. 47–
49) description of Constantinople consists of the catalogue of such relics
that can be found there—most notably, of course, the True Cross, but also
the sponge and reed with which the Jews gave drink to Christ on the cross,
and half of the crown of thorns. The crown of thorns is used as a dramatic
symbol not only of the propensity of relics to move, but of their divisibility
and consequently of their ability to radiate their power and their blessings
throughout the world. The other half of the crown of thorns, as it turns out,
is in Paris along with "one of the nails, and the spearhead [a rival spearhead
is in Constantinople, but Mandeville asserts the authenticity of the Parisian
relic, also noting that the emperor of Germany possesses the shaft of the
spear] and many other relics . . . in France in the King's chapel." (p. 48)
Mandeville even boasts that

> I have a thorn thereof . . for many of them are broken and have fallen down in
> the vessel in which is the Crown, for they break when men disturb the vessel
> to show the Crown to great lords and to pilgrims who come thither. (ibid.)

The journey of relics outward from the center of the world is the inverse
of the travel of pilgrims to the Holy Land. Mandeville dwells at length on
the sacred geography of Palestine. It is, in Greenblatt's (1991:41) judicious
phrase, "the place of sacred metonymy": each specific locale is not only
identified with one historical event, but rather constitutes a nexus of diverse
spiritual and temporal associations, extending time forward and backward
from the Incarnation. The Monastery of Saint Katherine, on Mount Sinai, is

not only the burial place of a Christian saint but also the place where Moses saw the burning bush and where later he received the tablets of the Ten Commandments (pp. 70–71). At the site of the former Temple in Jerusalem is a rock

> . . . where the Ark of God stood, and other holy things of the Jews. . . . And on this rock Jacob slept, when he saw the angels going up and down by a stair. . . . And on this rock Our Lord stood when the Jews wanted to stone Him to death; and the rock split apart and He hid Himself in the cleft, and a star descended and gave Him light. On this rock Our Lady sat and learned her Psalter. There Our Lord forgave the sins of the woman who was taken in adultery. There was Christ circumcised. . . . There David knelt, praying to Our Lord so that He would have mercy on him and his people. (pp. 82–83)

But nowhere are space and time more collapsed into a single center than on Calvary:

> The Cross was set in a mortice in the rock, which is white, streaked with red, in colour. Upon the rock blood dropped from the wounds of Our Lord when He suffered on the Cross. . . . And in that mortice Adam's head was found after Noah's flood, as a token that the sins of Adam should be redeemed in that place. And higher on that rock Abraham made sacrifice to Our Lord. There is an altar there, and before it lie Godfrey of Bouillon, and Baldwin his brother, and other Christian Kings of Jerusalem. (pp. 77–78)

The pilgrimage to the Holy Land, the journey to the center of space and time, constitutes a formidable means of spiritual renewal. But for Mandeville it also conveys a powerful sense of loss. As he notes ruefully, "it is a long time past since there was any general passage over the sea into the Holy Land" (p. 44). The "general passage" in question was, of course, the Crusades. The tombs of Godfrey of Bouillon, leader of the First Crusade, and his successors constitute a reproach to the Christian pilgrim that the Holy Land is once again in the hands of the "Saracens."

The point is hammered home in one of the most dramatic passages in Mandeville. The sultan of Egypt has just dismissed all his courtiers in order to have a private talk with Mandeville, who "lived a long time with the Sultan and was a soldier with him in his war against the Bedouins" (p. 59).

> And when they had all gone out, he asked me how Christians governed themselves in our countries. And I said, "Lord, well enough—thanks be to God."

And he answered and said, "Truly, no. It is not so. For your priests do not serve God properly by righteous living, as they should do. For they ought to give less learned men an example of how to live well, and they do the very opposite, giving examples of all manner of wickedness. And as a result, on holy days, when people should go to church to serve God, they go to the tavern and spend the day—and perhaps all the night—in drinking and gluttony, like beasts without reason which do not know when they have had enough. . . . Certainly it is because of your sinfulness that you have lost this land which we hold and keep. Because of your evil living and your sin and not because of our strength, God has given it into our hands. And we well know that when you serve your God properly and well, and serve Him with good works, no man shall be able to stand against you. . . . (pp. 107–8)

It is a masterful stroke of irony on Mandeville's part that he puts this sermon on the failings of Christendom in the mouth of the sultan, the archenemy of sorts. The uphill course of the pilgrimage, from the western edge of the world to the center, is both a sign and a consequence of the spiritual alienation of (anachronistically speaking) western Europe, the moral distance between Christendom and the Holy Land. Mandeville pursues the logic of his bitter irony relentlessly: "It seemed to me then a cause for shame that Saracens, who have neither a correct faith nor a perfect law, should in this way reprove us for our failings, keeping their false law better than we do that of Jesus Christ . . ." (p. 108).

Mandeville manages in his account of the pilgrimage to convey precisely a sense of time relatively commonplace in the fourteenth century: that of a sharp fall, of moral degeneration, of a disastrous break with a previously continuous past extending (as very literally embodied for Mandeville at Calvary) from Adam to Godfrey of Bouillon. The journey back to the center is an image not only of the individual quest for salvation, but of the imperative for a collective Christian spiritual renewal, a return to the sources of true religion. Once Christians recover their lost piety and good works, the Holy Land will once again be theirs.

The World Turned Upside Down

As we have seen, Mandeville's journey does not stop at the center, but continues all the way to the antipodes, to the realm of Prester John in the Indies. Mandeville's conception of the antipodes is organized around the basic principle that opposite ends of the earth are in fundamental ways opposite in nature. The paradigmatic opposition, in this case, is between the extreme

north and the extreme south. Mandeville mentions the far north in connection with a route to the Holy Land through Prussia and Russia. Here, he
notes, the rivers and marshes are only passable when they are frozen over;
one travels over them with sledges:

> For it is outrageously cold there, since it is the north side of the world, where
> the cold is usually more intense than in other places because the sun shines
> little there. And on the south side of the world in some places it is so hot that
> no man can live there for the appalling heat. (p. 104)

Revealingly, Mandeville's evocation of the south in this passage about the
far north seems virtually gratuitous. The mere mention of the frigid north
brings forth, through the free play of association, the thought of the torrid
south. Elsewhere, in any case, Mandeville has more to say about the far
south. Here, too, the emphasis is on what the climate does to the water. If in
the north water tends to freeze, the heat of the sun renders the water of Ethiopia so turbid and salty that it is undrinkable (p. 117); even further south
(presumably), the Sea of Libya is so close to boiling that not even fish can
live in it (p. 111). North and south correspond not only to the opposition
between freezing and boiling, but also between white and black. It is the
heat of the sun which blackens the people of the south, such as the Numid-
ians. But Mandeville pursues the logic of this opposition one step further,
arguing astutely that, for these black southerners, black is indeed beautiful.
Thus, observes Mandeville wryly, Numidian Christians paint angels black
and devils white (p. 64).

The antipodal contrast of north and south, derived from the Aristotelian
(and ultimately Hippocratic) humoral schema of hot and cold (Glacken
1967), conveniently defines the parameters of Mandeville's oppositional
framework, but this particular contrast is, in fundamental respects, secondary. The overall movement of the book, as we have seen, is rather from west
to east. The Far East, then, ought logically to be the opposite of "Western"
Europe. Stated in such terms, the proposition seems deceptively unambiguous. But what, in fact, constitutes the "opposite" of Europe? As readers of
Gulliver's Travels or of Voltaire's *Micromégas* are well aware (works which,
among others, owe a great deal, directly or indirectly, to Mandeville), opposition is of necessity relative. "We" may be the giant opposites of Lilliputians,
or else the diminutive opposites of Brobdingnagians. Both oppositions are
directly germane to Mandeville, who in one passage describes pygmies who
are two feet tall, who marry when they are a year and a half old and live to
the ages of eight or nine, and who have "men of our size who till the land

and dress the vines and do all the other heavy work that is necessary" and whom, moreover, they hold in great contempt (p. 140). Elsewhere, on the other hand,

> . . . the folk are as big in stature as giants of twenty-eight or thirty feet tall. They have no clothes to wear except the skins of beasts. . . . They eat no bread; but they eat raw flesh and drink milk, for there is an abundance of animals. They have no houses to live in, and they will more readily eat human flesh than any other. (p. 174)

These giant cannibals are a particularly salient example, precisely because they conflate the notion of "opposition" on several pertinent levels: physical constitution (they are giants compared to puny humans), material circumstances (they have no houses, eat no bread, and dress in wild animal skins), and morality (they eat human flesh). These three dimensions, united in this particular example, occur elsewhere in isolation or in various combinations. The range of possible permutations is, if not infinite, at least quite considerable. Mandeville's description of the East, of the antipodes, is at one level a kind of inventory of such permutations, an exploration of all the possible ways in which the people at the other end of the earth might be our "opposites."

The variegated repertory of monsters—men without heads, with one foot, with one eye, with the heads of dogs, to name only a few—are first and foremost physically opposite. Mandeville's descriptions of such peoples were in large measure responsible for the discredit he eventually earned among "rationalist" readers in later centuries, although their supposed existence can be traced back to classical sources, notably Pliny (Mason 2015:52–54). In any case, these physical "opposites" play a relatively minor role in Mandeville's overall scheme. He does not, for the most part, describe them at any length. Rather, from time to time the narrative includes an exuberant list of variations on a monstrous theme.

Oppositions in the realm of material conditions are in many respects more highly constrained. If the possibilities for describing humans who are physically "opposite" are seemingly endless, the material realm tends to generate extremes of either scarcity or opulence. The cannibal giants who have no houses, no bread, and almost no clothing constitute one prototype that recurs time and again with minor variations throughout the travels. For obvious reasons, descriptions of opulence can be far more elaborate, and none more so, of course, than that of the court of the Great Khan at Cathay:

. . . In the middle of the palace a dais has been made for the Great Khan, adorned with gold and precious stones. At its four corners there are four dragons made of gold. This dais has a canopy of silken cloth, barred across with gold and silver, and there are many large precious stones hanging on it. And below the dais are conduits full of drink, which the people of the Emperor's court drink from; besides the conduits are set vessels of gold which men can drink from when they wish. This hall is nobly and gloriously set out in every way. First, up on the top of the high dais, in the very middle, the throne for the Emperor is positioned, high up from the pavement, where he sits and eats his food. The table he eats on is made of jewels set in fine gold, and is bordered with gold set full of gems. The steps up which he goes to his throne are all of precious stone set in gold. At the left side of his throne is the seat of his chief wife, one step lower than his it is of jasper, bordered with gem-inlaid gold. (p. 142)

Mandeville tirelessly insists on the power and wealth of the Great Khan, "surpassing that of all earthly men" (p. 144).

Mandeville's description of the opulence of Cathay contains more than a hint of reproach towards his European contemporaries:

There is no such court here in this land. For here, kings and lords keep as few men in their courts as they can; but the Great Khan supports at his charge in his court each day folk without number. (p 144)

Not surprisingly, such a model ruler has model subjects to match:

All the people of that land are marvelously obedient to their rulers, and they never fight among themselves; nor are they thieves and robbers, but each one of them loves and respects the others. (p. 158)

The might, the riches, and the vast extent of the Khan's dominion are all, among other things, external signs of order, of the qualities embodied in good government, as depicted, for example, in Ambrogio Lorenzetti's famous fresco in Siena. Compared to this ideal Eastern state, Christendom—like Lorenzetti's bad government—is in sorry disorder, plagued by constant warfare and revolts.

As we can see, oppositions in the domain of material conditions almost inevitably shade into oppositions in the realm of morality. The moral domain is the most complex of all, and also at times the most ambivalent. Take, for example, Mandeville's description of the kingdom of Lamory (p. 127). The people go naked, not only because of the excessive heat but also because they declare that God made Adam and Eve naked, and that the wearing of clothing is consequently sacrilegious. They also practice sexual communism, which, they argue (as with the polygyny of the king of Calanok, cited above), is a fulfillment of the commandment to increase and multiply. They also hold all material possessions in common, but they have the nasty custom of relishing human flesh.

Indeed, "Eastern" anthropophagy is a stock opposite of "Western" practice (see Arens 1979), and cannibals of one sort or another appear and reappear in Mandeville's descriptions. At times, cannibalism serves a convenient function as a marker in a series of polar opposites: greatness and smallness, wealth and poverty, virtue and vice. Cannibalism is a convenient shorthand for viciousness: witness the giant breadless, hutless cannibals. However, there are other examples, such as the kingdom of Lamory, which are more unsettling, and where the absolute evil of the cannibals, as compared to Christendom, is not such a foregone conclusion. Perhaps the most spectacular example is the isle of Dundeya, where when a person is sick, his relatives go to consult the local idol, who either provides medicines to cure him or instructs his kin to kill him promptly and eat him. All the friends and relations of the deceased are invited to the feast, and it is considered an extreme breach of civility to decline such an invitation.

> They also say, when they find his flesh lean through long illness, that it would be a great sin to allow him to live longer or suffer pain without a cause. If they find his flesh fat, they say they have done well to have killed him quickly and sent him to Paradise, not allowing him to be tormented too long in this world. (pp. 136–37)

Even cannibalism, it would seem, has its own morality.

In any case, the moral "opposites" of western Europeans are not all cannibals by any means. As one might expect, Mandeville provides an idyllic portrait of a utopian society, the isle of Bragman.

> . . . they are not proud nor covetous, they are not lecherous nor gluttonous. They do nothing to another man they would not have done to themselves. They set no store by the riches of this world, or by possession of earthly goods. They do not lie, nor swear oaths for no reason, but simply say a thing is, or is not. . . . In this land, there are no thieves, no murderers, no prostitutes, no liars, no beggars; they are men as pure in conversation and as clean living

as if they were men of religion. And since they are such true and good folk, in their country there is never thunder or lightning, hail nor snow, nor any other storms and bad weather; there is no hunger, no pestilence, nor war, nor any other common tribulations among them, as there are among us because of our sins. (p. 178)

The antipodal logic of opposition is transparent in this whole passage. The Bragmans are defined almost entirely in terms of what they do not do, do not have, or do not endure, in terms of their freedom from typical European vices. The passage directly anticipates Montaigne's famous characterization of the "cannibals" (see below). The Bragmans outdo the cannibals, for they have no warfare and, of course, abstain from consuming human flesh. As a token of God's favor, they are even spared bad weather!

The Bragmans are a poignant reminder of our imperfections; their virtues make our vices all the more evident. When Alexander sets about conquering the world, he finally arrives at the land of the Bragmans and demands their submission. The envoy of the Bragmans points out to the conqueror that his people desire nothing at all beyond the bare necessities of life. "You can take nothing from us but our peace," he concludes. With all the graciousness and chivalry appropriate to a fourteenth-century pagan hero, Alexander accepts this scolding and leaves the Bragmans in tranquility, urging them to continue in their goodly ways (pp. 178–79).

Virtuous Pagans and the Ten Lost Tribes

The Bragmans constitute something of a theological problem. They are clearly virtuous, and Mandeville asserts with conviction that they are beloved of God. But he also makes it clear that they are not Christians. This is, in fact, not the first time in the book that Mandeville suggests that pagans can be more devout than Christians. Earlier, he cites the example of Job, whose kingdom he describes: "Although he was a pagan, [he] nevertheless . . . served God very devoutly according to the custom of his creed, and his service was acceptable to God" (p. 115). In fact, Mandeville pointedly reminds the reader of Job's example while extolling the virtues of the Bragmans.

Commentators (Letts 1949:165; Bennett 1954:73; Ginzburg 1982:9; Zacher 1976:148–49; Campbell 1988:155–57; Sobecki 2002) are almost unanimous in praising Mandeville's religious tolerance or openness. After all, Mandeville makes no attempt to conceal his admiration for the piety not only of pagans like the Bragmans, but even—more surprisingly, perhaps, for a fourteenth-century author—of Muslims. What is more, Mandeville is notably reluctant to condemn various Eastern Christian groups—Greek Orthodox, Syrians, Jacobites, Nestorians, and Arians, among others—who "keep and follow many articles of our faith, but in many points they vary from us and our faith" (p. 99). However, any characterization of Mandeville's religious attitude as "tolerant" is a thoroughly anachronistic reading of the text.

The motif of the "just pagan," of whom Job is the prototype, provides us with a basis for comparing Mandeville to contemporary texts that include similar characters. A notable example is Langland's poem *Piers Plowman*, which contains an account of the posthumous salvation of the Emperor Trajan, "a trewe knyght and took nevere Cristendom, / And he is saaf, seith the book, and his soule in hevene" (Langland 1978:145). Trajan is saved through the intercession of none other than Pope Gregory the Great, who, realizing what a virtuous man he had been, weeps for him and yearns for his salvation.

The story of Trajan's salvation is older than the fourteenth century.[13] Several versions are found in Jacobus de Voragine's (1969:184–85) thirteenth-century compilation, *The Golden Legend*. However, the striking differences between Voragine's and Langland's treatments of the same story reveal underlying changes in religious attitudes which illuminate Mandeville's use of a similar motif. In the first place, Voragine's compilation is an anthology of the lives of Christian saints. The whole point of the story is to demonstrate that Pope Gregory's charisma is so extraordinary that he can even save a pagan. The story is so problematic that Voragine conscientiously points out all the contradictions between different versions of the incident. As the story goes, Gregory was passing by Trajan's forum in Rome when he recollected how just an emperor he had been, weeping because he was damned, and, in some versions, also praying for him. A voice promptly and miraculously cried out that his request was granted. However, Gregory is scolded in some versions for praying for a damned soul, and warned never to do this again; he is punished in at least one version, and given the choice between two days of purgatory and living out the rest of his life in poor health. Needless to say, Gregory takes the latter option. In some versions, Trajan is actually brought back to life just in order to be baptized and saved as a Christian. In others, he is not fully saved, but merely relegated to limbo, where he is spared physical punishment but must endure eternal moral punishment, deprived of the sight of God. One way or the other, the thirteenth-century versions imply that Gregory's compassion for a damned soul, even the most virtuous of pagans, is misplaced.

In the fourteenth century, Langland draws a diametrically opposite moral from the same story: "Nought thorough preire of a pope, but for his pure truthe / was that Sarsan saved . . . Ac thus leel love and lyvyng in truthe / Pulte out of pyne a paynym of Rome" (Langland 1978:123). Langland not only minimizes Gregory's role, but even makes Trajan himself the hero of the story. He goes so far as to deny the very efficacy of papal intercession; salvation, he argues, depends directly on good works. What is more, Langland makes Trajan his mouthpiece for a surprising denunciation of law and of book learning in general. The scholastic niceties of theology, Trajan proclaims, would never have saved him. Only his own virtue could accomplish such a feat.

Langland's attitude is unquestionably more extreme than Mandeville's, but they definitely share certain religious sensibilities. Langland's adamant rejection of theology sheds light on Mandeville's attitude towards Eastern Christians. After all, the differences between the Roman Catholic Church and the Greek Orthodox Church, not to mention Nestorians and others, were above all theological. If, as both Mandeville and Langland argue, the piety of pagans is acceptable to God, then surely the piety of Christians, Roman Catholic or not, counts more than their theology. Heresy, seen in this light, is simply not an issue. This may well explain Mandeville's attitude not only toward Orthodox Christianity, but toward Islam. Islam—as Dante's description of Muhammad in Hell makes clear—was often categorized by medieval Catholics as a form of heresy, precisely because it acknowledged Christ's prophecy while denying his divinity. Mandeville's very indifference to the issue of heresy allows him to lavish the same kinds of praise on Muslims as on virtuous pagans—piety and good works.

It is important to point out, however, that the pagan piety which Mandeville admired might take rather extreme forms, most notably as regards his description of the juggernaut in the city of Calamy:

[Some] come in pilgrimage carrying sharp knives in their hands, with which they wound themselves in the arms and legs and other places, so that the blood runs from their wounds in great profusion. This they will do for love of that idol, and say that he who dies for love of that idol will be blessed indeed. . . . They set this idol with great reverence in a chariot . . . [followed by] all the pilgrims that have come from far countries, some of whom out of great devotion to that idol fall down in front of the chariot and let it roll over them. And so some of them are slain, some have their arms and legs broken; and they believe that the more pain they suffer here for the love of that idol, the more joy they will have in the other world and the nearer God they will be. And truly they suffer so much pain and mortification of their bodies for love

of that idol that hardly would any Christian man suffer the half—nay, not a
tenth—for love of Our Lord Jesus Christ. (pp. 125–26)

The comparison with Christian piety is a pointed one. The procession of
the juggernaut bears an uncanny resemblance to the processions of flagellant movements that spread throughout western Europe in the fourteenth
century, especially after the bubonic plague.[14] Mandeville's special interest
in the relics of the Passion, as we have already seen, is another manifestation of the same kind of religious sensibilities, a call for a direct and visceral
identification with Christ's suffering as a means of quite literally "recenter-
ing" Christian religion. The flagellants, like Mandeville and many others,
were highly critical of the institutional practices of the Church and relatively
unconcerned with doctrine; "pure" piety was seen to be a remedy for the
corrupt practices of the Church.

The corollary of such Passion-centered piety was a fierce hostility towards
the Jews, who were held collectively responsible for the murder of Christ.
The appearance of the flagellants coincided with massacres of Jews, particularly in Germany. Although it is far from clear whether the flagellants were
directly responsible for pogroms, [15] Mandeville fully shares this hostility,
a fact which, if nothing else, ought to call into question his reputation for
"tolerance."[16] For example, he mentions (p. 132) a foiled Jewish plot to poi-
son all Christendom. Tellingly, his account of the destruction of the Temple
in Jerusalem pits virtuous pagan Roman emperors—shades of Langland's
Trajan?—against diabolical Jews. Mandeville even ascribes Titus's motive
for the Jewish Wars to a desire to punish the Jews for the execution of Christ
without his leave (p. 81). In the same passage, Mandeville reviles Julian the
Apostate, not for attempting a revival of paganism, but rather for allegedly
favoring the Jews and attempting to rebuild the Temple for them. In another
passage, Mandeville pits Gog and Magog, who are none other than the Ten
Lost Tribes, against yet another virtuous pagan of classical antiquity, Alexander the Great, who—with God's assistance, no less—shuts them off in the
Caspian mountains:

If it should happen that any of them get out, they can speak no language
except Hebrew. . . . And so all the Jews in the different parts of the world learn
to speak Hebrew, for they believe that the Jews who are enclosed in those hills
will know that they are Jews (as they are) by their speech when they arrive.
And then they will lead them into Christendom to destroy Christian men.
(p. 166)

Gog and Magog, shut off by Alexander with God's blessing, are the diametri-
cal opposites of the Bragmans, beloved of God and who turn Alexander
away. Unlike virtuous pagans, who either ignore the Revelation or else hold
Christians in high esteem, second only to their co-religionists, the Jews are
guilty of actively rejecting the Revelation, crucifying Christ in the process.

The theme of the virtuous pagans provides a concrete link between
images of the heroes and emperors of classical antiquity, in the guise of idealized medieval rulers, and representations of the denizens of the antipodes,
the "polar opposites" of Western Christendom. Both, by their very virtues,
highlight by implicit comparison the sorry state of fourteenth century Christendom, and quite specifically of the Church. "Natural" piety, justice and
good works are contrasted both to corrupt institutional practices—simony
in particular—and to an undue stress on theological subtleties as opposed
to proper Christian conduct and to the cultivation of religious emotion
through the visceral identification with the suffering Christ.

It is not entirely surprising that Mandeville's views helped lead a simple
Italian miller towards heresy and ultimately the stake. Still, it is crucial to
bear in mind that the book is not a crypto-pamphlet, secret propaganda
for flagellants or other radicals of one "heretical" persuasion or another. In
the first place, the book was first and foremost intended as entertainment,
though, as with the best entertainment, this hardly precludes some serious
purpose. Moreover, there is no reason to doubt that it was intended as a
reasonably accurate representation of the world, consistent with a whole
body of written knowledge available at the time. Ultimately, the coherence
of Mandeville is not that of a tightly structured text (though it is hardly an
unstructured one either), but rather of a specific cosmological vision of the
world, literally in terms of center and periphery, and of specific sensibilities,
affinities with styles of religiosity that may find echoes in Langland, in the
flagellants, and elsewhere because they were, after all, reasonably commonplace in the fourteenth century. Pushed to extremes, as they sometimes were,
such sensibilities might lead to heresy. But religiously speaking, Mandeville
was at most a "fellow traveler."

Toward Modernity

Mandeville seems to encompass the dual heritage of anthropology: on one
hand, travel literature describing firsthand encounters with exotic "others,"
which might (anachronistically) be labeled "proto-ethnography"; on the
other, learned disquisitions on the place of such "others" within the broader

scope of humankind, "proto-ethnology" of sorts. Mandeville's claims, however transparently spurious in retrospect, to have witnessed what he recorded
have led modern readers to classify him, as an author of travel literature,
either as an "unredeemable fraud" (Greenblatt 1991:31) or as an "artist . . .
'ahead of his time'" (Campbell 1988:161). Such characterizations are misleading, not least because Mandeville was no doubt convinced of the general
accuracy of his representation of the world, pieced together from what most
learned men would have considered the most reliable sources available. At
stake was the relationship between the representation of the "journey" and
the representation of the "world." The modern bias (as postmodernists have
repeatedly pointed out; c.f. Clifford 1988:34–37) is to consider that the
"journey" authorizes the truth of the representation of the "world." Whether
or not this was Mandeville's intention (I do not see how we can be sure), the
relationship needs to be understood in very different terms. In Mandeville it
was precisely the image of the "journey," spurious as it might be in fact, that
turned knowledge of the "world" into allegory, passing from the western periphery of Christendom to the center of the world and finally beyond to the
antipodes. Within the confines of such an intrinsically meaningful world,
truth was situated in terms of the correspondence between its representation
and its ultimate significance, rather than between "experience" and "reality."

The most significant link between Mandeville's concerns and those
of modern anthropology is his systematic exposition of a worldview that
consistently takes account of the significance of exotic "others." Precisely
because Mandeville's world view is distinctly premodern, it provides a convenient point of reference with which to contrast later, more "modern" formulations. Specifically, for Mandeville, space and time radiated out from a
center (Jerusalem, the Incarnation). On one hand, spatial and temporal distance from the center served as an index of spiritual alienation; on the other,
true piety could bridge distances either in space or in time. Time, moreover,
was characterized by an idealized past as opposed to a devalorized present,
just as the virtues of the antipodes highlighted the vices of Christendom.
Mandeville's narrative abounds with ancient Greeks (Aristotle, Alexander)
and Romans (Titus, Julian the Apostate) in the absence of any notion of
"classical antiquity," qualitatively different from the relatively recent past,
as epitomized by the Crusades. Paradoxically, the sixteenth century was witness to the elaboration of a heliocentric model of the universe, a Eurocentric
model of the globe, and the "discovery" of classical antiquity (Weiss 1969).

Mandeville's cosmology consistently informed his vision of people literally and metaphorically at the other end of the world. The point is not that
such "others" appeared as the opposites of "us"; there was nothing at all new

in that kind of antipodal reasoning. Far more important, exotic "others" were used precisely in order to elaborate a scathing and thorough critique of the institutions of his own society. Mandeville's representations of the center of the world and of the antipodes were ultimately and intentionally used to elaborate a self-representation, and by no means a flattering one, of Christendom. Mandeville's literally "Christocentric" vision moralized the world very differently from a Eurocentric focus. Rather than judging others primarily in terms of the distance and difference between "them" and "us," it categorized everyone, "we" as much as if not more than "they," in terms of distance from the center. This was of necessity a vision deeply informed by a specific morality, in Mandeville's case by a conception of piety stressing both good works and a visceral emotional identification with the suffering Christ. Mandeville's world was seen through the lenses of this particular religious attitude, but, at the same time, its portrayal vividly confirmed the rightness of such a morality, depicted as the organizing principle of the world itself.

THREE

Between Two Saddles: Montaigne

"The century in which we live . . . is so leaden that it is difficult even to imagine (I won't say to practice) virtue; the word seems to be nothing but schoolboy jargon."

—Montaigne, *Essays*, I, 37

Two centuries after Mandeville, Michel de Montaigne was still deploring the present and extolling the past:

As concerns the lives of these heroes of times past, they sometimes display miraculous traits which seem to surpass by far our natural forces . . . It happens that we, who are but aborted humans, propel our souls, awakened by the discourses or the examples of others, far beyond the ordinary.[1]

But the similarities between such laments for the snows of yesteryear belie a revolutionary change in conceptions of time, in the very concept of an idealized past. For Mandeville the present was an abyss into which Christendom had only recently fallen; for Montaigne the past was located in antiquity, among the Greeks and the Romans, separated from the present by a gulf. The point is obviously not that Mandeville was unfamiliar with ancient Greece and Rome. As we have seen, Aristotle, Alexander the Great, and Julian the Apostate, among others, inhabit his book. What had changed by the sixteenth century was the notion that such characters lived in a world that had been qualitatively different from our own for more than a millennium. Indeed, Petrarch, the first of the great Italian humanists responsible for this reconceptualization of time, was a contemporary of Mandeville.[2] By the sixteenth century, classical antiquity had become the common standard by which the achievements of contemporaries were to be judged, in domains as diverse as the fine arts (Vasari's *Lives of the Artists*) and statecraft (Machiavelli's *Discourses on the First Ten Books of Livy*).

Conceptions of space had changed as radically as those of time. Jerusalem had ceased to be the center of the world, as the most cursory comparison of fourteenth-century and sixteenth-century maps reveals. Mercator was, after all, a contemporary of Montaigne. Most obviously, the so-called New World, the "Americas," was nowhere to be found in Mandeville's round world. Oddly enough, the effect of this "discovery" on sixteenth-century European intellectual life was rather less spectacular than one might imagine, far less radical than the effect on the European economy of the massive quantities of silver exported from Bolivia and Mexico to Spain. Europeans published and presumably read far more about travel to Asia than to the Americas. (Montaigne's personal interest in the Americas and relative lack of enthusiasm for matters Asiatic was definitely one of his many idiosyncrasies.)[3] Far more fundamental than the discovery of America was the simultaneous "discovery" of Europe.[4] While the idea of "Europe" was not entirely absent from the geographical imagination of Mandeville's contemporaries, it was decidedly marginal. Mandeville and his contemporaries located themselves in "Christendom" rather than in "Europe."

With the advent of the Reformation, any unitary idea of "Christendom" could hardly appear self-evident. This is hardly to say that medieval Christians were unaware of divisions within "Christendom"—Mandeville's text is ample proof to the contrary—but the Reformation represented a qualitatively different phenomenon. This was especially true in sixteenth-century France, beset by the Wars of Religion from 1562 to 1598. To identify oneself as a "Christian" in those circumstances was entirely beside the point: one was either a partisan of Rome or of the Reform. Ultimately, France was divided not simply in two but eventually in three factions, each led by one of the three Henris: Henri of Navarre, the future Henri IV, at the head of the Protestant faction; Henri of Guise, leader of the ultra-Catholic League, in open revolt against the crown; and Henri III, king of France, owing allegiance to the Church of Rome but desperately attempting to steer between Scylla and Charybdis.

To an extent, Montaigne's *Essays* represent a retreat from the turmoil of political and religious strife into the privacy of his study and of his own thoughts. The short preface to the work, addressed to the reader, warns immediately "that I set myself no goal other than a private or domestic one." Indeed, the preface insists that the book is a form of self-portrait, a memento for family and friends: "I want to be seen in my simple, natural and ordinary way, without artifice or guile. . . . Thus, reader, I am myself the subject of my

book: it is not reasonable that you expend your leisure on a subject so frivolous and so vain." Yet the *Essays*, though they reveal a wealth of personal and
sometimes intimate detail, are hardly autobiographical in any conventional
sense. Rather, as exemplars of his manner of discourse and of thought, they
are meant to convey a sense of himself, his tastes and distastes, his strengths
and weaknesses, and indeed his contradictions.

In fact, the book itself is a recurring subject of the *Essays*. In a striking
metaphor, Montaigne compares writing an essay and fording a river: "If it is
a subject that I do not understand, for this very reason I try it out [*je l'essaye*],
plumbing its depth from a safe distance; and then, finding it too deep for
my height, I stick to the bank. . . ."[5] The metaphor makes it clear that the
essay itself is a sort of test, a self-evaluation as well as an evaluation of
the subject matter. It is precisely this evaluative dimension that transforms
the *Essays* from an introspective project to a consideration of the author's
world. Montaigne can only judge himself in terms of his particular place
and time (sixteenth-century France in the midst of the Wars of Religion) and
even more precisely in terms of his station in society (the lower ranks of the
nobility). The spiral grows ever wider as Montaigne evaluates his own world
in terms of other places and other times. We are back, of course, to classical
antiquity, the yardstick by which Montaigne takes measure of himself and
of the world. (How far from Mandeville's focus on the incarnation of Christ
as the defining moment of humanity!) The judgment hardly stops here, as
Montaigne evaluates one ancient author or soldier in terms of some other.
As moralists go, for instance, he prefers Plutarch and Seneca to Cicero: "But,
to confess frankly the truth (since, once you have ventured beyond the barriers of impudence, there is nothing to hold you back), I find [Cicero's] style
boring. . . ."[6] Comparing Caesar to Alexander, though he admits that Caesar's ambitions were more modest, he concludes that his actions caused "the
ruin of his country and the universal worsening of the world," and that, as a
result, Alexander remains the more admirable in the balance.[7]

Not surprisingly, the world beyond Europe, and most particularly the
New World, was grist for Montaigne's evaluative mill. Montaigne's first es-
say/attempt to grapple with the problem of cultural difference, to phrase
the matter anachronistically, is in "Of Custom, and Not Easily Changing an
Accepted Law," written around 1572 or 1574.[8] Montaigne begins his essay
with a brief exercise in culinary relativism, citing "great peoples in markedly
diverse climates" of the New World who relish spiders, locusts, ants, lizards,
bats and toads, and for some of whom "our meats and viands were mortal
and venomous." In an untranslatable play on words, he adds that these
foreign (*estrangers*) examples are not strange (*estranges*). A few paragraphs

later, he emphasizes the point: "Barbarians are in no way more miraculous to us than we are to them." Strangeness, like foreignness, is all a matter of perspective. The overall theme of the essay, that humans are creatures of custom, is hardly of itself original. Montaigne predictably cites a famous anecdote from Herodotus, where Darius asks horrified Greeks to eat the corpses of their dead, and puckishly demonstrates that the ambassadors of the Callatiae are equally appalled at the prospect of cremating their deceased relatives. Each to his own, echoes Montaigne.

Montaigne's originality, though this is hardly the most original of his essays, is that he uses this apparently relativist premise to arrive at a set of decidedly unrelativistic conclusions. First of all, he rails against the miseducation of aristocratic boys, a subject to which he was to return later in one of his most famous essays.[9] He chides those parents who allow or even admire their children who wring the necks of chickens, torture dogs and cats, beat peasants and servants who dare not fight back, and trick or cheat their companions. "These are . . . the true seeds and roots of cruelty, tyranny, and treason." It must be pointed out that the word *coustume*, as Montaigne uses it, can mean not only "custom" but also "habit." The nasty habits we inculcate in our children become the vices of adults. The implication here is that *coustume* in this domain is malleable, that habit can be a moral force for good as well as for ill. Montaigne is not, of course, blaming all the ills of his century on the improper manner by which children are raised. But it is precisely the relationship between *coustume*—both as "habit" and as "custom"—and the ills of his century that is at the heart of Montaigne's essay.

If Montaigne's remarks on childrearing might suggest that some forms of *coustume* are more rational or more moral than others, the brunt of his essay argues quite the contrary, reverting to the sense of *coustume* as "custom." Much of the essay is devoted to a seemingly random and bewildering list of one strange or foreign custom after another:

There are [nations] where one finds public male brothels, indeed marriages [between males]; where women go to war along with their husbands, and have a rank, not only in combat but in command. Where rings are not only worn on noses, lips, cheeks and toes, but where heavy golden rods pierce nipples and buttocks. Where while eating one wipes one's fingers on the inside of the thighs and on the testicles as well as on the soles of one's foot. Where children are not heirs, but rather brothers and nephews; and elsewhere, only nephews except in the succession of a Prince. Where to administer the community of property which is observed, certain sovereign Magistrates have the universal responsibility for the cultivation of land and the distribution of

its fruits, according to the needs of every person. Where they lament the death
of children and celebrate that of the aged. Where they sleep ten or twelve to a
bed along with their wives. Where women who lose their husbands by violent
death can remarry, the others not. . . .

This is but a small sample. Such passages call to mind Renaissance compendia of customs, notably Johann Boemus' *Omnium gentium mores, leges,
& ritus ex multis clarissimis rerum scriptoribus* (translated into English as *The
fardle of façions, conteining the aunciente maners, customes, and lawes, of the
peoples enhabiting the two partes of the earth, called Affrike and Asie*), originally published in Latin in 1520 and translated into French in 1540 (though
Montaigne would hardly have needed a French translation of Latin works;
ancient Greek was an entirely different matter).[10] However, the purpose of
Boemus's text is to evoke a sense of marvel at the world's diversity; Montaigne, on the contrary, deliberately fosters a sense of bewilderment. The
domain of "custom" is radically irrational. Contradictory practices from
around the globe seem to cancel one another out. Worse, Montaigne suggests, "the laws of conscience, which we say are born of nature, are born of
custom. . . ." Simply put, morality itself would appear to be purely conventional, an assertion which might seem to be directly contrary to the teachings of the Church. Montaigne developed such radical skepticism at length
in his long "Apology for Raymond Sebond," calling into question the very
capacity of human judgment.[11]

If Montaigne's premise seems decidedly un-Catholic, the conclusions
that he draws, privileging faith over reason, were ultimately consistent with
Church doctrine at the time; only later was the Church to insist on the rational basis of its teachings. Montaigne's immediate moral is to stress conformity: ". . . the wise person should withdraw his soul within away from the
crowd, and hold it in liberty and power to judge things freely; but, externally,
he should entirely follow received ways and forms. . . . For it is the rule of
rule, and the general law of laws, that each should observe those of the place
where he is." There is a subtle, easily overlooked nuance in Montaigne's
formulation; he stresses conformity to the customs not of the place where
one is born, but of where one happens to be. This was not an empty distinction, as Montaigne was to make abundantly clear when he traveled through
Switzerland and Austria to Italy in 1580 and 1581, after completing the first
edition of the *Essays*: "M. de Montaigne, in order completely to try out [*es-
sayer*] the diversity of customs and ways, let himself be served everywhere
according to the fashion of the place, whatever difficulty he might thereby
encounter."[12]

Indeed, his curiosity to observe and absorb different customs led him to witness a Jewish circumcision in a Roman synagogue.[13] There is a striking disparity between the extreme social conformism that Montaigne advocates and the personal delight in experimentation which is evident both in his travels and in the *Essays*.

At the heart of this tension is Montaigne's attitude towards the Wars of Religion and especially towards the Reformation.[14] Change, however noble its motivations, is more likely to bring harm than good: "I am disgusted with novelty, whatever face it wears, and with reason, for I have seen its very damaging effects." Montaigne's support for the Church is based not on abstract reason, but rather on the devastating consequences of the civil strife occasioned by religious schism in France. "God knows, in our present quarrel, where there are a hundred articles [of faith] to remove or to put back, great and profound articles, how many are there who can pride themselves on having recognized the reasons and foundations of one or the other party? It is a number, if there were such a number, who would hardly be able to trouble us." Montaigne's cynicism about the Wars went far deeper than this, based on his personal acquaintance with the leaders of each of the three warring factions. This was more than a passing familiarity. Both Henri III and Henri of Navarre appointed him gentleman of the chamber. His trip to Italy was interrupted by a royal summons to assume the mayoralty of Bordeaux, to which he had been elected, presumably thanks to the king's support. Navarre twice spent the night at Montaigne's home, in 1584 and again in 1587.[15] Montaigne had even undertaken, at roughly the same period as he was writing the essay "Of Custom . . . ," the delicate and ultimately unsuccessful task of mediating between Navarre and Guise. He later confided to the historian Jacques-Auguste de Thou:

> That religion, which is alleged by both, is used speciously as a pretext by those who follow them; for the rest, neither one regards it. For Navarre, if he did not fear to be deserted by his followers, would be ready to return of his own accord to the religion of his forefathers; and Guise, if there were no danger, would not be averse to the Augsburg Confession [i.e., Lutheran articles of faith] . . .[16]

The *Essays* are as vociferous in their condemnation of the conduct of the Catholic as of the Protestant party. As the passage above suggests, he more than occasionally accuses partisans on both sides of using religion as a pretext for more narrowly political interests. Montaigne nonetheless blames the Reform for setting off the chain of events that was to lead to disaster, to civil wars that were to set neighbor against neighbor.

Montaigne's moral revulsion at the pointless violence of the Wars of Religion explains the apparent inconsistencies of his attitude towards *coustume*. As "custom," it is beyond the purview of reason and thus must be maintained as it is, lest its breach unleash, as an unintended consequence, the violent disturbance if not dissolution of the body politic. As "habit," on the other hand, it must be rationally conditioned in order to inculcate virtuous dispositions; to tolerate or even encourage bad habits is to predispose individuals to the vices of cruelty, tyranny, and treason—the very vices which characterized the extremists in both the Protestant and Catholic camps.

Montaigne's essay "Of Custom . . ." is hardly among his most remarkable or his most personal, though it certainly anticipates some of the themes which he was to develop in his more mature contributions. Of these, the justly famous essay "Of Cannibals" constitutes the most sustained reflection on the significance of non-European practices.[17] The cannibals in question were the Tupi-speaking neighbors of the abortive French colony of Antarctic France, located around what is now Rio de Janeiro. French interest in the region was centered on the trade in brazil wood, a tropical wood used as a dye. Before any attempt to establish a colony, some French traders had settled among the Brazilians, learning the language and taking local wives, much as the voyageurs were to do a century or more later in the North American fur trade. In 1550, some fifty Tupi were shipped to Rouen, where, along with prostitutes and sailors recruited for the purpose, they recreated a staged Brazilian village as a pageant for King Henri II.[18] Montaigne was present at the occasion, where he attempted with limited success to communicate with the "cannibals" through an interpreter, a *truchement*, one of the French traders who had settled awhile in Brazil. The colony of Antarctic France was established later, in 1555, under the patronage of Admiral Gaspard de Coligny, the most prominent of the leaders of the Reform party aside from Henri of Navarre. Ideally, it was hoped that the colony would help defuse tensions between Catholics and Huguenots by serving as a refuge for Protestants, simultaneously bolstering French commerce with the New World and fostering its pretensions as an imperial power. The leader of the expedition, Nicolas de Villegaignon, immediately proceeded to outlaw sexual relations between French colonists and Brazilian women on pain of death, alienating the trader-interpreters whose services were essential in brokering between the French and the local population. He then sent to Calvin in Geneva for a contingent of Protestant pastors who might presumably restore morality to the colony, but, upon their arrival, promptly quarreled with them about the significance of the Eucharist and expelled them to live with the neighboring

Tupi for a year, until they were able to find a ship to take them home. Under a more flexible leader, the colony might have survived, but by 1560—well before Montaigne began his *Essays*—the Portuguese expelled the colonists, though not the French traders.

At first sight, the subject seems even less likely to lend itself to autobiography than "custom." Yet one sentence of Montaigne's short preface to the *Essays*, written slightly after the first version of "Cannibals," suggests otherwise: "If I had been among those nations that are said to live still under the sweet liberty of the first laws of nature, I assure you that I would very willingly have painted myself in my entirety, and entirely naked." The cannibal, Montaigne is playfully suggesting, is his alter ego.

This playfulness is characteristic of much of the essay, which begins with a play on the meanings of the word "barbarian." Characteristically, Montaigne starts out with a reference to classical antiquity, recounting an anecdote about the Macedonian king Pyrrhus confronting a Roman army in Italy: "'I don't know,' said he, what barbarians these may be (for so the Greeks called all foreign nations) but the formation of this army I see is in no way barbaric." In the first place, this brings to mind Montaigne's punning in "Of Custom . . ." on *étranger* and *étrange*, "stranger" and "strange." To the extent that, as he points out, the original meaning of "barbarian" is simply "foreigner," this is another lesson in relativism. Yet in a deep sense, "Of Cannibals" is even less relativistic than "Of Custom" (which, after all, is a roundabout plea for loyalty to the teachings of the Catholic Church). "Strange," after all, is an intrinsically relative adjective; Montaigne points out already in the earlier essay that we are as strange to the cannibals as they are to us. "Barbaric," on the other hand, connotes both inferiority and cruelty. The cannibals cannot logically be both inferior and superior to us, more and less cruel. The very concept involves a moral dimension and calls for an unambiguous moral comparison.

The most famous passage of the essay leaves no doubt as to who is morally superior to whom:

> This is a nation, I would say to Plato, in which there is no sort of commerce; no knowledge of letters; no science of numbers; no word for magistrate or for political superiority; no condition of servitude, of riches or of poverty; no contracts; no wills; no division of property; no occupations other than leisure; no respect for any but common kinship; no clothing; no agriculture; no metal; no use of wine or wheat. The very words which signify lies, treachery, dissimulation, avarice, envy, backbiting, pardon, are unheard of.

This passage, as Hodgen has pointed out, is a string of negatives.[19] It bears an uncanny resemblance to Hobbes's famous depiction of the state of nature as a war of every man against every man, but also of Mandeville's description of the Bragmins. Indeed, for all three authors, the peoples or conditions described are in some sense "natural," though in each case the implications are significantly different. For Mandeville, the Bragmans are naturally virtuous, an example of the harmony of God and of nature, in the absence of revelation they spontaneously follow God's dictates. As a consequence, they are both pacific (hardly the case for Montaigne's cannibals!) and ascetic. Their lack, if lack it can be called, is clearly a consequence of voluntary renunciation rather than of ignorance. In any case, Montaigne's cannibals, who, he tells us elsewhere, spend much of the day drinking and dancing, exude a healthy and wholly unascetic joie de vivre. In any case, religious concerns are wholly absent from the passage; the cannibals are explicitly compared—favorably!—to Plato's *Republic*. After all, for Montaigne, classical antiquity and not contemporary France constitutes the yardstick of excellence, moral or otherwise.

Despite the superficial similarity, the string of negatives functions very differently in Montaigne and Hobbes, and not simply because "nature" furnishes a model for one and an antimodel for the other. For one thing, Montaigne supplies additional concrete details about how the cannibals live, whereas Hobbes's passage is explicitly the formulation of an abstract theoretical model. Most pointedly, the passage in question is primarily aimed at categorizing not the cannibals, but rather his own society. In a deliberate play of negatives and positives, the positive features of sixteenth-century France turn out to be morally negative.

But the rub is that the cannibals really do eat people. Significantly, Montaigne calls them "cannibals" and not "anthropophagi." André Thévet, later to become the royal cosmographer, in a description of Brazil, *Les Singularitez de la France Antarctique*, published in 1557, distinguished between these two varieties of man-eaters. The good "anthropophagi," allies of France, ate their victims as an act of vengeance; the bad "cannibals," the enemies, had a perverse taste for human flesh.[20] Montaigne, by refusing to make any such distinction and by deliberately choosing the stronger, more derogatory term, maximizes the force of the paradox. What if not this is "barbaric," in the sense of horribly cruel? Indeed, Montaigne's revulsion for cruelty is a recurrent theme in the *Essays*. Already, in "Of Custom," he singles out cruelty as one of the nasty childhood "habits" he most reproves. In his essay "Of Cruelty," roughly contemporaneous to "Of Cannibals," he remarks: "I hate, among other vices, cruelty cruelly, by nature and by judgment, as the most extreme of all vices."[21] By "by nature," Montaigne means that he is viscerally repelled by cruelty in all forms. He confides that he even dislikes watching chickens killed, not to mention hares tormented by hounds in the hunt. Tears, even feigned, move him to pity. For Montaigne, this is more a sign of "softness" than of virtue, to the extent that virtue consists of following the dictates of duty or reason rather than one's personal inclinations. Be this as it may, Montaigne was particularly appalled by the cruelty occasioned by the Wars of Religion—explicitly his point of comparison to the cannibals:

> I am not sorry that we remark the barbaric horror of such an action [killing and eating enemy prisoners], but indeed that, judging rightly their faults, we are so blinded to our own. I think it more barbaric to eat a man alive than to eat him dead, to tear apart by torture a whole body still full of feeling, to roast it slowly, to give it up to pigs and dogs to bite and torment (as we have not only read, but seen in fresh memory, not between ancient enemies but between neighbors and fellow citizens, and, what is worse, under the pretext of piety and of religion) than to roast and eat it after it is dead.

But Montaigne's horror of cruelty does not extend to a blanket condemnation of warfare. The warlike disposition of the cannibals, repeatedly stressed throughout the essay, is another point in their favor. Son of a father who was distinguished for his military service but who envied the accomplishment of men of letters, Montaigne was raised to remedy any such deficiencies. Paradoxically, Montaigne, who profoundly admired his father, repeatedly disparaged his own literary accomplishments—the *Essays* are full of self-deprecating remarks that cannot be written off as coyness or false modesty—and bemoaned his own inadequacies in the field of arms. Significantly, in his essay "The Most Excellent of Men" (all Greeks, who win out over the Romans; Montaigne's contemporaries are not in the running), of the three he chooses, only one, Homer, is a writer, The other two, Alexander and Epaminondas (his favorite of all), are soldiers.[22] The nobility of cannibal warfare (I use the word "nobility" advisedly, for the virtues are, for Montaigne, specifically associated with the aristocracy) resides in its motives. The cannibals fight not for land, not for political domination, and certainly not for religion, but only for revenge. The very fact of killing and eating prisoners of war is a form of vengeance. The crux of the matter is that revenge is a question of honor, and honor is precisely an aristocratic concern. So is courage, and the cannibal captive, about to be killed and roasted, who shouts defiance at his enemies and refuses to flinch is Montaigne's hero:

They ask no other ransom of their prisoners than the confession and recognition of their defeat; but there is not a single one, in an entire century, who does not prefer death to giving up, either by countenance or by speech, a single point of the greatness of invincible courage; not a single one is seen who would not prefer being killed and eaten then merely to ask to be spared.

Victory in combat, Montaigne adds, rests on advantages such as physical strength, agility, or skill that are morally neutral. A good fencer may be a coward and a cad. The cannibal remains morally undefeated, down to the last morsel.

Montaigne's emphasis on the aristocratic value of honor is, of course, profoundly old-fashioned. The development of modern artillery and of professional mercenary armies made such values redundant, replaced by a very different kind of court society.[23] Paradoxically, Montaigne was a perfect exemplar of this new nobility, the *noblesse de robe*, lawyers and administrators rather than soldiers. He studied law at Toulouse before serving, first in the Cour des Aides of Périgueux and from 1557 to 1570 in the parliament of Bordeaux.[24] Ultimately, Montaigne's values—though emphatically not his literary preferences—are not unlike Don Quixote's. (Montaigne discloses in passing that *Amadis of Gaul* and other chivalric romances, the staple reading of the hidalgo from La Mancha, held little attraction for him even in his childhood.[25]) Unlike Don Quixote, Montaigne held no illusions about the currency of such values in the contemporary world. It is with these values in mind, then, that Montaigne suggests that we, not the cannibals, are the true barbarians.

Montaigne not only plays with the meanings of the word "barbarian" but also, less consistently but just as significantly, with "savage." The pun does not translate easily from the French; *sauvage* means simultaneously "savage" and "wild." If cannibals are "savages," Montaigne puckishly suggests, this makes them rather like wild strawberries. (He doesn't actually mention strawberries, but rather wild fruit in general.) Wild fruit are, he adds, richer in taste and natural properties, whereas "those that we have altered by artifice and made to deviate from the common order should more properly be labeled 'savage.'" The implication Montaigne draws is that "wild" is "natural." He does not quite argue that the cannibals are entirely "natural," but he very definitely places them much closer to "nature" than his own society. It should be stressed that Montaigne unambiguously asserts the superiority of "nature" to "art"—in its earlier sense, not necessarily "fine" art but any product of deliberate human agency.

This "natural" state of the cannibals is first and foremost one of simplicity, specifically symbolized by their nudity. (This association between "savages," "nature," and "nudity" already appears in Montaigne's preface, when he projects himself depicted as such.) Nowhere does he make the point more starkly than in the ironic concluding sentence of the essay, where he dismisses the relevance of the cannibals' example because, after all, they don't wear *haut-de-chausses*—baggy, knee-length trousers in fashion at the time. Fashion is indeed one of Montaigne's bugaboos, a symptom of all that is wrong with the world around him: "The current fashion in clothing makes [us] condemn the previous one on the spot, with such great resolution and universal assent that you might say that it is a sort of mania that overturns reason."[26] If adherence to "custom," however irrational, is a stabilizing force, "fashion" dictates constant and even more irrational change, appealing to vanity and, worst of all, inviting invidious social distinctions. This relationship between clothing (or its absence) and social hierarchy is a constant theme of Montaigne's, particularly in the earlier essays contemporary with "Of Custom." Another essay, "Of Sumptuary Laws," suggests that such laws designed "to regulate the mad and vain expenses on foodstuffs and clothing would seem to be contrary to their purpose," valorizing the very things they purport to limit.[27] In the essay "Of the Inequality among Us," he ironizes: "We praise a horse for its vigor and adroitness . . . not its harness; a greyhound for its speed, not its collar. . . . Why, assessing a man, should you assess him all wrapped up?"[28] In yet another essay, "On the Practice of Clothing Oneself," he relates an anecdote about a nobleman in winter who confronts a scantily clad beggar and asks how he can bear the cold. The beggar answers that the nobleman, after all, leaves his face uncovered—as for the beggar, he is all face![29]

The cannibals, then, live in a state of natural equality, where individuals are distinguished by their moral qualities and not by artificial social distinctions. Montaigne gives the cannibals the last word, citing the remarks of some of the Tupinamba who were taken to Rouen for the king's amusement. They had expressed their amazement that hulking, strong, bearded men would docilely follow the orders of a child (Charles IX and his Swiss guard), and that the many indigent beggars did not slit the throats of their rich neighbors who flaunted their abundant possessions. The passage, however, is certainly not meant as a call to social revolution. There remains a constant tension in the *Essays*. On one hand, Montaigne constantly insists that social rank in no way corresponds to moral worth, occasionally by lauding the wisdom of the common folk, and more often by lambasting the mediocrity of the aristocracy. On the other hand, Montaigne makes it painfully clear that the lesson of the Wars of Religion is that it is always worse to rock the boat than to accept the established status quo, however flawed. The cannibals, like the ancient Greeks and Romans, are not so much an ideal to emulate (as if, he laments, he and his contemporaries would ever be capable of such a feat) as a standard by which to measure our own insufficiency.

But the simplicity of the cannibals is not only social but also intellectual, and Montaigne needs to take pains to argue that this is not merely stupidity: "Lest one think that all this is done by simple and servile obedience to their usage and by the impression of authority of their ancient custom, without discourse and without judgment, and that they have such stupid souls that they can take no other course, let me cite certain examples of their capacities." The examples he cites are songs—a song of defiance, sung by a captive about to be eaten, but also a love song, about which he finds "nothing barbarous." On the contrary, he characterizes it as "wholly Anacreontic"— that is, in the style of Anacreon, a Greek lyric poet much admired by Montaigne's contemporaries. Even the Tupi language sounds vaguely Greek to Montaigne. This is high praise indeed, though he also awards similar kudos to French popular songs: "Popular and purely natural poetry [he specifically cites "the villanelles of Gascony and the songs brought back to us from nations which have no knowledge of science, not even writing"] has naivete and grace by which it can be compared to the principal beauty of perfect poetry according to the rules of art."[30] The natural simplicity of the cannibals' poetry guarantees, as it were, the pertinence of their simple morality— "valor against the enemy and friendship for their wives" are the two essential maxims—and their simple religion: "They believe that souls are immortal, and that those which have deserved favor from the gods should be lodged in the place in the sky where the sun rises; the accursed, towards the west." The fact that their religious beliefs can be reduced to a single sentence speaks volumes. These articles of faith, broadly consistent with Christian morality, are enough, Montaigne implies. The Wars of Religion, fought over doctrinal issues, are proof of the evils of subtlety. To this, Montaigne adds that there are prophets who from time to time come down from the surrounding mountains, but if their prophecies turn out to be false, "they are hacked into a thousand pieces if they are caught." Montaigne heartily approves. One can only suspect that he has in mind the religious demagogues, Catholic or Protestant, of sixteenth-century France, the false prophets of his own day and age.

This taste for simplicity, one that assimilates the cannibals to the "simple" folk of Montaigne's France, is even reflected in Montaigne's account of the sources of his information. He claims to base the essay on the account of one of his servants who lived in Antarctic France for ten or twelve years,

presumably as a trader in brazil wood.[31] Montaigne qualifies his informant
as "simple and crude [*grossier*]," an ambivalent characterization. Simplicity
is a virtue, which the informant would presumably share with the cannibals
among whom he lived. Crudity is admittedly a less flattering trait; this is
not a word that Montaigne ever uses in reference to the Brazilians, though
he uses it in another essay to categorize himself: "All is coarse [*grossier*] in
me; I lack gentility and beauty."[32] Montaigne compares the reliability of
his informant to the testimony of "subtle people" (*fines gens*). Such subtle
people are more observant, but the problem is that they generally have axes
to grind. They will embroider a story to fit their theory, and consequently
they cannot be trusted.

It has been pointed out that, in this particular instance, Montaigne is as
disingenuous as the *fines gens* he criticizes. In fact, his account relies heavily
on previously published sources, the descriptions of André Thévet and especially of Jean de Léry.[33] Of course, by conveniently ignoring his published
sources, Montaigne uses his informant as yet another example of the virtues
of simplicity, the very virtues that condemn us as the real "barbarians" in
comparison to the cannibals. Yet the untutored informant, precisely because
he is a fellow Frenchman, allows Montaigne to introduce a more nuanced
appreciation of "simplicity" than his example of the cannibals would allow.
The "crude" informant is, after all, a "crude" observer. His testimony falls
distinctly short of the ideal; better a reliable account that lacks detail than
an elaborate account with spurious details. Indeed, the limited virtues of the
"crude" informant are offset at the end of the essay, when Montaigne relates
how, during the "visit" of several Tupi to Rouen, he spoke to one of them at
length, "but I had a translator [*truchement*] who followed me so poorly and
was so incapable of grasping my imagination because of his stupidity that
I could scarcely obtain any satisfaction." Apparently, simplicity sometimes
is stupidity.

The essay "Of Cannibals" is structured around this dichotomy between
"simplicity" and what one might label "subtlety," "cleverness," or "finesse"—
but *not* "complexity," the obvious inverse of "simplicity" in the nineteenth
or twentieth centuries. Other essays of Montaigne suggest a more complex tripartite scheme. The essay "Of Vain Subtleties" praises the religion
of "simple spirits, less curious and less educated," who obey the precepts
of the faith without question; and also of great minds—"*grands esprits*"—
those who "through long religious investigation, penetrate a deeper and
abstruse light of the scriptures." Error is the fruit of those who are no longer
simple and yet not wise. "The mixed breed who have disdained the first seat
of the ignorance of letters and who have not been able to reach the other

(their ass between two saddles, of where I, like so many others, find myself) are dangerous, inept, and importunate; they are the ones who trouble the world."[34] Montaigne applies similar strictures to his choice of historians. On one hand, simple historians who relate everything they see and hear (he cites the medieval chronicler Froissart as an example); on the other, those with the discrimination to choose the more plausible of two conflicting accounts, and who "know how to choose what is worthy of being known"— notably "virtually all the Greeks and Romans." In between the two are those "who give themselves the right to judge, and thus incline History to their fancy."[35] Poetry, too, as we have seen, obeys the same rules; Brazilian songs and popular ballads on one hand, Greek odes on the other, are worthy of appreciation. What lies between is "mediocre" in every sense of the word.

In short, Montaigne's moral, intellectual, and aesthetic universe is characterized by poles of naive simplicity and of accomplished excellence, with mediocrity in between. The first pole is epitomized by the cannibals, the second by the Greeks and Romans at their best. By either standard, Montaigne's world (and he resolutely includes himself) falls dreadfully short. Granted, "simple" French peasants and craftsmen are sometimes assimilated to the cannibal pole, though it is difficult for Montaigne to sustain any such assimilation too systematically. It is, after all, considerably easier to idealize people who live far enough away. Nor is Montaigne entirely contemptuous of his more distinguished contemporaries, but he readily admits his admiration for the likes of Machiavelli, Guiccardini, Bodin, Rabelais, and of course his dearest friend, Etienne de la Boetie, whose death left a void in Montaigne's life that the *Essays* could only partially replace. Within this system, the ancients are nonetheless superior to the cannibals, just as the truly learned are superior to the naive. In Montaigne's later essay "Of Coaches," where he deplores the conquest of Peru and of Mexico by the Spanish, he nonetheless regrets that they weren't conquered instead by Alexander the Great or some other distinguished Greek or Roman conqueror. The ancients would more gently have tutored their "savage" charges, fostering their "simple" virtues and teaching them their own. The Spanish, instead, have nothing to teach but their own corrupt ways—not that Montaigne would suggest that the French would be any better. In an image which to our tastes is disconcerting, he suggests that the "new" world is still in its infancy, still learning its ABCs.[36] The comparison evokes for us the egregious, hackneyed assimilation of so-called "savages" to "children," calling for paternalism at best, rough discipline (for their own good!) at worst. But such a point assumes that "childhood" is being compared to "adulthood." Montaigne has in mind, instead, the passage from "infancy" to "maturity" to "senescence." Montaigne's paradigm of maturity is embodied by the Greeks and Romans. His French and Spanish contemporaries are decrepit, "corrupt" in every sense of the word, decaying, and decadent.

If the *Essays* constitute a simultaneous self-representation and self-evaluation, Montaigne condemns himself, with the twin beacons of the cannibals and the ancients, to mediocrity. The *Essays* themselves, he insists, inhabit this middle world between two saddles: "If these essays were worthy of being judged, it would happen, in my opinion, that they would scarcely please common and vulgar minds, nor singular and excellent ones; the former would not understand enough, the second would understand too much; they could survive in the middle region."[37] He characterizes the essays more crudely as "the excrements of an old mind—sometimes hard, sometimes soft, always undigested," and suggests that there ought to be laws against "inept and useless writers" such as himself, just as there are laws against vagabonds. Still, he moderates his self-condemnation by adding that "in a time where acting wickedly is so common, just acting uselessly is almost praiseworthy."[38] Montaigne lacks the courage of the cannibals or of the Spartans at Thermopylae; he is no leader of men, in war or in statecraft; his thought is inconsistent and lacks real depth; his writing lacks the naive simplicity of the cannibals' songs without achieving the elegance of Virgil or Tacitus. The cannibals, along with the Greeks and Romans, are all that he is not. Above all, Montaigne finds the Europe of his own time to be profoundly unheroic, including its leaders, Henri III and Henri of Navarre, whom he knew personally and who seem to have had a higher opinion of Montaigne than he had of himself. Even his virtues are signs of weakness. His good nature is only a lack of ambition, his horror of cruelty a lack of nerve. "It is a boon to be born in a very depraved century; for, by comparison to others, you can earn a reputation for virtue at a bargain rate."[39]

FOUR

Climactic Harmonies: Bodin

"Jean Bodin is among the good authors of our time, with far better judgment than the crowd of scribblers of his century, and he merits our consideration."

—Montaigne, *Essays*, II, 32

The creation of anthropology as a modern discipline in the mid-nineteenth century was in large measure the work of lawyers—Maine, McLennan, Morgan—seeking to develop a comparative framework within which to evaluate European institutions, especially "family" and "government." This kind of perspective, comparing the institutions of "modern" Europe not only to those of the "ancient" world but also to non-Europeans, already had a long history, one in which lawyers and legal issues played an equally central role. Montesquieu's *Spirit of Laws* in the mid-eighteenth century is the most obvious example (see chapter 8), but this tradition of thought can be traced much further back, particularly to sixteenth-century France.

The remarkable development of a comparative perspective in sixteenth-century France grew out of the humanist critique of scholastic jurisprudence.[1] Initially, humanist scholars in fifteenth-century Italy, most notably Lorenzo Valla and Angelo Poliziani, had been concerned with challenging scholastic interpretations of Justinian's *Institutes* on philological grounds. In fact, the definitive and authoritative status of the code itself quickly fell prey to criticism on similar grounds. It became increasingly clear that the code was a sloppy and inconsistent compilation of laws that had been formulated at different times and in different contexts. While the aim of early critics, particularly in Italy, was to perfect the Roman code, such a critique ultimately challenged the universal authority of the code itself, notably in France, where the persistent application of common law in many domains called into question the relevance of Roman law for French jurisprudence.

Such issues of jurisprudence were directly relevant to the deep religious and political divides that split France in the sixteenth century. Most obviously, Huguenot intellectuals were particularly receptive to challenges to the universal authority of Roman law, just as they refused to accept the universal authority of the Roman Catholic Church. Moreover, Catholics in France were also deeply divided among themselves, with the ultra-Catholic League under the leadership of the duke of Guise eventually entering into an open revolt against the monarchy. Intellectuals loyal to the monarchy, especially those who were attempting to broker a compromise between Protestants and Catholics, were equally drawn to Gallican ideas of French legal specificity which would limit, without denying it, the authority of the Church, especially in the legal and political domain.

These controversies engendered a remarkable corpus of writings, not only about law and religion but also about history and politics. Out of these writings emerged the formulation of the notion of legal relativism, most clearly enunciated by François Hotman, one of the most radical Huguenot critics of the Justinian code:

> The learned men of every age have observed and voiced approval of the rule that the laws should be accommodated to the form and condition of the commonwealth, not the commonwealth to the laws . . . consequently, the laws of one monarchy are often useless to another, just as medicines are not all suitable to all men whatsoever without consideration of their sex, their age, and nationality (cited in Franklin 1963:46–47).

Admittedly, taken by itself, the doctrine of relativism was simply the ideological justification for the declaration of French independence from the religious, legal, and political interference of Rome. However, it could also constitute the conceptual framework for systematic comparative inquiry in the fields of history and, very anachronistically speaking, ethnology. After all, in a period of religious and political upheaval, in a bitter and often vicious three-way struggle for control in France, it hardly sufficed to assert that French laws were most suitable for France; one had also to demonstrate which laws and why. Presumably, a thorough comparative study of institutions across space and time could determine precisely which ones were best suited to any particular place or, alternatively, whether any principles of human society were universally applicable. Not surprisingly, in the humanist culture of the sixteenth century, classical antiquity occupied pride of place. At the same time, there was an explosion of travel accounts, and especially of compilations of voyages, beginning with Giovanni Battista Ramusio's three-volume *Delle navigationi et viaggi* (1550–53).[2]

Undoubtedly the most ambitious of all the French sixteenth-century thinkers to attempt such a broad comparative enterprise was Jean Bodin.[3] Comparison is central to three of his major works. The *Method for the Easy Comprehension of History*, published in 1565, details a program for reading history and evaluating historians with the aim of drawing useful examples and counterexamples. The *Six Books of the Republic* (1576), the most influential of all Bodin's works, attempts to define and evaluate principles of government from an entirely secular perspective. The *Colloquium of the Seven Sages about the Secrets of the Sublime* was written in 1588 but remained unpublished and unpublishable at the time; it is a dialogue about religion between five proponents of different religions, one skeptic, and one advocate of "natural religion."

The scope of the *Method* is intended to be nothing less than universal. Indeed, Bodin proposes a program of reading that moves from the most general to the most particular, from works of universal history to increasingly particular accounts. At the end of the book he meticulously and encyclopedically lists all the historians and works he has consulted and which he recommends. Not surprisingly, the list includes virtually all the historians of classical antiquity, along with ecclesiastical historians and chroniclers of the various western European nations, from Gregory of Tours to Macchiavelli and Guicciardini. More surprisingly, he includes works on Hungary, Poland, Bohemia, Slavonia, and Scandinavia; a considerable literature on Islam (including translations of the Qur'an), the Arabs, and the Turks. Finally, as concerns the rest of the world, he notes wryly, "We ought to collect the remnants of other works just as gems from the mud, if better are lacking" (1945:78). On central Asia, he cites Marco Polo and his contemporary, the Armenian Hayton, neither of whom he finds particularly reliable. On the Americas, he notes Columbus, Vespucci, and Cadamosto, among others. Bodin's interest in the New World is quite limited, certainly as compared to that of his contemporary Montaigne. No mention is made in the *Method* or subsequent works of the ill-fated French attempt to colonize Antarctic France, now Brazil; Bodin fails to cite André Thévet's *The Singularities of Antarctic France*, which was published in 1557, well before any of Bodin's major works.[4] Marco Polo notwithstanding, Bodin is equally indifferent to Cathay and the East Indies. Africa, on the other hand, was to excite his curiosity and imagination. Among the historians he cites most often and most favorably is Leo Africanus, a North African who traveled throughout the Maghreb,

Egypt, and West Africa before he was taken captive by pirates, sold as a slave, converted to Christianity, and ultimately acquired by the pope, in whose service he wrote his *Description of Africa*, which "holds the unwilling reader by the unceasing delight of new things" (1945:80).[5] Bodin heaps similar praise on Francisco Alvarez, a Portuguese Jesuit who, "with much greater faith and diligence [than Marco Polo], first wrote the affairs of the Ethiopians, which now are approved by foreigners and the best writers and are not read without great pleasure" (1945:79). He classes both Leo Africanus and Alvarez, along with Strabo and Pausanias, as "geographistorians" who "treat history along with geography" (ibid.).

Such praise from Bodin can hardly be taken for granted. In fact, much of the *Method* is devoted to guiding the reader in discerning bias on the part of historians, as a means of evaluating their reliability on any particular matter. It is in this context that he first elaborates his theory of climates. If different climates predispose their inhabitants to different temperaments, this can be used as a grid to evaluate different historians and the peoples they describe. The same theory is again exposed in the *Six Books of the Republic*, with even more explicitly relativist implications: different forms of government are suited to different peoples according, at least in part, to the climate in which they live.

Bodin's theory quite explicitly takes its inspirations from Greek thinkers, notably Hippocrates and especially Aristotle.[6] Like Aristotle, Bodin marks a major division between a cold north, a hot south, and an intermediate temperate zone, to which he assigns very precise latitudinal points of reference; unlike some subsequent writers who continued to adopt this kind of climatological perspective, he remained keenly aware that directional distinctions are reversed south of the equator. For Bodin, the dominant contrast between north and south is echoed by divisions between west and east, as well as between mountains and valleys. Bodin's explanation for these differences was that northern cold generated an interior bodily heat: ". . . The strength of inward heat brings it about that those who live in northerly lands are more active and robust than the southerners. . . . The further men move from the equator, the larger they grow, as in the land of the Patagonians, who are called giants, in the very same latitude as the Germans" (1945:92–93). Such differences in strength and military prowess explained why the English could so successfully invade France to the south, but always failed to subdue the Scots to the north. Their inner heat also enabled northerners to consume large quantities of alcohol. In general, "the northerners cannot control their appetites and furthermore are regarded as intemperate, suspicious, perfidious, and cruel" (1945:101).

If northern cold was favorable to the development of the body, southern heat had opposite effects: "Since the body and the mind are swayed in opposite directions, the more strength the latter has, the less has the former; and the more effective a man is intellectually, the less strength of body he has" (1945:98). This was not necessarily a contrast between southern virtue and northern vice; rather, the southerners had vices contrary to those of northerners. They were scheming, vengeful, parsimonious if not avaricious, relentlessly jealous of their wives, and prone to melancholy fits of madness. One way in which Bodin's grid can be read is consistent with Aristotle's consistent preference for the mean: temperate zones, presumably, balance the virtues and vices of excessive heat or cold. Bodin identifies such a zone quite precisely as running from the fortieth to the fiftieth parallel, including "Further Spain, France, Italy, Dacia, Moldavia, Macedonia, Thrace, and the best part of Asia Minor, Armenia, Parthia, Sogdiana, and a large part of Greater Asia" (1945:96). This zone, mediating between the excessive physicality of the north and the excessively abstract intellectuality of the south, is characterized by a sense of practical intelligence, "of men who possess the fine arts of obeying and commanding, who can blunt the cunning of the southerners with their strength and withstand the attack of [northerners] through their wisdom" (1945:98). Admittedly, they also are given over to excessive litigiousness—perhaps not such a terrible vice after all, in the eyes of a lawyer like Bodin. Predictably, France is situated squarely within this ideal temperate zone. On the other hand, it is important to point out that Bodin's scheme does not at all distinguish Europe from the rest of the world. On the contrary, parts of Europe lie within the northern and southern zones, while the temperate zone includes much of Asia. The scheme as such is arguably Gallocentric, but hardly Eurocentric.

In any case, aspects of Bodin's scheme tend to subvert any neat Aristotelian reading. In fact, "north" and "south," as "body" and "mind," are by no means equally evaluated: ". . . Since the mind does excel the body and greater force of genius exists in the south than in the north, there is no doubt that the more able part of the world extends to the south, and that greater virtues [but also, Bodin adds, greater vices!] are found in the southerners than among the Scythians" (1945:109). The same contrast applies, to a lesser degree, to "east" and "west"; here, of course, the categorization is evidently Eurocentric, at least in the literal sense of establishing a point of reference. In the *Republic*, Bodin also, if only in passing uses this east/west scheme in comparative and evaluative terms: "The Spanish have remarked that the peoples of China, the easternmost who exist, are really the most ingenious of men and the most courteous in the world; and that those of

Brazil, the westernmost, are the most barbarous and cruel" (1993:426; my translation).

Southerners are particularly remarkable for their learning: ". . . The southern people, through continued zeal for contemplation . . . , have been promoters and leaders of the highest learning. They have revealed the secrets of nature; they have discovered the mathematical disciplines; finally, they first observed the nature and the power of religion and the celestial bodies (1945:111). . . . It should not seem strange to those who have read history that the ablest philosophers, mathematicians, prophets, and finally all religions in the world have poured forth from those regions as from the most plenteous spring" (1945:113).

Strikingly, Bodin illustrates the religiosity of southerners with examples drawn from his African sources citing the "seven hundred temples [mosques]" of Fez as well as "what Alvarez reported in the history of the Abyssinians about the unheard-of size of the temples, about the infinite number of monks, who walk around, not only in isolated areas but also in the countryside, in crowds, in the market place, and in the camps" (1945:114). Indeed, the entire passage contains an uncharacteristically long evocation of Ethiopian piety, notably of "fasts of the whole people that are plainly incredible if anyone compares them with ours" (ibid.). Admittedly, Bodin continues by declaring "how stupid they are in managing affairs and governing the country," proof that "men of this type [i.e., southerners] are little suited to manage affairs" (1945:114–15); the next passage goes on to suggest, however, that "Scythians"—northerners—are even worse at governing.

Even in the domain of statecraft, Bodin's comparisons between Ethiopia and European nations are by no means invariably to the disadvantage of Africans. In several passages of the *Method*, Ethiopia as well as the Ottoman Empire constitute positive examples, particularly in comparison to Germany. For instance, Bodin extols the merits of hereditary dynasties, such as those of France, as opposed to elective monarchies like that of the Holy Roman Empire. The issue was by no means an empty abstraction at a time when the French monarchy was actively challenged by Protestants on one hand and by the Catholic League on the other. In support of his claim, Bodin asserts: "I suppose, though we seek everywhere, we shall find no better evidence of a well-constituted state than its long continuance. The Abyssinians, who for eight hundred years have held the greatest empire of all Africa, have always sought their kings from one and the same family" (1945:285).

In another passage, Bodin's contrast of Asian and African monarchies to the pretensions of the Holy Roman Empire is even starker. Bodin devotes an entire chapter of the *Method* to the refutation of the claim, based on an interpretation of a passage from the Book of Daniel, that the world has known and will know only four great monarchies: Assyria, Persia, Greece, and Rome. The point of such an assertion was to claim that Germany was the legitimate heir to the Roman empire. To this, Bodin ironizes:

> . . . What has Germany to oppose to the sultan of the Turks? Or which state can more aptly be called a monarchy? This fact is obvious to everyone—if there is anywhere in the world any majesty of empire and of true monarchy, it must radiate from the sultan. He owns the richest parts of Asia, Africa, and Europe, and he rules far and wide over the entire Mediterranean and all but a few of its islands. . . . I shall not discuss the prince of Ethiopia, called by his people Jochan Bellul, that is, precious gem, whose empire is little less than all Europe. What of the emperor of the Tartars, who rules tribes barbarous in their savagery, countless in number, unconquered in strength? If you compare Germany with these, you compare a fly to an elephant. (1945:292–93)

It might seem that Bodin's comments about the "northerly" Germans are a typical example of Gallic Germanophobia. On the contrary, Bodin uses the German case in order to refute any theory of strict climactic determinism. If climate furnishes a set of given predispositions, these can either be reinforced or counteracted by human volition, especially through the effects of systematic training. Witness the Germans, "who as they themselves confess were once not very far from the level of wild beasts. . . . Nevertheless, they have now so far advanced that in the humanities they seem superior to the Asiatics; in military matters, to the Romans; in religion, to the Hebrews; in philosophy, to the Greeks; in geometry, to the Egyptians; in arithmetic, to the Phoenecians; in astrology, to the Chaldeans; and in various crafts they seem to be superior to all peoples" (1945:145). Statecraft remains conspicuously absent from this list of German achievements, but the list is nonetheless impressive.

Ultimately, Bodin rejects strict climactic determinism, for better but also for worse, commenting that "there is no natural goodness so unbounded that it may not be corrupted by a perverse training" (145:146). Even so, his scheme seems alternately to privilege the South (as "mind") over the North (as "body"), or else the temperate zones over northerly and southerly extremes. Yet there remains another way in which Bodin's scheme can be understood, and which does not privilege one region over another. From a global point of view, the virtues of northerners, southerners, and denizens of temperate zones—strength and manual dexterity, speculative intelligence and religiosity, and commercial and political acumen—are complementary. Bodin explicitly relates this complementarity to a literally universal scheme, with analogs in terms of parts of the body, balance of humors, faculties of the soul, social components of the body politic, and the influence of the planets, inter alia. Taken together, the regions taken together constitute "the universal Republic of this world" (1993:424), the virtues and vices of each balancing out those of the others. In the *Republic*, he develops the theme of complementarity:

> . . . The rich commoner agrees better with the poor gentlewoman, and the poor gentleman with the rich commoner woman, and he who has a certain perfection of mind with she who possesses a gracious body, than if they were equal in every respect, just as among merchants there is no association more certain than that of a rich, lazy man with a poor, diligent one, because there is equality and similarity between them: that is to say, equality, because one and the other have some good quality, and similarly, because each has a defect. . . . And so the principal foundation of marriages and of human society rests in amity, which can not be durable without the harmony and mutual concord mentioned above. (1993:568–70)

The notion that harmony is both literally and metaphorically the marriage of opposites is quite consistently applied by Bodin to the intermarriage of peoples from different regions, with potentially salutary effects. For example: "Danes, Saxons, and English mingled with Britons, making them more ferocious, while they themselves became more kindly" (1945:144). He even speculates about what new type of human would result from the intermarriage of Scythians and Ethiopians.

Bodin's dominant metaphor for felicitous complementarity is harmony, specifically music. He makes very literal claims about the power of music, specifically the ability of harmonies in the Lydian and Ionic modes to domesticate the natural savagery of northerners (1993:350). But his most daring expression of the power of harmony and complementarity is the *Colloquium*, a series of six dialogues between seven sages, each of whom represents a different religion or religious viewpoint: a Catholic, a Lutheran, a Calvinist, a Jew, a Muslim, a skeptic, and an advocate of "natural religion"— rather akin to a deist. The book begins with an allusion to Plato, in which the narrator, who is in the service of Coronaeus, the Venetian and Catholic host, reads from Plato's *Phaedo* to the assembled group. But the dialogues are anything but Platonic; there are no clear winners or losers to any particular argument. Indeed, scholars disagree about which character, if any, represents Bodin's own point of view (Kuntz 1975:xliv). Each speaker puts forth his position forcefully and cogently. Bodin's erudition in the domains not only of Catholic and Protestant theology but also of Judaism and Islam, is phenomenal. Bodin is not entirely free from Christian misconceptions about Islam—most notably, he tends to assimilate religious differences among Muslims to Christian "sectarianism"—but on the whole his treatment of Islam is not only sympathetic but accurate. Throughout the book, different clusters of sages agree or disagree with one another, depending on the issue at hand; but, in the end, none of them is swayed from his initial position. From time to time they may all express consensus about one matter or another, but this hardly suggests that the solution would be to seek the common denominator of all faiths; such a solution would be the "natural religion" advocated by the character Toralba, but his is only one voice among the seven.

Bodin's solution is even more heterodox. At one level it would seem to constitute a plea for tolerance. Venice, where the dialogues are set, is clearly meant to be taken as an example: the open practice of Judaism and Orthodox Christianity are permitted, and "it is possible for each man to enjoy liberty provided he does not disturb the tranquility of the state, and no one is forced to attend religious services or prevented from attending" (1975:467). Turkey and Persia are similarly lauded for their tolerance; it is certainly an intentional irony of Bodin's part that the Muslim spokesman, Octavius, is in fact a convert from Christianity, and as such is liable to pursuit by the Inquisition for apostasy. But the conclusion of the *Colloquium* transcends such a vision of tolerance, where in each case one religion is after all given pride of place. Instead, it ends with a utopian vision of "harmony" in the religious sphere that can only arise out of the simultaneous expression of different voices. The book ends with a song, sung to the participants on the order of their host: "Lo, how good and pleasing it is for brothers to live in unity, arranged not in common diatonics or chromatics, but in enharmonics with a certain, more divine modulation" (1975:471). Afterward, the disputants all embrace and continue to live together in harmony and piety, each adhering to his own religion.

This conclusion, that different voices in the religious domain are ultimately the source of a higher form of harmony, remains startling. However, it is fundamental to point out that the musical analogy is quite the opposite of a policy of religious laissez-faire. On the contrary, different voices may just as well create dissonance as harmony, and Bodin is concerned with the exclusion of dissonant voices—those of witches and atheists, those who attempt to deny or subvert the divine order rather than to express it in one register or another. In fact, he wrote an entire book in 1580 titled *The Demon-Mania of Witches* (1995), attempting to refute skeptical arguments contesting the reality of witchcraft and suggesting stratagems for its effective repression. "Harmony" was precisely not an all-inclusive paradigm.

Bodin's grand scheme was intended as an answer to the urgent problems of his era: order and difference. In a France racked by civil war and religious strife, he offered a radical solution, one that sought to distinguish between disorder and diversity in terms of a global scheme that reflected the ultimate order of the universe as divinely created. Disorder—witchcraft and atheism in the religious domain, sedition but also tyranny in the political sphere— was to be suppressed as effectively as possible. However, the diversity that remained, far from threatening order, expressed a "harmonic" order of the highest kind, born of complementarity as opposed to likeness, arguably foreshadowing Durkheim's distinction, centuries later, between "mechanical" and "organic" forms of solidarity.

Bodin's attempts to theorize difference, both in the geographical and the religious domains, are strikingly novel and challenging. His division of the globe into northern, southern, and temperate zones emphatically fails to differentiate Europe from the rest of the world. France, it is true, may lie in the temperate zone—but so do Turkey and Persia. By situating the realm of "mind" as opposed to "body" to the south and to the east, Bodin privileges Africa and Asia in general, and most specifically Turkey, Persia, Morocco, and Ethiopia, all of which compare favorably to Europe in many respects. Bodin's ultimate vision of harmonic complementarity embraces all the world, and hardly suggests pride of place for Europe. In the religious domain it admittedly privileges "Abrahamic" monotheistic religions: Judaism, Islam, and variant doctrinal expressions of Christianity. Even here, "pagan" forms of worship are by no means rejected out of hand, even if they are relegated to relative theological inferiority. In any case, for the sixteenth century, Bodin's scope is about as far-reaching as one could expect. His solution is strikingly different from that of Montaigne, who uses difference in his essay "Of Custom" to portray a bewildering panoply of contradictory practices, only to conclude that, in the absence of any rational standard for judging, it is wisest to stick with one's own established tradition—or, in "Of Cannibals," to use Brazilians as a foil for the failings of sixteenth-century Europe. In his refusal to reduce difference to the contrast of "We" and "They," Bodin is ultimately more disconcerting; his utopian vision of a harmony of peoples and religions, literally in tune with the harmony of the universe, was hardly to find an echo in the following centuries, although the project of a comparative universal history was to be resurrected in the eighteenth century, and ultimately by another generation of lawyers in the construction of Victorian anthropology.

FIVE

St. Confucius: The Jesuits in China

"Now the Chinese Empire, which challenges Europe in cultivated area and certainly surpasses her in population, vies with us in many other ways in almost equal combat, so that now they win, now we."

—Gottfried Wilhelm Leibniz, preface to the *Novissima Sinica*

The grand project of a comparative and historicist theory of society that flourished in late-sixteenth-century France disappeared abruptly from the horizon in the seventeenth century. Arguably, its eclipse coincided with the triumph of absolutist monarchies. The idea that different forms of law and government were appropriate to different times and places implied that the monarchy itself was a contingent institution—hardly a message that monarchs wanted to hear. Some of the conclusions of sixteenth-century historians and social theorists were deliberately suppressed. As late as 1714, Nicolas Fréret was imprisoned in the Bastille for challenging the Trojan origins of the French monarchy.[1]

But it is not fair to lay all the blame at the feet of monarchs. Prevailing intellectual currents were explicitly hostile to this kind of enterprise. This is the lesson that Descartes draws from human diversity:

It is true that, while I devoted myself to considering the mores of other peoples, I hardly found anything to reassure me, and I remarked therein as much diversity as I had previously in the opinions of philosophers, so that the greatest profit that I obtained thereby was that, seeing several things which, however ridiculous and extravagant we consider them, do not fail to be commonly accepted and approved by great peoples, I learned not to believe in anything too firmly that had only persuaded me through example and custom, and in this way I freed myself from many errors which can obscure our natural reason, and which render us less capable of rational understanding.[2]

The bewildering diversity of custom which had led Montaigne to despair of human reason was, for Descartes, a justification for trusting to reason alone. Though Descartes may not have applied his radical deductivism to social theory, the principal social philosophers of the seventeenth century adopted precisely such an a priori approach. Beginning with Hobbes, social contract theorists developed a hypothetical model of the "state of nature" which corresponded only very tangentially, if at all, with empirical cases. Locke's "natural" rights to life, liberty, and property were in principle rationally intelligible to all reasonable people of good will. The opponents of social contract theory, the adherents of the theory of the divine right of kings, were even less inclined to any empirical, historicist, or comparative approach. The outstanding counterexample to this trend is Spinoza's *Theological-Political Treatise*, in which he applies to scripture the same kind of critical perspective to which the Italian (and later French) humanists had applied to Roman law. But Spinoza's theories in this and other domains were almost universally reviled, not only in his own time but throughout the following century.[3]

Paradoxically, this aversion to comparative theory in no way signaled a lack of interest in the rest of the world. The late sixteenth century had seen the emergence of a new genre, encyclopedic compendia of voyages: Ramusio in Venice, Hakluyt in England, De Bry and Hulsius in Frankfurt.[4] These works continued to be re-edited in the seventeenth century, and the enterprise was continued, notably by Samuel Purchas in England and by Melchisédech Thévenot in France. Among the most assiduous and influential contributors to this genre of travel literature were the Jesuits.

Needless to say, the Jesuits had no truck for the kind of comparative theory elaborated by the likes of Bodin, much less of Spinoza. Yet, in spite of their ideological commitments to the contrary, there was a real, if sometimes submerged, "elective affinity" between Jesuit strategies of proselytizing and the comparative perspective. In the first place, the Jesuits, precisely because they were such a recent order, needed to resort to more aggressive tactics to make their mark on the Church. The opening up not only of the New World but of the sea route to Asia provided them with a signal opportunity to assert their leadership, if not their importance, by bringing Asians and Americans into the fold of the Church, additional recruits to the army set against the recalcitrant Protestants of northern Europe. Of course, the Jesuits were hardly the only order engaged in the process of attempting to convert the peoples of the non-European world. Yet, from the very beginning, they were spectacularly successful in outpublishing their rivals.

It is instructive to compare sixteenth-century accounts of Mexico, where the Jesuits were in fact late arrivals following on the steps of Franciscans, Dominicans, and Augustinians, some of whom left extremely detailed (and for modern historians indispensable) accounts of the peoples they encountered. The most notable of these—the works of the Dominican Diego Duran and of the Franciscans Diego de Landa and, above all, Bernardino de Sahagun—were left in manuscript form and were never meant for publication.[5] Indeed, they were unpublished until the nineteenth century, and entirely escaped the notice of avid seventeenth- and eighteenth-century consumers of travel literature. This was no accident. The detailed accounts of pagan religious practices were intended for in-house consumption. Their purpose was precisely to help preachers identify concealed attempts to perpetuate those practices, so that they could stamp them out more effectively. De Landa, whose account provides us with much of what we know about the religion of the Maya of Yucatan at the time of the conquest, personally presided over the burning of Maya manuscripts.[6] At the same time, in 1590, a Jesuit, Jose de Acosta, published his *Historia natural y moral de las Indias*, describing both Mexico and Peru—the section on Mexico based, in part, on Duran's manuscript (Acosta 2002).[7] The work was promptly translated into Italian in 1596; into French, German, and Dutch in 1598; and into English in 1604.[8]

As propaganda, Jesuit publications served multiple purposes. They might serve to attract the attention of influential persons who could serve as patrons to the Jesuits at royal courts of Catholic monarchs. More generally, they could incite donations to further the effort to convert the populations of Asia and the Americas. (Africa, with the important exception of Ethiopia, largely escaped their attention.) Last but not least, the Jesuits carefully cultivated a heroic image, attracting some of the best and the brightest of their pupils as missionaries ready to risk martyrdom to bring the faith to the remoter parts of the globe. (Since they were the only order without a female branch, such appeals were intended exclusively for men, but they sometimes inspired women's vocations anyway, notably the Ursulines who came to Quebec in the seventeenth century.) Indeed, Jesuit accounts of their failures, appealing to the mystique of martyrdom, could be as effective as testaments of their triumphs. And there was no lack of failures, most spectacularly the explusion of the Jesuits from Japan and the massacre of their converts. This stream of publications continued throughout the seventeenth and eighteenth centuries, at least until the order itself was suppressed by papal decree in 1773. From 1702 until 1776, the order regularly published an annual edition of *Edifying and Curious Letters, Written in Foreign Missions by Several Missionaries of the Company of Jesus.* The edifying parts related the progress of the missionaries in converting their charges—or their heroic attempts in spite of their lack of progress, as the case might be. The curious parts, on the other hand, contained information about all these peoples—in the Far East, in India, in Ethiopia, in the Levant, and in North as well as South America.[9] The quality of the information was such that the *Edifying and Curious Letters* found a place in the libraries of many of the Enlightenment intellectuals— Montesquieu, Turgot, Voltaire—who were more often than not hostile to the Jesuit cause. It is no accident that Acosta's work was translated in England and Holland as well as in France and Italy. Protestants were as likely as Catholics to accept the scholarly authority of the Jesuit accounts of Asia and the Americas. Indeed, Protestants were sometimes more likely to endorse the authority of the Jesuits, as they were unconcerned by quarrels internal to the Catholic Church: attacks on the Jesuits by Jansenists on one hand, supporters of rival orders on the other.

This sustained Jesuit interest in the peoples they were attempting to convert, as evidenced by the number and quality of their publications from the mid-sixteenth to the mid-eighteenth centuries, was hardly entirely disinterested. It was their deliberate strategy to adapt their message to their audience. Such a strategy called for a comparative approach, at least implicitly. Of course there was no question of suggesting that different societies called for different forms of government, much less different religions; rather, the Jesuits called for different modes of proselytizing. Acosta, for example, distinguished between settled states and empires, notably the Mexica and the Inca, on one hand and nomadic populations, the Chichimec and the Otomi, on the other. If Acosta, like so many after him, was convinced that nomads had to be sedentarized and domesticated in order to prepare them for conversion, he also suggested that the institutions of settled people provided a useful, indeed admirable foundation: "The most diligent and learned men who have penetrated and attained their secrets, their ancient style, and their government judge them in a very different way [from the false opinion that is commonly held about them, that they are brutes and bestial folk], amazed that there could have been so much order and reason among them."[10] Moreover, such peoples had notions of a supreme god, even if they also practiced idolatry; their religious practices included sacrifices, priests, sacraments, and prophets, admittedly simulacra of the institutions of the true faith, instruments of the devil to deceive their practitioners, but such practices could be turned to good use and serve to prepare such peoples for received religion.

In passing, Acosta also compared the Mexica and Inca to the Chinese and Japanese, specifically in terms of knowledge and systems of writing. However, the situation of Jesuits in the Far East was entirely different from Mexico and Peru. The political institutions of the Chinese and Japanese were hardly subject to European overrule. Jesuits—and other orders, for that matter—needed permission to preach in the first place, even before deciding how best to pitch their message. Until the establishment of a Portuguese enclave in Macao in 1557, it was impossible for the Jesuits (or any other preaching order) to gain a foothold in China. After unsuccessful attempts to obtain permission to reside elsewhere, the Jesuits established a mission in Macao in 1565. Initially, the aims of the mission were modest indeed, ministering largely to Europeans and a handful of Chinese closely associated with Europeans who were encouraged to speak Portuguese and dress in European attire.[11]

Clearly, such a missionary strategy was ill-suited to converting the entire population of China to Roman Catholicism. The fact did not escape the attention of the Jesuit hierarchy, notably Alessandro Valignano, visitor of the Indian missions based in Goa, with authority over all the Jesuit missions in Asia. Valignano spent ten months in Macao in 1557 and 1558 (not by design; he was waiting for favorable winds to sail for Japan) and proceeded to recruit missionaries who would be capable of adopting a more enterprising stance, in particular by learning to speak, read, and write in Chinese. The first of these was Michele Ruggieri, who arrived in Macao in 1579. Ruggieri was immediately faced with the question of how he should integrate himself into Chinese society, and of what kind of persona he should assume in order to make his mission both comprehensible and acceptable to his potential converts. He arrived at a solution, apparently suggested by a Chinese official, which was as ingenious as it proved ineffectual: the garb of a Buddhist monk.[12] By shaving his head and wearing a simple robe, Ruggieri simultaneously communicated the religious nature of his vocation and his consequent commitment to a life of asceticism. But in order to proselytize, the missionaries needed at the very least the permission to establish themselves in locations outside the enclave of Macao, and this required the intercession of relatively high-ranking officials whose patronage could vastly improve the mission's chances of success, but whose opposition could put the missionaries in a very delicate if not untenable position. In late Ming China, Buddhist monks were not for the most part highly respected in official circles, and, partly as a result, the mission's progress remained modest indeed.

Matteo Ricci, another protégé of Valignano, arrived a few years later in 1582. Ricci eventually adopted a very different garb (and persona): that of a Confucian scholar. This was in effect the dress and manner of the elite, and specifically of the officials whose backing he needed.[13] The strategy proved successful and effectively provided a paradigm for Jesuit involvement in China for the next century. The ties which Ricci cultivated among the literati allowed the Jesuits to expand their activities farther and farther away from their base in Macao, until Ricci was eventually admitted to present his respects to the throne, though the emperor Wanli was not actually present at the time. In addition, Ricci was able to convert a few literati to Catholicism. It must be emphasized that this adoption of the persona of a Confucian scholar was by no means simply a matter of apparel. Ricci needed to demonstrate a thorough knowledge of the written and spoken language, and of the Confucian classics, not to mention the elaborate etiquette of the elite. The hope, of course, was to convert Chinese society from the top down, beginning, if not with the emperor himself, at least with a significant number of members of the most influential strata of society.

The enterprise hinged in no little measure on the Jesuit attitude towards the core Confucian texts. Mastery of these texts was the defining character of the literati with whom Ricci mingled, not to mention the basis for the system of examinations providing access to official positions. Not only did Ricci have to know and understand the texts thoroughly—a task for which his particular interest in the arts of memory turned out to be indispensable[14]— but in a profound way he had to accept them. Ricci was to reach an understanding of the Confucian classics such that they could be fully compatible with Roman Catholicism. As Ricci was well aware, such an interpretation was at odds with the interpretations of many of his Chinese contemporaries. Be this as it may, the very possibility that Confucianism and Catholicism could be reconciled allowed the Jesuits to preach Christianity without in any way calling into question the ideological underpinnings of the empire.[15]

Ricci died in 1610 before publishing his account of his mission in China. The task was entrusted to Nicolas Trigault, who had arrived in China the year after Ricci's death, only to be sent back to Europe two years later in order to secure more backing for the mission in the form of missionaries, funds, and independence from the jurisdiction of the Jesuit mission in Japan. In the process, he translated Ricci's book from Italian into Latin, at times amending it substantially if not somewhat tendentiously,[16] and prefacing the diary with a very extensive description of China based on Ricci's and others' observations. The book was rapidly translated into German, French, Spanish, and (paradoxically!) Italian, with excerpts in English included in Samuel Purchas's popular anthology of travel literature, *Purchas, His Pilgrimes*. It was "the most influential description of China to appear in the first half of the seventeenth century," and, perhaps more importantly, it "provided European readers with more, better organized, and more accurate information about China than was ever before available."[17] The book established the reputation of the Jesuits as European experts on China, not only for the duration of the seventeenth century but for most of the eighteenth. Anyone who chose to write about China—Leibniz, Montesquieu, and Voltaire, among others—either echoed the Jesuits or deliberately contradicted them.

The Ricci/Trigault description was published,[18] it must be stressed, as part of a propaganda campaign to rally support for the Jesuit mission. As such, its depiction of China was hardly disinterested. The image of China was globally favorable, especially as concerned the governing elite whose support the Jesuits so assiduously cultivated. Indeed, a century later, Samuel Johnson, translating the journey of yet another Jesuit, Jeronimo Lobo, to Ethiopia, prefaced his volume by praising Lobo's account, suggesting that "the reader will here find . . . no Chinese perfectly polite, and completely skilled in all sciences. . . ."[19]

In all fairness, Ricci and Trigault were by no means naively enthusiastic about all things Chinese, but this lent all the more plausibility to the narrative. Trigault's account begins by emphasizing China's vast size and population: [20]

> Considering its vast stretches and the boundaries of its lands, it would at present surpass all the kingdoms of the earth, taken as one, and as far as I am aware, it has surpassed them during all previous ages.[21]
>
> [In 1599], the adult population, of which every member was subject to royal taxes, numbered 58,550,801. This number does not include the women of the country, nor does it include the men who are exempt from taxation, such as soldiers, eunuchs, the relatives of the king, magistrates, scholars, and many others.[22]

There follows a long assessment of Chinese agriculture and food in which Trigault compares China to Europe in a surprisingly understated way. He notes that rice is the staple crop and that "the Chinese harvest two and sometimes three crops of such plants every year, owing not only to the fertility of the soil and the mildness of the climate but in great measure to the industry of the people" (p. 16). He notes the abundance and variety of fruits and vegetables, but also the absence of olives, and the use of sesame oil instead of olive oil. (One cannot help suspecting that this was more likely remarked by the Italian Ricci than by the Flemish Trigault, who might not so readily miss olive oil.) He remarks that the Chinese cultivate an abundance of beautiful flowers unknown in Europe, but also that they take more delight in their visual than in their aromatic properties, and are unskilled in making perfumes. He prefers European to Chinese wines, conceding nonetheless that rice wine is "not at all unpleasant, though it does not produce the same feeling of warmth as our wines of Europe" (p. 18). Trigault refers to tea as "cia," an Italianized version of the Chinese name; tea was not yet an item of household consumption in Europe, and he finds it "not unpleasant to the taste, being somewhat bitter" (p26). He notes the Chinese preference for pork, but also that, "in spite of this plentiful supply of meat, the flesh of horses, mules, asses, and dogs finds equally as much favor as other meats, and this equine and canine meat is exposed for sale in all the markets. . . . The flesh of game animals, especially that of deer, hares, and other small animals, is common and may be had cheaply" (p. 18). (Such game, in Europe, where poaching was a serious crime, would have been reserved for the aristocracy.) Trigualt underplays the implications for European readers of this ready availability of either dog or deer meat, blandly asserting in another passage that "The Chinese eat about everything that we do, and their food is well prepared" (p. 111). He goes so far as to assert that "the similarity of customs [between Chinese and Europeans] is rather remarkable when we consider their methods of eating and sitting and sleeping, in which they alone of all the nations outside of Europe are quite in accord with the West. Their use of tables, chairs, and beds is wholly unknown to any of the peoples of the states that border on China . . ." (pp. 40–41).[23] This is to say not that he did not meticulously describe the Chinese use of chopsticks, but that he did not use such customs to insist on radical difference.

His comparison of Chinese and European industry is equally nuanced. If, generally speaking, he considers European production to be of superior quality, he furnishes an interesting and astute explanation:

> It should be noted that because these people are accustomed to live sparingly, the Chinese craftsman does not strive to reach a perfection of workmanship in the object he creates, with a view to obtaining a higher price for it. His labor is guided rather by the demand of the purchaser who is usually satisfied with a less finished object. Consequently, they frequently sacrifice quality in their productions, and rest content with a superficial finish intended to catch the eye of the purchaser (p. 30).

In fact, although this is hardly Trigault's intent, his description suggests that production in China in the early seventeenth century was more thoroughly industrial than in Europe, most notably in the cloth trade: "Silk is manufactured on so large a scale that it can readily compete with the European product, though perhaps the latter may be of a higher quality. . . . Their other woven fabrics also find a ready market in Europe, and the price they receive for them is about one third or one fourth of what we pay for a similar product in the West" (p. 20). Thus, for example, Chinese paper is cheaper and more easily available than its European equivalent, though "the best variety here is inferior to many of our own brands" (p. 25). However, Trigault is very impressed with Chinese printing technology and its adaptability to the numerous characters of Chinese script: "The simplicity of Chinese printing is what accounts for the exceedingly large numbers of books in circulation here and the ridiculously low prices at which they are sold" (p. 34). The Jesuits themselves, he is quick to point out, were able to profit from the cheap production of books in order to produce their own literature for the purpose of spreading their message. If Trigault is unimpressed by Chinese glass blowing (or perhaps this is Ricci's voice; this is after all an Italian specialty), his praise for Chinese porcelain foreshadowed the extent of demand for the product in Europe.

This comparison of the material cultures of China and Europe avoids the pitfalls both of rampant Sinophilia and of Eurocentric dismissal of anything alien, but also of the temptation to exoticize China too radically. The description establishes a sort of parity between Europe and China while at the same time maintaining a space for difference. The Chinese eat more or less the same kinds and variety of foods as we do (plus dog, and minus olive oil), on tables and chairs, no less, but with chopsticks.

But such issues are ultimately secondary to the discussions of scholarship, government, and of course religion—all issues that were particularly sensitive, and which touched directly on the strategies the Jesuits employed. Specifically, Ricci's adoption of the persona of a Confucian scholar as a model for Jesuit involvement in China could not help but inflect the ways in which Confucius and his teachings were portrayed. Trigault's first mention of Confucius sets the tone:

> The most renowned of all Chinese philosophers was named Confucius. This great and learned man was born five hundred and fifty-one years before the beginning of the Christian era, lived more than seventy years, and spurred on his people to the pursuit of virtue not less by his own example than by his writings and conferences. His self-mastery and abstemious ways of life have

led his countrymen to assert that he surpassed in holiness all those who in times past, in the various parts of the world, were considered to have excelled in virtue. Indeed, if we critically examine his actions and sayings as they are recorded in history, we shall be forced to admit that he was the equal of the pagan philosophers and superior to most of them (pp. 48–49).

Confucius is first and foremost presented as a moral philosopher, and any association of Confucianism with religious teachings is, in this passage at least, overlooked. He is not only ranked with the best of the pagan philosophers, presumably Plato and Aristotle—high praise indeed from a Jesuit!—but is actually their precursor by a century or so. He qualifies as a righteous pagan, someone whose natural understanding has led him to the truth, at least to that portion of the truth accessible to human understanding alone. Indeed, in another passage, Trigault goes so far as to assert that Confucius and some of his disciples may even have achieved salvation:

One can confidently hope that in the mercy of God, many of the ancient Chinese found salvation in the natural law, assisted as they must have been by that special help which, as the theologians teach, is denied to no one who does what he can toward salvation, according to the light of his conscience. That they endeavored to do this is readily determined from their history of more than four thousand years, which really is a record of good deeds done on behalf of their country and for the common good. *The same conclusion might also be drawn from the books of rare wisdom of their ancient philosophers. These books are . . . filled with the most salutary advice on training men to be virtuous.* In this particular respect, they seem to be quite the equals of our own most distinguished philosophers. (pp. 154–155; my emphasis)

(Note here that the philosophers in question are not necessarily qualified as "pagan.") This is an absolutely remarkable assertion. It suggests not only that Confucius himself may have been saved, but that in the absence of revealed religion his teachings may have led others to salvation.

Not surprisingly, Trigault hastens to add that "he was never venerated with religious rites, however, as they venerate a god" (p. 49). This is no offhand remark, but a crucial assertion for the Jesuits. Indeed, in his discussion of Chinese religious sects, Trigault identifies the "literati" as one of three indigenous varieties, along with the "Sciequia" (Buddhists) and "Laucu" (Taoists). Trigault and subsequent Jesuit writers have little but contempt for the Buddhists and Taoists, responsible in Trigault's opinion for the spread of idolatry and superstition to China, especially but not exclusively among the popular classes. The fact that both Buddhist and Taoist practices included monasticism, and that, as we have seen, Jesuits were initially classified as an analogous sort of monks, no doubt made them even more eager to distinguish themselves from those whom they very definitely considered their rivals.

Confucians, on the other hand, were at least potential allies rather than rivals. As such, Trigault definitely downplays any possible conflict between Confucian and Christian values and practices, as in his detailed description of the rites by which the literati honor (but not, he insists, worship) Confucius:

> The Temple of Confucius is really the cathedral of the upper lettered and exclusive class of the Litterati. The law demands that a temple be built to the Prince of Chinese Philosophers in every city, and in that particular part of the city which has been described as the center of learning. . . . In the most conspicuous place in the temple there will be a statue of Confucius, or if not a statue, a plaque with his name carved in large letters of gold. . . .
>
> With the coming of each new moon and also at the time of the full moon, the magistrates congregate in this temple, together with those of the baccalaureate order, to do honor to their great master. The ritual in this instance is made of bowing and of bending the knees, of the lighting of candles, and the burning of incense. Each year on his birthday and at other times fixed by custom, they offer him dishes of food elaborately prepared and assert their thanks for the doctrines contained in his writings. . . . *They do not recite prayers to Confucius nor do they ask favors of him or expect help from him. They honor him only in the manner mentioned of honoring their respected dead.* (pp. 159–160; my emphasis)

The assertion that these rites have no religious significance was hardly disinterested. Any literati who converted to Christianity were nonetheless required to participate in these rites, or else lose rank and office. Indeed, as the last sentence indicates, Trigault interpreted commemorations of family ancestors in exactly the same way:

> . . . they consider this ceremony as an honor bestowed upon their departed ancestors, just as they might honor them if they were actually living. They do not really believe that the dead actually need the victuals which are placed upon their graves, but they say that they observe the custom of placing them there because it seems to be the best way of testifying their love for their dear departed. . . . This practice of placing food upon the graves of the dead seems

to be beyond any charge of sacrilege and perhaps also free from any taint of superstition, because they do not in any respect consider their ancestors to be gods, nor do they petition them for anything or hope for anything from them. (p. 159)

These assertions turned out to be extremely controversial.

But, of course, it is not enough for Trigault to point out that Confucians worship neither Confucius himself nor their family ancestors. He still must address the question of what they do worship; if nothing at all, this suggests that they are really atheists at heart, an accusation that was readily leveled by European detractors of the Chinese and of their Jesuit admirers. He resorts to depicting Confucianism as a variety of monotheistic natural religion:

> Of all the pagan sects known to Europe, I know of no people who fell into fewer errors in the early ages of their antiquity than did the Chinese. From the very beginning of their history it is recorded in their writings that they recognized and worshiped one supreme being whom they called the King of Heaven, or designated by some other name indicating his rule over heaven and earth. . . . Nowhere do we read that the Chinese created monsters of vice out of this supreme being or from his ministering deities, such as the Romans, the Greeks, and the Egyptians evolved into gods or patrons of the vices. (p. 154)

In other words, if the moral philosophy of the Chinese is the equal of that of the ancients, their religion is indeed superior. However, the pristine nature of ancient Chinese religion did not insulate it from error. For the Jesuits, human knowledge was subject to human error. Over time, "real" Confucian truths were subject to deleterious interpretations and modifications. The irony is that the Jesuits, warriors of the Counter-Reformation, found themselves advocating a sort of Confucian reform in China, a return to the "pristine" texts unadulterated by later generations of interpreters. The utopian result would be a wedding of reformed Confucianism and Roman Catholicism: "One might say in truth that the teachings of this academy, save in some few instances, are so far from being contrary to Christian principles, that such an institution could derive great benefit from Christianity and might be developed and perfected by it" (p. 162).

Religious considerations aside, Trigault makes it clear that the "moral philosophy" of the Confucian literati is intimately connected to the administration of the empire. He describes the examination system in considerable detail, noting what "to Europeans might seem to be a rather strange and perhaps a somewhat inefficient method": that "philosophers" judged examinations not only in their own subject, but also "in military science, in mathematics, or in medicine" (p. 67). Trigault's remarks here are ultimately ambivalent. On one hand, he clearly implies that the Chinese have limited respect for technical expertise, much less practical experience. To suggest that Europeans would find the subjection of military decisions to moral philosophers "strange and perhaps somewhat inefficient" is a considerable understatement. On the other hand, it echoes the Platonic dream of a state under the guidance of philosophers, and it is not difficult to imagine Jesuits seduced by a vision of a realm under the aegis of moral philosophers who had been converted to Christianity.

Indeed, "while recording a few more things in which [Chinese] people differ from the Europeans" (p. 90), Trigault seems to suggest that the predominance of moral over military concerns might have its advantages:

> . . . it seems quite remarkable, when we stop to consider it, that in a kingdom of almost limitless expanse and innumerable population, and abounding in copious supplies of every description, though they have a well-equipped army and navy that could easily conquer the neighboring nations, neither the king nor his people ever think of waging a war of aggression. They are quite content with what they have and are not ambitious of conquest. In this respect they are much different from the people of Europe, who are frequently discontent with their own governments and covetous of what others enjoy. While the nations of the West seem to be entirely consumed with the idea of supreme domination, they cannot even preserve what their ancestors have bequeathed them, as the Chinese have done through a period of some thousands of years. (p. 90)

This is a stunning denunciation of imperialist ambitions. It is quite transparent that Trigault's sympathies in this respect lie entirely with the Chinese, or at least with the idealized version of them he presents, as opposed to his fellow Europeans. Of course, the conversion of the Chinese to Roman Catholicism can itself be understood as a sort of colonial project.[24] Be this as it may, the passage certainly indicates that the relationship between conversion and colonialism needs to be seriously nuanced.

Trigault explicitly relates this aversion to conquest with the preeminence of the literati over the military, "marking a difference from the West [in] that the entire kingdom is administered by the Order of the Learned, commonly known as The Philosophers." As a result, "policies of war are formulated and military questions are decided by the Philosophers only and their advice and counsel has more weight with the king than that of the military leaders" (p. 91). Needless to say, this spurs the ambitious to "prefer the lowest rank in the philosophical order to the highest in the military" (p.92). Trigault suggests that it is perhaps the Chinese temperamental aversion to imperial expansion that explains the subordination of the military to the literati. In any event, he is inclined to see these two phenomena in terms of cause and effect.

The depiction, at least in this section of the text, is of a remarkably orderly government. High office is determined by a strictly regulated system of examinations. Successful candidates are guaranteed a government position for life unless they are found guilty abusing their office. They are promoted and demoted in accordance with regular triennial inspections. All weapons are prohibited within city limits, making the towns, and presumably the realm as a whole, remarkably free from violence, certainly by European standards of the time. In general:

> The order and harmony that prevails among magistrates, both high and low, in the provinces and in the regal Curia is also worthy of admiration. Their attitude toward the king, in exact obedience and in external ceremony, is a cause of wonderment to a foreigner. The literati would never think of omitting certain customary formal visits to one another or the regular practice of freely offering gifts. In the courts and elsewhere, inferiors always bend the knee when speaking to a superior, and address him in the most dignified language. (p. 92)

Other passages in the text serve to qualify, if not subvert, this idealized portrayal. The Jesuits had to master the art of giving and receiving the "customary formal visits" mentioned in the passage above in order to mingle with the literati, not to mention to enjoy any access to the imperial court, and their exasperation at the degree of formality occasionally shows through: ". . . They make so much of urbane ceremonies that a great part of their time is wasted in them. To one acquainted with their customs, it really is a source of regret that they do not rid themselves of this external show, in which they far surpass Europeans" (p. 98). Chinese cities are admittedly far safer than European ones, at least as far as physical violence is concerned, but on the other hand "thieves are numerous everywhere . . . it frequently happens that houses are thoroughly ransacked by night marauders. This probably happens because the watchmen themselves are robbers or are in league with the robbers and the result of frequent thieving is that others are engaged to watch the watchmen" (pp. 134–35). As far as theft is concerned,

Trigault finds the Chinese authorities culpable of laxity; in particular, it is never a capital offense.

Indeed, Trigault's description of the administration of justice by the magistrates casts serious doubt on the idealized portrayal of China as an orderly and well-governed realm: "The penal laws of the country do not seem to be too severe, but it seems that as many are illegally put to death by the magistrates as are legally executed" (pp. 144–45). This, he suggests, is because magistrates are relatively free to administer floggings, but these are so vicious that they frequently result in death. Consequently, "the accused will buy off his life by paying a high price to the magistrate, contrary to all law and justice." Indeed, "so great is the lust for domination on the part of the magistrates that scarcely anyone can be said to possess his belongings in security, and everyone lives in continual fear of being deprived of what he has, by a false accusation. . . . [These people} have very little regard for the truth, acting always with great circumspection and very cautious about trusting anyone" (p. 145).

Despite the hesitations and contradictions, this remains overall a positive depiction of China, a paradigm that Sinophiles would repeatedly echo and Sinophobes would consistently contest for the next century and a half.[25] Such a depiction was hardly disinterested. To portray China as an orderly realm and the literati as principled scholars was clearly meant to vindicate the Jesuit strategies of emulating the literati in order to infiltrate their ranks and cultivating close ties with the imperial court. This is not to suggest, however, that the portrait was deliberately dishonest. A consistent feature of Trigault's description is the recurrent if not systematic comparison of Chinese and European ways, whether in the realm of material production, statecraft, philosophy or religion. Only in the domain of religion does Europe (and not all of Europe) detain the ultimate truth, the inevitable yardstick by which Confucian, Buddhist, and Taoist doctrines are measured. In other matters, the comparison is remarkably open-ended, with Trigault sometimes preferring Europe and sometimes China. In this respect, the assessment is remarkably thoughtful and far more balanced than most of its successors.

The approach to converting the Chinese that Ricci pioneered was very rapidly contested within the Catholic Church, and to some extent even within the Jesuit order. In fact, Ricci's hand-picked successor, Nicolò Longobardo, the very man who sent Trigault back to Europe to seek additional funds and manpower for the mission, had serious reservations. However, any such internal disagreements were dwarfed by attacks on the Jesuit mission by its rivals, the Dominicans and the Franciscans. Theological disputes were compounded by international rivalries. The Chinese (and, while they lasted, the Japanese) Jesuit missions were under the authority of the oldest of the Jesuit missions in Asia, the Portuguese enclave of Goa. The Dominicans and Franciscans, on the other hand, were based in the Spanish colony of the Philippines. However, such turf wars involved genuine disagreements over fundamental issues of mission policy revolving around translation and toleration. This issue of translation concerned how, if at all, one might translate "God" into Chinese. The issue is not, of course, a trivial one. It makes a difference whether one prays to "Heaven" or to "the Sky." The fact that the issue was ultimately submitted to the arbitration of persons who were entirely ignorant of the Chinese language did not help.

More concretely (and certainly more accessibly), the debate also came to be centered on what is now known as the Chinese Rites Controversy. Trigault had forcefully asserted that the ceremonies during which all Chinese offered food to their ancestors, and in which literati made similar offerings to Confucius, were strictly commemorative. But if such offerings are understood as "sacrifices," then such rites must be construed as a form of worship, a form of behavior entirely unsuited to Christian converts. The most important critic of the Jesuits was a Dominican friar, Domingo Navarrete, who published a description of China in 1676 based on his own travels.[26] (Whatever his opinions of Jesuit theology, Navarrete was, like his opponents, quite favorably impressed by China and the Chinese. It is noteworthy, and much to Navarrete's credit, that he did not resort to the obvious stratagem of demonizing or disparaging the Chinese in order to discredit the Jesuit depiction.) In fact, critics objected to the very core of the Jesuits' strategy, in Europe just as much as abroad, which was to attempt to adapt the message to the audience.[27] For the Jesuits' opponents, the divine word was a single, unalterable truth; any attempt to adapt it in different ways to different audiences risked its distortion. In the Jesuits' eagerness to win over converts, especially powerful and influential ones, they risked introducing error at best, or heresy at worst, into the Church itself. The Jesuits, of course, were convinced that their own faithfulness to the Church as an institution, but also to its teachings, was beyond question, but also that the refusal to adapt the message to the audience was a certain recipe for failure. Maintaining the absolute purity of the word served no useful purpose if it won over no converts.

In 1688, a contingent of French Jesuits sent over by Louis XIV arrived in Beijing, in the process changing the nature of the missionary turf wars. The "Portuguese" Jesuits (not all of whom were Portuguese by any means, but who depended on the Portuguese mission in Goa) were by no means enthralled, and for good reason; they were quickly muscled out by their French colleagues. But it turned out that the Jesuits were not the only French missionaries with the ambition of establishing themselves in China. The Société des missions etrangères (Society of Foreign Missions) had similar aspirations. The Jesuits had may detractors in France, most prominently the Jansenists. The Rites Controversy fell into the lap of the anti-Jesuit camp, and so a quarrel which had initially pitted Portuguese against Spanish now became a rallying point for different factions within the Church in France. If Spain and Portugal were on the periphery of the seventeenth-century western European intellectual world, France was in the center, and the controversy could not fail to attract the attention of intellectuals outside France and indeed outside the Roman Catholic orbit. Most notably, Gottfried Wilhelm Leibniz, though a Protestant, not only corresponded extensively with the Jesuits but weighed in publicly on their side.[28]

In 1696, one of the members of the early French Jesuit mission, Louis Lecomte, published a long description of China, *Nouveaux mémoires sur l'état présent de la Chine* (New Memoirs on the Present State of China), very deliberately with the intention of supporting the Jesuit cause in the controversy.[29] Lecomte, who had only spent five years in China, was less knowledgeable about it than some of his Jesuit colleagues, though his account nevertheless "contains much accurate information about Chinese history, religion, and culture."[30] However, some of its more contentious assertions, notably about Chinese religion, hardly escaped the attention of censors hostile to the Jesuit cause, and the book was condemned by the Sorbonne. The condemnation cut short Lecomte's career at court as confessor to the Duchess of Burgundy, but the book's notoriety contributed to its reputation, and it was quickly translated into several languages.

If Trigault's portrait of Confucius depicts him as a philosopher equal to or superior to the ancients, Lecomte's sketch of his life is virtually a hagiography: "He resolved to preach everywhere an austere morality, to inspire contempt for riches and pleasure; an infinite esteem for justice, for temperance, and for the other virtues; an uncompromising greatness of soul, a sincerity incapable of the slightest disguise, even towards the greatest of princes; and last of all a kind of life which combated all the passions and which only cultivated reason and virtue."[31] However, it was Lecomte's depiction of the ancient religion of the Chinese, rather than his veneration of Confucius, that got him into such trouble: his assertion that "for over two thousand years, China conserved the knowledge of the true God and practiced the purest moral maxims, while Europe and almost all the rest of the world was in a state of error and corruption."[32] Indeed, Lecomte claimed that the Chinese had built a temple to the creator even earlier than the one in Judea.[33] Granted, he admitted that China was eventually "infected" by idolatry, first in the form of Taoism and later, and worse, by Buddhism (or the religion of Fo, as it was labeled by the Jesuits). Lecomte's assertion that the natural religion of the Chinese, a legacy of the descendants of Noah, was in the absence of revelation the spiritual equivalent of Judaism, if not Christianity, did not go over well with the authorities.

If Lecomte's theological assertions were initially the most controversial parts of his account, other facets of his description of China were ultimately far more influential in molding the image of China throughout much of the Enlightenment, paradoxically sowing the seeds for both utopian and dystopian portrayals of the Chinese empire. This is not to suggest that Enlightenment thinkers all drew indirectly, if not directly, on Lecomte's work, though it was certainly not unknown to many of them. Rather, in crucial respects Lecomte's account is representative of Jesuit writing on China, as well as one (but only one) of its cardinal sources. In particular, there were three issues where Lecomte's (and more generally the Jesuits') account of China fueled Enlightenment discourse: the chronology of the world; the administration of the empire; and the comparison between Chinese and European accomplishments.

By the middle of the seventeenth century, Jesuit scholars had come to realize that Chinese historical accounts dated, in Lecomte's words, "further back than any of our profane histories, and even the time that is marked by the Vulgate is not long enough to account for their chronology."[34] Bluntly put, either the Vulgate or the Chinese annals had to be wrong, or the Chinese empire would antedate the world itself. Lecomte delicately hinted that it would have been politically impolitic, if not suicidal, for the Jesuits to contest the Chinese chronology, at least openly. However, even more awkwardly for the Jesuits, they had reason to find the Chinese annals plausible. The Chinese chronicles duly noted the occurrence of eclipses, dates which the Jesuit mathematicians and astronomers were able to verify. Indeed, one of the very reasons why the Jesuits had managed to find favor at the imperial court—as the Jesuits were vociferous in proclaiming—was that they could predict eclipses better than the Chinese astronomers. Indeed, the Jesuits were commissioned with building a royal observatory, which Lecomte describes in loving detail, replete with illustrations.[35] The rub—according to Lecomte, himself a mathematician—was that the Chinese astronomers were not knowledgeable enough to have been able to predict (or, properly speaking, to retrodict) the eclipses mentioned in the Chinese chronicles, which the Jesuit astronomers could verify (assuming, of course, that the world had

existed at the time). In other words, according to Lecomte, the eclipses mentioned in the early parts of the chronicles must have been the product of
empirical observation, rather than later interpolations. The Jesuits resolved
this apparent contradiction ingeniously. and arguably disingenuously, by
calculating Biblical chronology based on the Septuagint rather than the
Vulgate, adding about five hundred years to the age of the universe in the
process—just enough time in order to be able to fit in the Chinese.

In the long run, the Jesuits' pious ruse had absolutely the opposite effect
from what they intended, undermining rather than restoring faith in biblical chronology of any sort. By the same token, and equally inadvertently,
they set a new standard for the longevity of political institutions. Until then,
Rome had been the yardstick for the durability of the state; no other European state came remotely close to rivaling its longevity, much less its grandeur. Now China suddenly threatened to challenge Rome's supremacy. It
had been a powerful empire long before Romulus and Remus had ever (presumably) suckled at a she-wolf's teat; and despite the inevitable dynastic
ups and downs, it was still formidable in the seventeenth century.

The secret of China's apparent power, wealth, and longevity was presumably the quality of its administration:

> Among all the ideas of government formed in antiquity, there is perhaps none
> which establishes a more perfect monarchy than that of the Chinese. The
> ancient legislators of this powerful State proposed it in their time more or
> less as it is still nowadays. The other empires . . . have had, so to speak, the
> weaknesses of childhood; they were born unformed and imperfect; and they
> needed, like men, to pass through all the stages of age before arriving at per-
> fection. Chine seems to have been far less subjected to the laws of nature; as
> if God himself had been its legislator, the force of its government had scarcely
> been more perfect in its origin than it is at present, after more than four thou-
> sand years that it has lasted.[36]

Here, Lecomte's lavish praise is far less nuanced than Ricci's initial appraisal.
Not surprisingly, there are considerable parallels (though Lecomte certainly
does not formulate them outright) between France under the Sun King and
China under the Celestial Emperor:

> . . . the first sentiment that was inspired in the people was a respect for the
> prince that is almost tantamount to adoration. He is called the Son of Heaven
> and the Unique Master of the World. He orders are considered holy, his words

function as oracles, everything that issues from him is sacred. He is rarely seen, and spoken to only on bended knee.[37]

Only the emperor has the power of life and death; he must approve any death sentence in the realm. He has the power to remove anyone from office, and unlimited powers to impose taxes and tributes, from whom no one, be they priests or mandarins, is exempt. There is no hereditary nobility, and consequently no hereditary privileges of tax exemption. Indeed, "the amounts [of taxes] decreed by law are so considerable that if the lands of China were not so fertile and the people so industrious, the Empire would soon be nothing more than an assembly of beggars and paupers, like most of the kingdoms of the Indies."[38]

Lecomte is acutely aware that such a system of absolute authority could easily seem excessive and tyrannical. While he admits that abuses have certainly occurred (as a theologian, he notes that no human system is without its failings), he suggests that "as long as the prince cares for his reputation, or his interests, or the public good, he cannot systematically abuse his authority."[39] For Lecomte, the true underpinnings of order and stability in China are its principles of government and morality. He cites ten maxims of good government. First, no one should hold office in his native province. Second, the children of the most prominent officials should live in the emperor's court, if only as hostages of a sort. Third, the emperor can try anyone, of whatever rank, by an official of his choice. Fourth, offices should be never sold but always awarded for merit, on the basis of examinations. Fifth, foreigners are prohibited from living permanently within the empire. Sixth, there should be no hereditary nobility. Seventh, the empire should always maintain a large standing army in peacetime as well as in war. Eight, rewards as well as punishments should be meted out justly. Nine, women should be excluded from worldly affairs. And, finally, commerce within the empire should be systematically fostered. [40] It is indeed striking to note the extent to which Lecomte's description of the underlying principles of Chinese government resembles the aims of Louis XIV's administration to curb the influence of the nobility and foster the power of the state bureaucracy. It is no accident, as we will see in chapter 8, that in the next century those Enlightenment thinkers who admired Louis XIV—Voltaire, most notably—would depict Chinese government in ideal terms. Those who, like Montesquieu, considered the reign of Louis XIV disastrous would be equally critical of China.

For Lecomte, good government in China relied not only on sound principles of government, but also on three principles of morality. The first

. . . recommends to children a love, a complaisance, a respect for fathers which neither ill treatment nor advanced age nor a superior rank the child may have acquired can ever change. . . . Their children are obliged to nourish them all their life, and after their death to mourn them continually. They prostrate themselves a thousand times before their corpse, they offer them viands as if they were still alive to show that all the family goods still belong to them, and that they wish with all their heart that they were still capable of enjoying them. They bury them with excessive pomp and expense; they shed tears regularly over their graves; they often perform the same ceremonies before portraits which they religiously keep in their house, and which they honor with offerings. . . .[41]

Chinese filial piety is at one sweep removed from the realm of religion—how could Jesuits condone ancestor worship?—and squarely placed within the domain of morality. Indeed, as a moral principle it occupied a critical place within the discourse of absolutist rule in Europe; arguments for the divine right of kings placed an explicit parallel between the divinely sanctioned authority of a king over his subjects with the equally sanctioned authority of a father over his children. The second principle of morality that Lecomte cites, which is that the people should venerate officials as representatives of the emperor, demonstrates an even more transparent link between morality and absolute rule.

The third, and indeed the most surprising, principle of morality cited by Lecomte is the scrupulous observation of rules of politeness. No one however lowly, he emphasizes, is exempt: ". . . I have been astonished a thousand times to see lackeys kneel one before the other to bid farewell, and villagers give one another compliments in the course of festivities that we would not make in our public ceremonies."[42] Rules of protocol are so exacting that foreign ambassadors must receive forty days of training before an audience with the emperor, to ensure that they do not omit any of the required formalities.[43] Lecomte devotes several pages to the description of a formal banquet:

But the banquets outdo anything one can imagine. You are not invited to eat, but rather to make faces. You don't place a morsel in your mouth or drink a drop of wine without it costing a hundred contortions. There is, as in our musical performances, an officer who beats the measure so that all the guests coordinate when they take something from their dish, when they place it to their mouth, when they raise the little stick which they use as forks or put them down regularly and correctly in their place. Everyone has his own table, without tablecloth, napkin, knife, or spoon; since everything is cut into pieces, and nothing is touched other than with two small silver-plated sticks which the Chinese use very adroitly and which is their universal implement.[44]

If Lecomte admittedly finds such ceremony a bit excessive and sometimes exasperating—he complains that one would leave formal banquets hungrier than when one arrived!—he nonetheless concludes that "one cannot dispute that these customs, so precisely observed, inspire the people with sentiments of gentility and a sense of order."[45] All in all, Lecomte's argument about the political significance of morality is remarkably astute: the little ceremonies of everyday life, he suggests, such as filial piety and rules of politeness, are fundamental constituents of the order and stability of the entire Chinese realm because of the kinds of dispositions they inculcate in ordinary subjects.

All in all, in Lecomte's description, China compares very favorably with Europe. Admittedly, it was not (yet) a Christian realm, a situation which the Jesuits were doing the best to remedy and a prospect for which Lecomte had the most optimistic. if not realistic. hopes. Chinese achievements lay especially within the intertwining realms of morality and government, thanks partly to the wise dispositions of the earliest Chinese emperors,[46] and in equal measure to the sage teachings of Confucius. This politico-moral excellence had, after all, accounted for the longevity of the Chinese empire, a longevity that dwarfed Europe's greatest and most admired political achievements. The one glaring defect of the Chinese, in Lecomte's eyes, was that they were "mediocre in the sciences," even if "they succeed much better in the Arts."[47] (By "arts," Lecomte did not have the fine arts in mind so much as crafts such as porcelain and silk, in which the Chinese were acknowledged to excel.) As we have seen, the very presence of the Jesuits in China was at least partly due to the superiority of their mathematical and astronomical knowledge over the Chinese. The Jesuits had every interest in touting the superiority of European science. However, Lecomte published his account of China in the very midst of the famous Quarrel of the Ancients and the Moderns.[48] The relative importance of scientific achievements, as opposed to literary but also moral and political excellence, was at the very center of the quarrel. In principle at least, partisans of the ancients should have found China's achievements impressive indeed. Moderns, on the other hand, were less likely to be enchanted.

SIX

Distant Relations: The Jesuits in New France

The Chinese Rites Controversy demonstrated how acrimonious, even vicious, was the struggle between different Catholic orders to establish spheres of influence outside Europe where they could best compete for converts. Needless to say, China was the greatest prize, given its huge population, its wealth, and its geopolitical and economic importance. However, even where the stakes were far lower, such rivalry was far from absent.

If the sixteenth-century French attempts to establish colonies in the New World, first in Brazil and then in Florida, both ended in disaster, they finally managed to gain a foothold in the early seventeenth century in Acadia (now Nova Scotia) and Quebec.[1] Missionaries followed closely on the heels of the colonists: two Jesuits, Fathers Biard and Massé, arrived in Acadia in 1611. The missionaries did not always enjoy smooth relations with their compatriots, the French colonists. In any case, the mission was cut short when the priests were captured by an English vessel sailing from Virginia. In 1616, Biard published *Relation de la Nouvelle France, de ses terres, naturel du pais, et de ses habitans* (*Relation of New France, of its Territory, the Nature of the Country, and of its Inhabitants*), an account of the mission and a call to continue the work of evangelization there.[2] However, it was by no means clear at the time that such evangelization was to be left to the Jesuits. In 1615, at Champlain's invitation, four Recollect fathers arrived in Quebec; the Recollects were a Franciscan order. Not surprisingly, four missionaries were hardly enough to evangelize Quebec, and the Recollects asked the Jesuits for reinforcements. The mission was once again cut short by the English, who took possession of New France in 1629, expelling the missionaries along with the French administration.

The territory was restored to France in 1632. This time, the Jesuits managed to procure exclusive rights to the mission, edging out the Recollects, who were unable to return until much later. (Hennepin, who accompa-

nied La Salle on his exploration of the Mississippi River, was a Recollect.)
Too late, the Recollects attempted to assert their moral claim to primacy by
publishing in 1632 *Le Grand Voyage du pays des Hurons* (*The Long Journey to
the Country of the Hurons*), Gabriel Sagard's account of his mission to the
Huron in 1623 and 1624.[3] It is striking to note that the Recollects only published an account of their mission as a rearguard action, a response to what
they considered Jesuit maneuvering to muscle them out of the missionary
field in New France. By contrast, Paul Le Jeune, head of the Jesuit mission
in Quebec, immediately began publishing "relations" of the mission, the
first being *Brière relation du voyage de la Nouvelle France* (*Brief Relation of the
Journey to New France*) in 1632.[4] Thereafter, for the next forty years, the Jesuits published an annual "relation" of the mission's accomplishments, and
sometimes of its setbacks. These publications were part of a concerted effort
to rally moral, political, and financial support, not to mention volunteers,
for the missions. The Jesuit *Relations* of the mission to New France, much like
Jesuit publications about China, were a rich source of information about
the peoples whom the Jesuits were trying to convert; but they were also very
carefully crafted as a means of conveying impressions which fostered the
Jesuits' long-term aims.

The *Relations* were narratives of setbacks as well as of triumphs. After all,
accounts of their tribulations allowed the Jesuits to depict themselves—not
entirely without justification, in all fairness—as heroes of the faith. The early
Relations were all the less triumphant because the pace of conversions was
deliberately slow. The Jesuits were determined to ensure that converts were
thoroughly instructed in the articles of faith and that they demonstrated a sincere and long-term commitment before they were baptized. This demanded
of the Jesuits, first and foremost, a command of the local languages, which
belonged to two distinct families, Algonquian and Iroquoian. The Jesuits
were acutely aware of the problems of conveying complex and unfamiliar
theological constructs in languages they had mastered only imperfectly. At
least the total absence of competitors preserved them from the kinds of accusations they faced in China—namely, that their translations were inaccurate
and apt to give rise to unacceptable or even heretical interpretations. On the
other hand, unlike in China, they had to deal with an entirely oral culture in
New France. If mastery of Chinese literacy ultimately conferred prestige on
the Jesuits, they realized that in New France the equivalent was oratory. They
found themselves obliged not only to be accurate, but to be eloquent.

The major exception to their principle that only those educated in the
faith were to be baptized was in the case of the moribund. The missionaries actively sought to baptize anyone who was at death's door, at times

aggressively seeking them out. The strategy was advantageous whether the convert lived or died. Those converts who died shortly after baptism were assured of going to heaven, especially as they did not have the occasion to backslide. If, on the other hand, the convert survived in the face of everyone's expectations, those of the Jesuits included, this could be ascribed to the miraculous power of the Catholic faith, and induce other mortally sick individuals to seek material or spiritual succor from the missionaries. Most of these converts were in fact young children, and almost all of them died immediately. The record of early conversions was decidedly morbid. The glaring exception was Manitougache, alias "La Nasse" ("the fish trap"), who chose to convert and settle next to the Jesuits in Quebec; in the early *Relations* he is often simply called "nostre sauvage" (our savage).

La Nasse's decision to take up permanent abode with the Jesuits represented more than a public demonstration of religious preferences. From their very beginnings in New France, as early as Biard's first *Relation*, the Jesuits identified the seminomadic ways of their intended converts as a major obstacle. This was specifically true of the Algonquian-speaking groups who were the Jesuits' immediate neighbors in Quebec. While they settled down to grow crops during the summer months, they dispersed in small hunting bands throughout the winter in search of game. Le Jeune, in his *Relation* of 1634, despaired of ever converting such nomads:

> . . . it seems to me that we have little to hope from the Savages as long as they are nomadic [*errants*]; you teach them today, tomorrow hunger will steal away your auditors, forcing them to go seek their livelihood in the rivers and the woods. Last year, I stutteringly taught the Catechism to a good number of children . . . my birds flew off, one here, one there. This year, now that I speak a bit better, I thought I would see them again, but as they camped on the other side of the great St. Lawrence River, I was frustrated in my expectations. To follow them, you would need as many missionaries as they have bands [literally huts, *cabanes*],[5] and even then you wouldn't achieve your goal; as they are so busy seeking their livelihood in the woods that they don't have the leisure to be saved, so to speak. Moreover, I don't believe that for a hundred missionaries you could find ten who could resist the work it would take to follow them.

Le Jeune had higher hopes for the mission to the Huron, further inland. For the French colonists, the Hurons were of particular strategic importance because of their role in the fur trade. For the Jesuits, however, the fact that the Huron lived in large, permanent settlements made them a particularly attractive target. Le Jeune envisioned sedentarizing the nomads as a precondition for converting them. However, the French authorities in New France had neither the means to carry out such a project nor the slightest interest in doing so. In the meantime, ministering to the nomads was a cross to bear, an occasion for heroic suffering:

> . . . you must suffer running after the Savages, which you must do of necessity if you want to save them. . . . You don't suffer such inconveniences staying within the mission house, what you endure there is tolerable; but when you must become a Savage with the Savages, you must take your life and everything you have and throw it to the winds, so to speak, contenting yourself with a very fat and heavy cross for all your wealth. It is very true that God does not suffer defeat and that the more you leave behind, the more you find; the more you lose, the more you gain; but God hides himself sometimes, and then the chalice is most bitter.

The Sorcerer's Reluctant Apprentice

Whatever his reservations about ministering to nomadic bands, Le Jeune set out in the fall of 1633 with a band of Montagnais hunters in order to perfect his skills in their language and his knowledge of their beliefs and customs, an expedition he related in considerable detail in the *Relation* of 1634. His host was the brother of Pierre Pastedechouan, a Montagnais who, as a young boy, had been taken back to France by the Recollects to be educated in French as well as the Catholic faith. In principle, on his return, Pastedechouan was to have served as an interpreter and intermediary between the French and the Montagnais. Le Jeune took him on as a language tutor. Not surprisingly, Pastedechouan resented the subservient role he was given, whether by the French administration or by the Jesuits, who in turn found him unreliable and uncooperative. He eventually left the French settlement to stay with his brothers, but he was equally unhappy among the Montagnais, where he was clearly a misfit. Growing up in France, he had never learned to be a proper hunter. Because of his mediocre skills, his several marriages quickly failed and he was generally considered by his fellow Montagnais as a man of little worth.

By the time Le Jeune set out with the band, Pastedechouan had entirely ceased to practice Catholicism, and Le Jeune referred to him in the *Relation* simply as "the apostate." The leader of the band and Le Jeune's host was not, of course, the apostate, but rather one of his older brothers, a man of far more standing among the Montagnais. To Le Jeune's short-lived relief, when the band set out, it did not include another of the apostate's brothers, a prominent shaman whose company Le Jeune resolutely sought to avoid. Soon after their departure, to Le Jeune's great chagrin and despite his entreaties, the shaman joined the group and was to remain Le Jeune's nemesis for the duration of the journey. Le Jeune referred to the shaman as "the Sorcerer" (*le Sorcier*, which can also be translated as "the witch"; the French language makes no distinction between witches and sorcerers). The choice of name was significant. The Jesuits referred to Native American shamans as either "sorcerers" or *jongleurs*. The latter term literally means "juggler," but it has the broader connotation of "entertainer" or "showman," especially one who specializes in sleights of hand. By depicting shamans as *jongleurs*, the Jesuits were implying that they were charlatans who unscrupulously duped their clientele. On the other hand, to the extent that their powers were strictly imaginary, they were seen as relatively harmless. By calling them sorcerers, however, the Jesuits made them out to be much more sinister. Accusations of sorcery and witchcraft were still taken very seriously in France. Indeed, the trial and condemnation of Urbain Grandier, held responsible for the demonic possession of Ursuline nuns at Loudun (and their exorcism at the hands of a Jesuit), took place in 1634, making it exactly contemporaneous with Le Jeune's *Relation*.[6] The powers of sorcerers were diabolical and real.

Indeed, of all the hardships Le Jeune endured during his journey, the company of the Sorcerer was, in his opinion, among the worst:

> . . . This miserable man, and the smoke, were the two greatest torments I endured among these Barbarians; neither the cold, nor the heat, nor the inconvenience of the dogs, nor sleeping outside, nor sleeping on the ground, nor the posture you need to adopt in the huts, cuddled into a ball, or lying down, or sitting down without a seat or a mattress, nor hunger, nor thirst, nor the poverty and filth of their meat, nor sickness, all this seemed a game by comparison to the smoke and to the malice of the Sorcerer, with whom I have always been on bad terms.

The passage alludes to the discomforts of the makeshift shelters of the Montagnais that Le Jeune describes in less than loving detail. Their bark exterior was not very efficient in keeping out the wind and the snow, while the fire in the center of the hut was always extremely hot, so that half of Le Jeune would freeze while the other half was burning hot. A tiny shelter would accommodate the entire band—including the dogs—and it was difficult finding enough space to sleep. Worst of all, in Le Jeune's opinion, was the smoke from the fire, which could not escape very effectively through the roof, making it impossible to stand up in the hut and often choking him even when he lay on the ground; at times, he complained, he would try to sleep outside in the snow rather than face the smoke in the huts. When Jean de Brébeuf, in his earliest account of his mission to the Huron in the *Relation* of 1635, described their longhouses, he laconically commented:

> The huts of the country are neither Louvres nor palaces, in no way similar to the rich buildings of our France, not even the smallest cottages; they are nonetheless better and more comfortable than the hovels of the Montagnais.

In fact, the physical hardships of Le Jeune's journey were hardly limited to the radically uncomfortable lodgings and unpalatable food. It was a very bad hunting season, and the men in the band were hard put to find enough food to subsist. On many days there was nothing whatsoever to eat. Moreover, his band was relatively lucky; none of its members starved to death, the fate of several other bands that winter. In these circumstances, Le Jeune was at a total loss to comprehend the Montagnais practice of feasting on whatever they had managed to hunt, gorging themselves to finish everything rather than storing anything for later. He was particularly disconcerted by ritual feasts where it was incumbent on all participants to finish absolutely everything they had been served. In one instance, he was thoroughly rebuked for surreptitiously attempting to feed some of his portion to the dogs, on the grounds that any dog who partook of the meat of such a feast would prove useless in the hunt. The Montagnais were quick to comment on his attitudes about food:

> It is a kind of insult to a savage to refuse the morsel he presents you. One man, seeing that I tried to politely decline some food that my host had offered me, told me, "You don't like him, since you rejected his offer." I answered that it is not our custom to eat at any hour, but I would nevertheless take what they gave me, provided that they didn't offer it too often. They all burst into laughter, and an old woman told me that if I wanted to be loved by their nation, I would have to eat a lot.

Le Jeune's attitude towards Montagnais food practices is a fairly typical example, not only of his incomprehension of the culture, but of the confrontation between two sometimes irreconcilable sets of values. It was this confrontation that was to set him against the Sorcerer, his principal rival for the spiritual leadership of the band. At one point, he was even convinced that the Sorcerer was planning to kill him, "seeing that he hated me for several reasons . . . notably because I attempted to demonstrate that all he did was nothing but jest and childishness." The Sorcerer, it must be said, replied in kind:

> "Your God," he said to me, "has never come to our country, this is why we don't believe in him, make me see him and I will believe in him." "Listen to me and you will see him," I answered. "We have two sorts of sight, the sight of the body's eyes and the sight of the soul's eyes. What you see with the soul's eyes can be as certain as what you see with the body's eyes." "No," said he," I see nothing except with my body's eyes, if not while I am asleep, but you don't approve of our dreams."

The issue of dreams was indeed a thorny question. According to Le Jeune, the Montagnais

> . . . have a great belief in their dreams, imagining that what they have seen must happen to them, and they must execute what they have dreamed. . . . Our savages asked me every morning, "Didn't you see any beavers or moose in your sleep?" and as they saw that I ridiculed dreams, they were astonished and asked me, "What do you believe, if you don't believe in dreams?" "I believe in He who has created everything and can do everything." "You have no sense. How can you believe in him if you can't see him?"

The Montagnais freely expressed their skepticism not only of a God they couldn't see, but also of books and prayers that seemed to them of no utility, and especially no protection against hunger:

> "Ask Him," they said, "for moose, bears, and beavers, tell Him that you want to eat some." And when I told them that this was a trifling matter, that there were other riches to ask for, they burst out laughing. "What," they answered, "could you wish for that is better than eating all you want of such good meats?"

Theology aside, Le Jeune was not invariably unsympathetic to Montagnais values, even when they were diametrically opposed to European ones. He was impressed by the Montagnais ethic of reciprocity, with their willingness to give freely whatever they possessed, although he was occasionally confounded by his own reluctance to conform to these norms when asked for tobacco. His behavior must have seemed all the more peculiar in that he did not indulge in the habit himself, but rather hoarded his tobacco to dole it out as gifts to the apostate in return for language lessons, or to young children in return for small favors. Even so, his depiction of the Montagnais attitude towards French possessiveness seems to reproach his own compatriots rather than the "savages":

> . . . One insult that the savages give to the French is that they love what they possess. When you refuse to give something to a savage, he will immediately tell you *Khisakitan*, "You love it," *sakhita, sakhita*, "Love it! Love it!" as if to say that one is to attached to what one likes, and that one prefers it to their friendship.[7]

On other occasions Le Jeune was either unwilling or unable to understand the Montagnais point of view, and on such occasions, the Sorcerer was all too willing to call him to order. For example, Le Jeune egregiously misconstrued the Montagnais practice of matrilineal inheritance. Given what Le Jeune considered their rampant philandering, Montagnais men could not be sure of the fidelity of their own wives and the paternity of their own children, he argued. They choose their sister's sons as heirs, he suggested, only because in this case they could be sure of the blood connection. Indeed, one day Le Jeune told the Sorcerer in his son's presence that he could not be sure the child was really his own.

> He answered, "You have no sense. You French only love your own children, but we, we love all the children of our nation." I broke out in laughter, seeing as he philosophized like a horse or a mule.

On another occasion the Sorcerer borrowed the Jesuit's robe for a month, returning it "so ugly and dirty that I was ashamed of it, because the spit and other garbage that covered it gave it another color." It is important to point out that in seventeenth-century France, and of course in New France, the state of one's clothing was the most important criterion for determining "cleanliness," far more than how often, or even whether, one bathed.[8] For Jesuits, the cleanliness of one's clothes was a fundamental moral virtue and not just a social one. But when Le Jeune unfolded the robe in front of the Sorcerer in order to demonstrate his displeasure, the Sorcerer answered him pithily: "You say that you want to be a Montagnais and a Savage like us. If that is the case, don't be so upset to wear the costume, because that is how we keep our clothing."

Laconically commenting on the ridicule to which he was subjected, particularly though not exclusively by the Sorcerer, Le Jeune concluded:

Believe me, if I brought back no other fruit from the savages, I have at least
learned many insults in their language. At the slightest occasion, they told me
eca titou, eca titou nama khitirinisin, "Shut up! Shut up! You have no sense";
Achineou, "He is proud"; *Moucachtechiou,* "He is a hanger-on"; *sasegau,* "He is
vain"; *cou attimou,* "He looks like a dog"; *cou mascoua,* "He looks like a bear";
cou ouabouchou ouistoui, "He has a beard like a hare's"; *attimonai oukhimau,* "he
is the chief of the dogs"; *cou oucousimas ouchitgonon,* "His head is like a pump-
kin"; *matchirinou,* "He is difformed, he is ugly"; *kichcouebeon,* "He is drunk."
These are the colors in which they depicted me, and there are many others I
have chosen to omit.

Given that, in another passage, Le Jeune complained bitterly about the Montagnais propensity to resort to obscene language, one can easily imagine the
kinds of insults that he left out of his account.

Surprisingly enough, Le Jeune's portrait of the Montagnais is far from
entirely negative. If he writes a whole chapter on "what one must suffer
wintering with the savages," he also devotes a whole chapter to "the good
things that are found among the savages," admittedly followed by a chapter
on "their vices and their imperfections." His praise of the savages begins
with their physical appearance, which he compares favorably to that of the
ancient Romans, quite to the detriment of Le Jeune's own compatriots, *"pe-
tits damoiseaux"* (little, and by implication effeminate, gentlemen).

> I used to think that the busts of Roman emperors represented the idea of
> painters rather than men who ever existed, so great and mighty were their
> heads, but I see here on the shoulders of the people the heads of Julius Caesar,
> Pompey, Augustus, and Otho, and others I have seen in France sketched on
> paper or in relief on medallions.

Nor is there the slightest hint in Le Jeune that this physical excellence comes
at the expense of deficiencies ether in the intellectual or the moral realms.
Their minds, he claims, are *"de bonne trempe"* (of good caliber), and their
souls likewise. He ascribes their errors to lack of education rather than to
malice or stupidity, comparing them in this respect to French peasants—
admittedly a less flattering comparison than to Roman emperors.

> . . . nevertheless I have not seen anyone until now among those who have
> traveled to these lands who does not frankly confess and avow that the savages
> have more wit [*plus d'esprit*] than our ordinary peasants.

So much for the French peasantry.

While their egalitarian ideology and lack of hierarchical authority are hardly features of Montagnais society that Le Jeune endorsed as a general rule—as we have seen among the Chinese, the Jesuits had a healthy respect for hierarchy—he admitted that it preserved the savages from the ravages of greed and ambition which plagued his own society. *Macbeth* would clearly be lost on the savages; the office of chief conferred so little authority that it was not worth murdering for. Moreover, as the Sorcerer, of all people, pointed out to Le Jeune, the Montagnais were far more capable of self-control than the French, who easily lost their tempers. Admittedly, Le Jeune was reluctant to take at face value the Sorcerer's claim that "as for me, nothing is capable of making me lose my calm; if famine menaces us, if my close friends and family pass on to the other life, if our enemies the Iroquois massacre our people, I never get angry." Although Le Jeune commented that he had seen the Sorcerer angry more than once, he added more charitably that "it is true that he often held back, and forcefully reined in his temper, notably when I exposed his imbecilities." It apparently took more than this to make the Sorcerer blow his cool.

Not surprisingly, this kind of self-restraint was accompanied by a patience that in times of famine could be heroic, and an aversion to complaining, whether about fate, the weather, or someone else's behavior. Even more surprising for Le Jeune, the Montagnais did not seem to bear grudges. He tells the story of how, in midwinter when the band was close to starving, a hunter killed a moose and buried it in the snow so that a party could fetch it the next day. When he returned that evening to inform the others, there was a visitor present who promptly found a pretext for returning home forthwith. When the party set out to retrieve the moose the following morning, they found that a good part of the meat had already been removed. Clearly, the visitor had hurried to take the meat before the hunters returned. When this same visitor turned up on another occasion, Le Jeune began to harangue him for the theft of the meat, but his host, who was the brother of the apostate and the Sorcerer, immediately motioned for him to cease, and the visitor was warmly welcomed. By the same token, Le Jeune praises the Montagnais' generosity, their willingness to share whatever they have (and to make fun of any people, particularly the French, who seem too attached to their possessions), and to care for orphaned children as their own.

On the negative side, it is clear that what irks Le Jeune the most about the Montagnais is their total lack of respect for authority:

> They imagine that by birthright they should enjoy the freedom of wild asses
> [*anons Sauvages*; Le Jeune, like Montaigne, plays on the meanings of *sauvage*,
> though for opposite rhetorical effect], subjecting themselves to no one, unless
> they so desire. They reproached me a hundred times that we fear our Chiefs,
> but they mock and make fun of theirs; all the chief's authority is at the tip
> of his lips, he is only as powerful as he is eloquent; and when he has killed
> himself talking and haranguing, he will not be obeyed unless it pleases the
> savages to do so.

Indeed, to Le Jeune's perpetual annoyance, they seemed to make fun of
everything and to turn everything to derision, being foul-mouthed in the
process. Le Jeune's ears were clearly offended by much of what he heard, and
more than occasionally he simply pretended not to understand. Le Jeune
clearly understood that such mockery served to deflate all pretensions to
authority, whether political or religious, and definitely threatened the kind
of spiritual authority that the Jesuits wished to impose, albeit by persuasion
rather than force.

The very importance of eloquence and persuasion in establishing authority, in the absence of hierarchical institutions, made Le Jeune and other
Jesuits extremely conscious of the importance of language. Unlike in China,
they enjoyed an official monopoly over their flock and did not, at least,
have to worry that members of rival orders might challenge the accuracy of
their translations and suggest that they were effectively purveying heretical
ideas, if only inadvertently or through negligence. The exactness of their
translations was of little comfort if no one was going to listen to them. Indeed, on one occasion, when Le Jeune's host was giving a feast, the guests
requested that Le Jeune make a speech: ". . . They wanted to laugh, since I
pronounce the Savage language like a German speaking French. Wanting to
please them, I began a discourse, and they broke out laughing." This was
perhaps a way to win friends, but hardly to influence people.

Le Jeune devoted an entire chapter to the language, which he characterized as "very rich and very poor." He begins the chapter by specifying in
what respect the language is "poor": its lack of terms for "piety, devotion,
and virtue," and the absence of "the language of theologians, philosophers,
mathematicians, doctors, in a word learned men," and of "all the words
that concern the policing and government of a city, a province, and empire."
Not surprisingly, the religious and political concepts and institutions that Le
Jeune finds sorely lacking in Montagnais society have no counterpart in their
language, either. Far more unexpectedly, Le Jeune devotes the lion's share of
the chapter detailing the riches of the Montagnais language rather than its

deficiencies. For example, he notes that "I find an infinity of proper nouns among them that I can only explain in French through circumlocution." It would seem, then, that for all the French concepts lacking in Montagnais, there are Montagnais concepts absent from French. But this is not the least of it:

> . . . they have such an importunate [linguistic] wealth that it almost propels me to believe that I will all my life be poor in their language. When you know the parts of speech in the languages that flourish in our Europe, and you know how to put them together, you know the language. It is not the same for the language of our Savages. Fill your memory with the words which signify each thing in particular, learn the syntax or how to tie them together, and you are still but an ignorant person; You may well be able with this to make yourself understood by the Savages, and even then not invariably, but you won't understand them. The reason is that, in addition to the name of each thing in particular, they have an infinity of words which signify several things together.

Le Jeune gives the example of the sentence "The wind blows the snow." In French, if you know the words for "wind," "to blow," and "snow," and you know the rules of grammar, you can make the sentence. In Montagnais, however, according to Le Jeune, the word for wind is *routin*; for "to blow," *yakhineou*; for snow, *couné*. However, if you say *"Routin yakhineou couné,"* your savage interlocutor will either not understand you or will burst out laughing. For them, "The wind blows the snow" is denoted by a single word, *piouan*, different from all the other three.

What is so striking about this chapter is that the very features of the language that present the most problems for Le Jeune are depicted not as weaknesses but as riches. Le Jeune marvels at the complexity of the language, but in admiration. There is never a supercilious hint that the language is in some strange sense irrational, that his difficulties in learning it are in some way the fault of the Montagnais rather than of the missionary. However disgruntled Le Jeune could be with the Montagnais, he was never dismissive.

Le Jeune's description of the Montagnais provided a template for future Jesuit descriptions of native populations in the *Relations*, and first of all with Brébeuf's depiction of the Huron in 1636, only two years later. Brébeuf had already lived for a while among the Huron, having served as a Jesuit auxiliary to the earlier Recollect mission. When he returned, he was already acquainted with numbers of his flock. He had at least some knowledge of the language and, according to Le Jeune, had a special gift for languages. Le Jeune, Brébeuf's superior, had more hopes for the mission to the Huron

than for his own to the Montagnais, not least because the Huron were seden-
tary. Granted, for three months in the summer, everyone went off to work in
the fields and no one had time to listen to the preaching of the missionaries.
Even so, unlike the Montagnais or other hunters, the Huron always came
back to the same place, and it was possible to build a stable and permanent
mission without perpetually having to follow the people in their wander-
ings. Last but not least, the Huron were a powerful confederacy, rivals to
the Iroquois for control over the fur trade. (Brébeuf himself would later be
twice captured and tortured, the second time to death, by the Iroquois.) If in
the long run this was to spell doom for the Huron, in the short run it made
them more approachable for the missionaries, who were glad to find some
relatively stable structures of political authority:

> I won't pretend here to establish a parallel between our savages and the Chi-
> nese, Japanese, and other perfectly civilized nations, but only to extricate them
> from the status of beasts to which the opinion of certain people has reduced
> them, and to give them a rank among men and make apparent that, even
> among them, there is some kind of political and civil life.

The Huron, it would seem, were at least a little less intractable than the
Montagnais.

Brébeuf's passing comparison of the Huron and the Chinese points to one
very important if entirely inadvertent contribution of Jesuit ethnography to
European comparative discourse. As we can see clearly in Bodin,[9] the dominant geographical topos for comparing peoples had been the Aristotelian
schema of north (cold), temperate, and south (hot) climates. This particular
schema was by no means to disappear. Climate continued to figure prominently throughout the seventeenth and indeed the eighteenth centuries,
systematically in the theories of Montesquieu and Buffon, and even more
often in passing, where "Laplanders" and "Hottentots" were often lumped
together as specimens of the equally deleterious effects of extreme cold and
heat.[10] Jesuit ethnography proposed an alternative scheme, based on the polarity between east and west. Admittedly, Mandeville had also organized his
world in terms of east and west, but, placing Jerusalem in the center, his west
was situated in England. For the Jesuits, now thoroughly Eurocentric, China
was East and America West. The polarity was between hierarchy and empire
on the one hand, savagery and anarchy on the other. (The contrast was admittedly never absolute. Peru in the Americas was generally the "western"
equivalent of China, whereas Asian nomadic pastoralists—"barbarians"—
were in many respects akin to "savages.") Quite unintentionally, the Jesuits

provided the Enlightenment with a culturo-spatial vocabulary with which to dispute political values.

Le Jeune's Sorcerer provided a prototype of another sort: that of the dialectical (one is tempted to say "uppity") savage, the savage who talks back.[11] Le Jeune's examples of the Sorcerer's retorts provide one of the best examples of the indigenous voice in early narratives of non-European societies. Paradoxically, Le Jeune transmits the Sorcerer's disparaging comments more or less verbatim precisely because for the missionary, his antagonist's barbs are so transparently unreasonable. The insults Le Jeune suffers are a testimony to the cross he has to bear, to the indignities that a pious missionary must learn to endure. The Sorcerer's jibes are clearly meant by Le Jeune to contribute to a genre of heroic narrative, a form of verbal martyrdom that prefigured the all-too-real martyrdom that Brébeuf among others was to endure. However, it was all too easy for anticlerical intellectuals in the eighteenth century to read the text subversively. They could easily sympathize with anyone who ridiculed the Jesuits and expressed what they considered a healthy skepticism towards established religion, Christianity in particular. The Montagnais rejection of hierarchical authority and material wealth in favor of liberty and equality was an attractive, if extreme, position. It is impossible to assert that Le Jeune's Sorcerer was the literary prototype of Lahontan's Adario.[12] But it is equally certain that Lahontan, as well as later Enlightenment authors, read the Jesuits assiduously, if critically; the portrait of the Sorcerer clearly lent authenticity to the dialectical savages of Voltaire, Diderot, and company.

Long Lost Lycians

If Le Jeune's account of his winter's journey among the Montagnais inaugurated the Jesuit descriptions of the "savages" of New France, Joseph-François Lafitau's massive *Moeurs des sauvages Américains comparés aux moeurs des premiers temps*, published in 1724, represents their final and perhaps their crowning achievement. Lafitau's tome has been masterfully translated into English by William Fenton and Elizabeth Moore, but the title of their translation, *Customs of the American Indians Compared with the Customs of Primitive Times*,[13] is somewhat misleading. Clearly, the academic politics of euphemism are hardly an invention of comtemporary "political correctness." By changing Lafitau's title from "American Savages" to "American Indians," Fenton and Moore assuage the sensibilities of their audience at the expense of squarely placing the text within a broad discourse on "savagery" in the early modern period to which, as we have seen, the Jesuits contributed substantially. "Primitive Times" is misleading for very different reasons, as it obviates the vast difference between Lafitau's chronology and our own; the "earliest times" would be a better and more neutral translation. For Lafitau, human time begins with the Garden of Eden in the first instance, with the dispersal of mankind after the Flood in the second. The *"premiers temps,"* the earliest times, are recorded in the Bible and in Greek and Latin texts. There was no room in Lafitau's scheme for "prehistory"; savages were just like the French, historical beings. Indeed, the very aim of Lafitau's book was to restore them their place in universal history. To accomplish such a goal, he systematically related his own inquiries among the Iroquois as well as the accounts of other Jesuits (particularly Le Jeune and Brébeuf) to his encyclopedic knowledge of the Bible and the classics.

Lafitau's account consequently begins with the Creation, the expulsion from the Garden of Eden, the Flood, and the dispersal of humankind after the collapse of the tower of Babel. There was obviously no space in such a chronology for "prehistory." Lafitau suggested that, before the dispersal, humans were privy to divinely transmitted moral principles, natural religion for all intents and purposes. Given the intrinsic sinfulness of human nature after the Fall, these principles were bound to be violated or distorted in the absence of revealed religion. This said, such an Augustian perspective hardly qualifies Lafitau as a "degenerationist," as Hodgen (1971:380) and Trigger (1985:23) have alleged. On the contrary, Lafitau's central concern was to demonstrate how traces of the divine teachings were never totally abandoned, and could be found throughout the world's peoples. As we have seen, Jesuits had already described the Chinese literati as exemplary in how they had maintained these principles relatively intact over the centuries. But if such traces could be found among the Iroquois, their universality was confirmed. Such an assertion was an essential tenet of Jesuit humanism. Lafitau's account of the Native American migration from Asia was also a flat denial of polygenesis, an assertion of the essential oneness of human nature. The Iroquois, indeed all Native Americans, were moral beings who could and should be converted to Christianity.

Given Lafitau's postdiluvian paradigm, the Iroquois—indeed all Native Americans—had to have their origins in the Old World. In his efforts to uncover the mystery of their origins, Lafitau, very much like his nineteenth-century successors, focused on the Iroquois system of matrilineal descent or, in his terms, gynococracy. Lafitau's extensive classical education had in fact prepared him for such a discovery. Herodotus had described such a system among the Lycians of Asia Minor. On these grounds, Lafitau speculated that the Iroquois were none other than long lost Lycians who had migrated across Asia through Siberia to America. (He dismissed the idea that they might be one of the lost tribes of Israel as preposterous.)[14]

In a short and early chapter where he sketched out a general "Idea of the Character of Savages in General," Lafitau catalogued the virtues and vices of savage existence. Admittedly, at first glance they appeared to be "coarse, stupid, ignorant, ferocious, without sentiments of religion or humanity, given to all the vices, the natural product of a complete freedom which is troubled neither by any sentiment of the divine or of human laws, nor by principles of reason or education." But such stereotypes, he insisted, were misleading if not flatly wrong. "They have good sense, a vivid imagination, an easy grasp of ideas, and an admirable memory. All possess at least the traces of an ancient and hereditary religion, and of a form of government" (vol. 1, p. 90).[15] Indeed, the centerpiece of Lafitau's argument was the assertion of the universality of three fundamental human institutions: religion, marriage, and government. Nearly half his book is devoted to a demonstration that the American savages in general, and the Iroquois in particular, possessed all three of these institutions in one form or another. However, the way in which Lafitau constructed his arguments was radically different for each of these three institutions. In the first instance, he constructed a generalized account of "pagan" religion amalgamated from miscellaneous classical sources, his own experience of the Iroquois, and other (mostly but not exclusively Jesuit) descriptions of Native American religious practices. In the second, he (generally favorably) compared the Iroquois practices he observed with an absolute template of marriage as a divinely ordained institution. Third, he provided a sort of functional analysis of Iroquois institutions to demonstrate the effectiveness of their form of government. In short, he provided three radically different analytical and rhetorical strategies for "humanizing" the savages.

Lafitau's chapter on religion is far and away the longest in the book. His composite picture of the religious system that was carried from Europe through Asia to the Americas includes examples from classical antiquity, Zoroastrians, Mexico, Peru, Guiana, Brazil, Virginia, and of course New France. This is the only chapter, however, in which his own observations play a relatively marginal role. His concern was ultimately to separate the wheat from the chaff, to uncover the core of eternal truth that lay beneath the accretion of superstition and error. The key tenets of this religious system were, minimally, belief in the divinity, in the soul, and of life after death. This is hardly to say that Lafitau's discussion limits itself to any such bare minimum. The sun, he suggests, is a "natural" symbol for the divinity; consequently, the worship of fire, "pyrolatry," is a common feature of its cult.

Lafitau's use of the comparative method to create a single paradigm out of composite sources taken out of context bears remarkable similarity to later constructs—Tylor's "animism," or Frazer's "homeopathic" and "contagious magic—even if his creationist message is diametrically opposed to their evolutionary scenarios.

Unlike Tylor and Frazer, however, for whom "animism" and "magic" epitomized the logical confusion of the savage mind, Lafitau expressed considerable sympathy for this ancient-cum-savage religion as he understood it. It is instructive to compare Lafitau's attitude toward self-mortification to that of previous Christian writers. Of course, for Roman Catholics in the seventeenth century and earlier, self-mortification was both readily comprehensible and potentially praiseworthy. In the fourteenth century Sir John Mandeville was impressed with the readiness of South Asian Indians to throw themselves beneath the cartwheels of the "juggernaut."[16] For him, it was a scandal that idolaters were prepared to go to such lengths for false gods while Christians were unwilling to display the same level of self-sacrifice for the true God. The practices of others were, in this respect, largely a foil for what he considered the egregious inadequacy of his coreligionists. In the sixteenth century, José de Acosta saw the religious practices of the Mexicans and Peruvians in a rather different light: "Because the religious life . . . is so acceptable in the eyes of Divine Majesty, and so greatly honors his holy name and beautifies his church, the father of lies has not only tried to imitate that life but in a certain sense tries to compete with it and to make his ministers vie with it in austerity and observance."[17]

The monasteries of the virgins of the sun in Peru, the bloodletting of Mexican priests who would pierce their bodies with spines of maguey, were so many manifestations of the devil's imitation of religious virtue, a form of satanic parody. Nonetheless, such practices served not only "to demonstrate Satan's accursed pride and shame" but also "to waken the sense of our own lukewarm efforts in the service of Almighty God."[18] It was hard for Acosta to repress a begrudging sense of admiration.

For Lafitau, however, such self-mortification was in fact divinely inspired rather than a devilish travesty. His long discussion begins with a description of the pagan mysteries of classical antiquity, which clearly expressed "the truth of religion" in spite of the later introduction of various "abominations and shameful things" which "were diametrically opposed to their initial spirit which was a spirit of death to oneself, of penance and sanctification":

> In the state of expiation which was truly one of penance, they [the initiates] kept themselves in retreat and silence; they fasted rigorously, abstained from

the allowed pleasures of matrimony, made a confession of their sins, passed through many purifications representing the state of a mystical death and regeneration: finally, they underwent penalties which appeared to be a penance and an atonement for past sins. (vol. 1, p. 180)

Lafitau insisted on "the conformity of these initiations and mysteries of the ancients with the religions of the East Indies, of Japan and China, or even with those of such highly organized American nations as the Mexicans and the Peruvians,"[19] and notably "in the perfection to which they [the priests of these religions] aspire by the profession of a penitent, austere life, passed in fasts, abstinence, chastity, poverty, mortification [of the flesh] and finally in the practice of virtues, virtues of which they possess in truth only the external appearance, but, in this appearance, they find the claim of an entirely holy origin."[20] Here, Lafitau was careful to resort to an extremely subtle distinction. He could not assert that such practices of self-mortification in other religions were valid in any ultimate sense, for this would have made them equal to Roman Catholic Christianity; rather, these practices, invalid in themselves, nonetheless expressed a valid and holy truth.

Lafitau's interminable chapter on religion is the one which corresponds most closely to Duchet's (1985) and de Certau's (1985) characterization of his use of the comparative method. He draws remarkably little on the ethnography of New France, either from his own observations or those of his predecessors, and instead cites extensively from descriptions of other parts of America, from Virginia to Peru, in order to supplement his classical sources. If anything, it is not his Iroquois ethnography that illuminates the silences of his classical sources, but quite the reverse:

I have no doubt at all that their initiations and tests were almost like those of the Virginian tribes of which we spoke at first but, whether they had already lost many of their customs when the Europeans began to visit them, or whether they carefully concealed their mysteries . . . or, finally, whether the Europeans were not careful enough in questioning them or capable of penetrating adequately the spirit of the rites which they saw performed, we lack any detailed account of them in the old Relations. . . .[21]

Lafitau suggests that the "savages" of New France had lost or abandoned their initiation rites—the equivalents of ancient Greek and Roman "mysteries"—relatively recently. Ultimately, Lafitau's purpose is to amalgamate classical and ethnographic sources to reconstruct a sort of ur-paganism, a refraction rather than a reflection of the original divine spark.

Unlike his treatment of religion, Lafitau's discussion of marriage and the family relies very centrally on his own observations. For Lafitau marriage, like religion, was a divinely inspired institution. As one might readily imagine, marriage was ideally monogamous and permanent, between individuals who were not closely related to one another. Lafitau's account of Iroquois kinship terminology was actually part of his argument for the universal applicability of incest prohibitions. Indeed, he resorted to Iroquois kinship in order to explain—or, more exactly, to explain away—an embarrassing passage in Genesis (20:12) that seemed directly to contradict the entire thrust of Lafitau's universal history. Abraham, who has asked Sarah to pass herself off as his sister rather than his wife in the kingdom of Gerar, justifies himself to the king, Abimelech, on the grounds that Sarah is indeed his half-sister, child of the same father by a different mother. For Lafitau the Hebrews, as God's chosen people, were the only ones to keep intact the knowledge of God's commandments, the incest prohibition among them. How could Abraham, apical ancestor of the Hebrews and a holy prophet, flout the incest prohibition so flagrantly? Lafitau's excursus into the intricacies of kinship terminology provided a perfect answer: Sarah was only Abraham's classificatory sister *à la manière des Iroquois*. In this instance, Lafitau resorts to the comparative method not to fill in the gaps of his knowledge of the past, but rather to cover up its scandals. Iroquois classificatory kinship terminology serves as a convenient fig leaf for Abraham.

Lafitau (and Brébeuf before him) heartily approved of the Iroquois avoidance of marriage between relatives on all sides, even distant ones—regulations that seemed to echo those of the Catholic Church (which could, unlike the Iroquois, accord dispensations). The Iroquois were also monogamous, another trait that easily won approval from the missionaries. The one spot on the Iroquois record, in the eyes of the missionaries, was the frequency of divorce and the ease with which it could be obtained. It is hardly surprising that missionaries would find Iroquois marriage somewhat short of perfection. Still, except for the issue of divorce, their overall tone was one of approval. Unlike in Le Jeune a century before, there is not the slightest hint in Lafitau that Iroquois matriliny was a sign of marital laxity. In short, Lafitau measured Iroquois institutions of kinship and marriage in terms of what he considered universally valid, divinely decreed standards. If these practices fell short of perfection—a human rather than "savage" predicament—they were anything but degenerate.

Finally, Lafitau insisted, the Iroquois savages definitely had a system of government. He named such a system "gynecocracy," the rule of women, to underscore its matrilineal basis, though he pointed out that governmental affairs were "in the men's hands only by way of procuration" (vol. 1, p. 287). Thus the office of chief always passes from a man to "his aunt's children or his sisters' or his nieces' on the maternal side" (vol. 1, p. 292). The successor is chosen by the matron of the group, who confers with the members of her own longhouse (*cabane*). As for the chiefs, "Their power does not appear to have any trace of absolutism. It seems that they have no means of coercion to command obedience in case of resistance. They are obeyed, however, and command with authority; their commands, given as requests, and the obedience paid them, appear entirely free" (vol. 1, p. 293). Lafitau reserves the highest praise for their councils:

> After their deliberation on whatever subject it may be, there is almost no reason, for or against, which they have not seen or weighed and, when they want to take account of their decision, they make it so plausible that it is difficult not to interpret it in the way that they do. In general, we may say that they are more patient than we in examining all the consequences and results of a matter. They listen to one another more quietly, show more deference and courtesy than we toward people who express opinions opposed to theirs, not knowing what it is to cut a speaker off short, still less to dispute heatedly: they have more coolness, less passion, at least to all appearances, and bear themselves with more zeal for the public welfare. Also it has been by a most refined policy that they have gained the ascendancy over the other nations, that they have gained the advantage over the most warlike after dividing them, rendered themselves formidable to the most distant, and maintain themselves today in a state of tranquil neutrality between the French and English by which they have been able to make themselves both feared and sought after. (vol. 1, p. 297)

They managed to keep quarrels to a minimum, and to have a system of justice for resolving disputes, including the payment of compensation for homicide.

While Lafitau drew parallels between Iroquois government and examples from classical antiquity—Lycian "gynecocracy" was after all an absolutely critical element of his argument concerning the ultimately European origins of the Iroquois—his account differed in striking ways from his treatment of marriage and religion. Specifically, he made no argument that Iroquois government conformed in any degree to some divinely mandated paradigm. Of course, the most theologically oriented political argument, in the seventeenth if not the eighteenth century, was the divine right of kings. This would hardly have suited the Iroquois case, where kings were notably absent. In any

case, by Lafitau's time, the argument for the divine right of kings was no longer taken very seriously. As a result, this implied that Iroquois government
was an entirely human achievement, and that the Iroquois rather than God
could take direct credit for its very real successes. All in all, Lafitau's account
of the Iroquois moves from chapter to chapter, quietly but inexorably, from
divine creation towards human achievement, from universally valid tem-
plates drawn from an amalgam of classical sources and travel narratives to
an increasingly straightforward firsthand account of Iroquois practices.

By focusing either on Lafitau's ethnographic representation of the Iroquois or on the nature of his comparative project, critical assessments of his
contribution have failed to take into consideration the articulation between
these two facets of his work, and most particularly the different ways in
which they articulate with one another in different sections of his book. The
section on marriage comes closest to wedding Iroquois ethnography with
Lafitau's quest for evidence of traces of the divine plan. Not only are many
if not all Iroquois practices divinely sanctioned, but they even serve to "rec-
tify" readings of Holy Scripture. As far as religion is concerned, in order to
compensate for real or perceived lacunae in the ethnography of New France,
Lafitau has abundant recourse to classical sources as well as descriptions
of other "American savages" in order to compensate for real or perceived
lacunae in the ethnography of New France. Finally, aside from the putative
Lycian origins of Iroquois gynecocracy, the governmental institutions of the
Iroquois do not neatly conform either to a classical paradigm or to the ideal
of an absolutist monarchy with which the Jesuits were most comfortable, yet
they nevertheless demonstrate that they can function legitimately.

A century after Lafitau, Lewis Henry Morgan (1985) would use his own
ethnographic research among the Iroquis to suggest that the institutions of
their society in the realms of government, family, and property provided a
glimpse of the "prehistory" of the Greeks and Romans. There is a brief passage where, for a moment, Lafitau also self-consciously rereads the Greeks
in the light of his direct experience of the Iroquois:

> I took particular pleasure in reading Apollonius of Rhodes' poem on the ex-
> pedition of the Argonauts, because of the perfect resemblance which I find
> in all the rest of the work between these famous heroes of antiquity, and the
> present day barbarians, in their voyages and military undertakings. Hercules
> and Jason, Castor and Pollux, Zetes and Calais, Orpheus and Mopsus, and
> all those other half-gods, who rendered themselves immortal, and to whom
> people have burned incense only too readily, are so well represented by a
> troop of rascals and miserable savages that I seem to see [pass] before my eyes

those famous conquerors of the Golden Fleece, but this resemblance lowers the conception which I had formed of the glory [of these heroes], and I am ashamed for the greatest kings and princes in the world that they have thought themselves honoured to be compared to them.

The famous ship Argo which has for anchor a stone tied to a laurel root cord, to which Hercules' weight alone served as ballast and which the Argonauts carried on their shoulders for twelve days and twelve nights in the Lybian fables, has nothing to distinguish it from a dugout or at most from a long-boat [chaloupe]. This Hercules himself who chose his place on the benches with the others and took an oar in his hand, who plunged into the woods to make an oar of a little fir tree after breaking his; who, every time that they selected land to camp, lay on the shore, in the open air, on a bed of leaves or branches, is a savage in all ways and is not superior to them [the Indians]. (vol. 2, pp. 116–17)

In this remarkable passage where Lafitau relates his epiphany, his fleeting impression that the Argonauts were far more like the Iroquois than like the sculptures of the Parthenon, we can catch a glimpse of *The Golden Bough*.

By the time Lafitau published his work, theologically inspired universal histories were out of fashion, though Montesquieu's *Spirit of Laws* and Voltaire's *Essai sur les Moeurs*, attempts to understand the sweep of human history in purely human terms, had yet to be published.[22] Lahontan's description of the Huron and Algonquians was already in print—indeed, Lafitau included objections to Lahontan's account in his book—and it was to provide a far more influential portrait of the "savage" than Lafitau.[23] Although French Enlightenment theorists relied heavily on Jesuit narratives (and no doubt took great pleasure in using them in ways absolutely contrary to Jesuit ideas), Lafitau was largely left aside, whether because of his overly theocentric conception of history or his pedantic array of classical references. Ultimately he made his mark in Scotland. Adam Ferguson and John Millar drew very heavily on Lafitau for their portrait of "savages."[24] Paradoxically, it was to his sections on government and warfare to which they turned, neglecting his accounts of marriage and especially religion. Once again, the Jesuit narratives were used against the grain, and Lafitau served to buttress universal histories in which God was absent and humans alone were the principal actors.

SEVEN

Ancients, Moderns, and Others:
Fontenelle and Temple

On January 22, 1687, a commotion broke out on the floor of the Académie française. Charles Perrault, best known nowadays for his witty and cynical book of fairy tales, *Contes de Ma Mère l'Oye* (Mother Goose Tales), read a long poem in which he claimed that the accomplishments of France under the Sun King, Louis XIV, outshone those of the ancients. There was an immediate outcry. Many leading literati staunchly denied the possibility of equaling, much less excelling, the accomplishments of the Greeks and the Romans. So began the Quarrel of the Ancients and the Moderns, which eventually crossed the English Channel and continued to rage throughout the early years of the eighteenth century.[1]

Such self-conscious comparison of "ancients" to "moderns," much less of Europeans to non-Europeans, was astonishingly muted throughout most of the seventeenth century, as opposed to the era that preceded it and, even more, to the one that succeeded it. Indeed, participants in the Quarrel looked back very self-consciously to the Renaissance; at issue was whether "the restoration of learning, almost extinguished in the western parts of Europe"[2]—the phrase is Sir William Temple's (1963:66)—ultimately allowed that learning to be surpassed. At the same time, by pushing the comparative agenda back squarely into the forefront of intellectual debate, the Quarrel articulated a series of issues that were to remain at the core of the Enlightenment.

The Quarrel raised questions that were both broadly and narrowly "anthropological." The relevance of "anthropology" in the older sense of the word—theories of human nature—is obvious enough. For example, it might have been possible to argue that ancients were superior human beings to moderns, that the human race as a whole was degenerating, and that consequently moderns could never hope to equal, much less excel, the achievements of the ancients. As it happens, this particular argument was never invoked on the side of the ancients; but the counterargument, that the ancients and moderns were for all intents and purposes identical kinds of beings, and that consequently all the advantage was on the side of the moderns who could build on the ancients' achievements, was a central tenet of Fontenelle. The debate was not only about human accomplishments but about human potential in the past, present, and future. One way or the other, both sides had to take "human nature" into account, and did so quite explicitly.

However, "anthropology" in the sense of the consideration of non-Western societies was by no means entirely absent from the Quarrel, for the same reasons that it had appeared in sixteenth-century comparisons of "ancients" and "moderns." In any case, while the "moderns" were distinctly western European, this was hardly the case for the "ancients." At the end of the seventeenth century, the limits of the "ancient world" were far more comprehensive than they were to become a century or so later, when they were largely restricted to the Greeks and Romans.[3] The Egyptians, Assyrians, Chaldeans, and Persians were all quite conventionally included within the purview of classical antiquity. For example, these were all described at length in Bossuet's *Discours sur l'histoire universelle*, a book derided a century later by Voltaire for its Eurocentrism, and most notably for its omission of any mention of China. Indeed, Bossuet lavished particular praise on Egypt, depicted as a virtual model for the court of the Sun King in France.[4] More important, the Quarrel, in its attempt to define and evaluate "modern" Europe in comparative terms, came to demarcate it in contrast not only to the ancient world but also to non-Europeans, to those who apparently constituted the periphery not only of modernity but of antiquity.

While the "anthropology" of the Quarrel, if by that one means theoretical discussions about human nature, has hardly escaped the attention of its historians, the importance of non-Western societies has (not surprisingly) generally remained unremarked. Yet non-Europeans figure prominently in the writings of two key participants in the Quarrel, one "ancient" and one "modern," one Briton and one Frenchman: William Temple and Bernard de Fontenelle. Fontenelle's short "Digression sur les anciens et les modernes," penned in 1688, was no doubt the single most influential formulation of the "modern" position. Temple's "Essay upon the Ancient and Modern Learning," written two years later explicitly as a rejoinder to Fontenelle, was the spark that ignited the Battle of the Books, the British version of the Quarrel. Both texts elaborate theories of "human nature"; both also allude, at important junctures, to non-European societies. Indeed, such concerns with human nature and with non-Europeans characterize other works of Fontenelle and Temple; their invocation, in the context of the Quarrel, is by no means simply circumstantial, but rather the product of systematic reflection. Consequently, the rest of this chapter will focus on these "anthropological" concerns of both authors, not only in their respective polemical contributions to the Quarrel itself, but more generally in their writings.

Indeed, these concerns of Fontenelle and Temple have not gone entirely unnoticed.[5] Temple's description of Chinese gardens in his essay "The Gardens of Epicurus" occupies a special place in the history of gardens:

> . . . their greatest reach of imagination is employed in contriving figures, where the beauty shall be great, and strike the eye, but without any order or disposition of parts, that shall be commonly or easily observed: and though we have hardly any notion of this sort of beauty, yet they have a particular word to express it; and where they find it hit their eye at first sight, they say the *Sharawadgi* is fine or is admirable, or any such expression of esteem.[6]

Temple's short passage was the herald of a new aesthetic in European, especially English, gardens; and it incidentally sparked much scholarly speculation about what Chinese word he might conceivably (and apparently rather unintelligibly) have rendered as "sharawadgi." More generally, Temple was noted for his Sinophilia.[7] Nevertheless, the relationship of these particular facets of their thought has not been systematically related to the issues raised more broadly by the Quarrel itself.

The Upstart and the Curmudgeon

When he wrote the "Digression" at the age of thirty-one, Fontenelle had only recently established his reputation. The nephew (and later biographer) of the great tragedian Pierre Corneille, he began his literary career writing relatively undistinguished poetry and opera librettos. His first success was *New Dialogues of the Dead* in 1683, a series of short and witty exchanges pitting two ancients, two moderns, or one ancient and one modern against one another. By 1686, with the publication of *Conversations with a Lady on the Plurality of Worlds*, an urbane exposition of Copernican astronomy, he demonstrated his capacity for explaining "modern" scientific ideas in lucid and indeed entertaining prose. His reputation, both as a littérateur and as a "popularizer" (the term is flagrantly anachronistic with reference to the seventeenth century, since Fontenelle's audience was hardly "popular") of science were to earn him election to the Académie française in 1691 and to the Académie des sciences, where he was named "perpetual secretary," in 1699. In the eighteenth century he became a senior mentor to the major figures of the French Enlightenment, dying at the ripe old age of almost one hundred in 1757.[8]

Temple, by way of contrast, entered the fray only at the very end of his career. He had distinguished himself primarily as a diplomat and statesman during the Restoration, most notably by arranging the marriage of William of Orange to Charles II's niece, Mary. His consistently pro-Dutch sympathies eventually put him at odds with the attempts of Charles II to strike an alliance between Britain and France. When his name was struck from the list of privy councilors in 1681, he retired definitively from public life until his death in 1699, devoting himself to gardening and to letters.[9]

It is hardly surprising, then, that on the side of the moderns we find the brash young man of letters, nephew of one of the greatest writers of the century, just beginning to make a name for himself in Paris; and on the side of the ancients, the disillusioned if not bitter elder statesman who, one might uncharitably suspect, would readily attribute his own failures to the failings of the age. Yet to contrast a young optimist fascinated by science with an old pessimist disgruntled with politics, while not entirely off the mark, is far too simple. Specifically, such a contrast ignores underlying similarities between the men. To begin, both were educated in elite institutions: Temple at Cambridge, Fontenelle in the Jesuit Collège de Bourbon in Rouen. Such "polite" learning implied reasonable fluency in Latin, though not in Greek. If Temple was known at Cambridge for preferring tennis to the classics, he also, at the end of his life, rendered passages from Virgil in English verse. Fontenelle, a more brilliant student in his youth, composed a Latin poem on the Immaculate Conception at the age of thirteen.

This kind of familiarity with the classics was, of course, common to virtually all the literary figures of the age. Paradoxically, Temple, the "ancient," was more fluent in modern languages, no doubt because of the many years he spent abroad before and during his diplomatic career. Temple's "Essay upon Ancient and Modern Learning" specifies that he read Fontenelle's "Digression," and indeed his *Conversations with a Lady on the Plurality of Worlds*, in their original French; a subsequent essay on the same subject, "Some Thoughts upon Reviewing the Essay of Ancient and Modern Learning," cites (in French) satirical verses of Boileau apropos of the Quarrel. Fontenelle the "modern" seems less cosmopolitan; he can perhaps be forgiven for mistaking Paris during the siècle de Louis XIV for the center of the world, or at least the world of letters. This is by no means to imply that his intellectual horizons were limited to France; for example, he translated a treatise of a Dutch scholar into French, but the treatise had been written in Latin, not in Dutch. Whereas Temple kept abreast of the progress of the Quarrel in France, there is little evidence that Fontenelle was even aware of, and certainly not concerned by, Temple's rejoinder to his "digression."

It is appropriately ironic that Temple's contribution to the Quarrel was (and was titled as) an *essay*, a distinctly modern genre. Toward the end of the essay, Temple openly acknowledges his admiration for Montaigne as well as a variety of other modern "wits," among them Machiavelli, Rabelais, Cervantes, and Bacon, another essayist. There can be no doubt that his essay extolling the superiority of ancient learning consciously takes as its formal model the works of Montaigne. Conversely, the first work in which Fontenelle addresses the issues of the Quarrel—his *New Dialogues of the Dead*—is even more self-consciously modeled after an "ancient" writer, Lucian. Indeed, Fontenelle opens the *Dialogues* with a dedicatory epistle addressed "A Lucien, aux Champs Elysiens" ("To Lucian, in the Elysian Fields"), which concludes:

> Pour moi, je n'ai garde de prétendre à la gloire de vous avoir bien imité; je ne veux que celle d'avoir bien su qu'on ne peut imiter un plus excellent modèle que vous.
>
> [As for me, I have no intention to claim the glory of having imitated you well; I only want that of having realized that one cannot imitate a more excellent model than you.]

Arguably, Fontenelle's rhetoric here calls for an appropriate degree of false modesty, and one can hardly take his statement about the inimitablilty of his ancient model very literally. Even so, the readiness of the "modern" Fontenelle to resort to an ancient genre, and of the "ancient" Temple to resort to a modern one, in arguing their respective causes suggests the extent to which they inhabited a common literary culture.

Over and above this common culture composed of strange mixtures of "ancient" and "modern" elements, Fontenelle and Temple shared other attitudes. Most tellingly, both acquired on the basis of their writings a sometimes dubious reputation as *libertins*—freethinkers if not, worse, atheists. (Both conformed fairly scrupulously, however, whether out of prudence or conviction, to the conventional religious practices of their respective nations.) Temple's avowed Epicureanism, as expressed in his essay "Upon the Gardens of Epicurus," led Bishop Burnet to condemn him as "a corrupter of all that came near him," and who "delivered himself wholly to study, ease and pleasure."[10] Temple's Sinophila in his essay "Of Heroic Virtues" was another target for the bishop's outrage, on the grounds that "he thought religion was fit only for the mob. He was a great admirer of the sect of

Confucius in China, who were atheists themselves, but left religion to the rabble."[11] Despite the bishop's invective, however, Temple's genteel Epicuro-Confucianism hardly put him at great risk, at least in this world.

Fontenelle's libertinism, coming as it did at the end of the reign of Louis XIV, was not nearly so safe. In 1686, he published *History of Oracles*, a translation and adaptation of a Latin treatise by a Dutch Calvinist, Van Dale. The work refutes the notions that the oracles of the ancient world were the work of demons, and that consequently they were silenced by the coming of Christ. Instead, Fontenelle, following Van Dale, argues that the oracles were all too human products, conjurer's tricks perpetrated by cynical priests at the expense of the credulous masses; and that, at any rate, classical sources are quite explicit that such oracles persisted well into the Christian era. It was fairly obvious to contemporary readers that the priestly chicanery Van Dale depicted in ancient Greece and Rome was also intended to apply to Roman Catholicism. Even more daringly, Fontenelle had published earlier that year a short text titled "Curious Relation of the Island of Borneo, Extracted from a Letter Written in Batavia, 27 November 1684, Pertaining to the Civil War Which Has Erupted on the Isle of Borneo, Contained in a Letter of M. de Fontenelle." The text, which Fontenelle did not and could not openly avow as his own, was a transparent allegory à clef, the story of the struggle between the queen of Borneo, Mréo (an anagram of Rome), and her rival claimant to the throne, Eénégu (i.e., Genève). The point of the piece was to protest the revocation of the Edict of Nantes. By publishing these texts—even if he prudently, if disingenuously, distanced himself from the ideas they expressed by stressing in the first case that he was only a translator, and refusing in the second to admit to its authorship—he ran the very real risk of being sentenced to the Bastille.[12] As much as thirty years after the fact, a satirical poem would insinuate that "The historian of Borneo / The learned and pious Fontenelle . . . / embraces instead of a crucifix / The portrait of Spinoza."[13]

However shrill the accusations of their detractors, they were hardly baseless, most obviously in Fontenelle's case but also, to an important extent, in Temple's. Be this as it may, the real nature of Fontenelle's and Temple's religious convictions is beside the point. What matters is that their view of history—and the Quarrel of Ancients and Moderns hardly makes any sense outside of some historical perspective—is fundamentally anthropocentric and secular. Most specifically, the Quarrel precluded any providential vision of history, as developed most notably in Bossuet's *Discours sur l'histoire universelle*. If human accomplishments were to be explained in terms of God's providential design, how could one possibly presume to predict whether God would allow future achievements to equal or surpass those of the past?

Fontenelle and Temple, by excluding all considerations of divine providence and focusing instead on human nature, shared a common outlook
that in profound ways went beyond a simple zeitgeist or even an end-of-
seventeenth-century elite culture.

Even more strikingly, Fontenelle and Temple, on opposite sides of the
Quarrel, shared a common view of human nature as unchanging over time
(though not always, as we shall see, over space). After all, a progressive view
of human nature would have conveniently bolstered the "modern" position,
though such a view would only emerge in its most radical forms much later,
in the nineteenth century, when, for example, Herbert Spencer—a "modern"
among moderns, with a profound contempt for classical education—would
link biological evolution with cultural superiority. For that matter, the "ancients" never propounded a degenerationist view of humanity, which would
have been a more plausible alternative in the late seventeenth century. Nor
were these the only imaginable alternatives, the most notable and pertinent
of which was developed by Vico (1968) half a century later. Vico's cyclical
vision of human history linked changes in human institutions to changes
in mental processes as well as, literally, in bodily form. For Vico, the people
of Homer's age thought poetically just as we think prosaically. For this very
reason, Homer's poetry was matchless; but it was equally absurd to attempt
to extract, through allegory, essentially prosaic secrets supposedly hidden
in the wisdom of the ancients. Vico's "solution" to the Quarrel, that the
achievements of the ancients and the moderns were ultimately incommensurable in kind, was as far removed from Fontenelle and Temple as was any
resort to divine providence.

Indeed, Fontenelle's "Digression" begins by raising the issue of "human
nature," asking rhetorically whether the trees of bygone eras were larger than
those of today.[14] In other words, if one assumes that the trees of antiquity
were in no way "naturally" different from those of modern times, it follows
that human beings, too, were equivalent in their natures. But Fontenelle
takes this botanical comparison one step further. Trees may not change from
century to century, but they do vary from place to place; orange trees (the
example is Fontenelle's) grow more readily in Italy than France. The implication is that

> Perhaps the soil of France is not appropriate to the reasonings of the Egyp-
> tians, any more than to their palm trees. . . .[15]

Ultimately, Fontenelle minimizes the importance of climate. First of all,
"the ideas of a country travel more readily than its plants."[16] This point is ab-

solutely fundamental to Fontenelle's vision of human knowledge, to which we will return later. However, he also supports his argument by resorting to theories of the effects of climate on human nature and particularly on "mentalities." As we have seen, these theories derive from the Hippocratic and Aristotelian scheme of hot, cold, and temperate climates, the mean being characteristically preferable to the extremes. (Fontenelle had already treated the contrast rather whimsically in fantasizing about the inhabitants of other planets in the "Plurality of Worlds," imagining that the ebullient denizens of Venus might find the inhabitants of Earth's torrid zones remarkably placid, whereas grave Jupiterians would consider earthly northerners far too vivacious.) Fontenelle's argument in the "Digression" is that the advantages and disadvantages of vivacity and gravity, the respective effects of heat and cold, would compensate for one another. Still, Fontenelle is willing to consider the possibility that such climatological relativism has its limits:

> . . . perhaps it has not been by chance that [the sciences] have restricted themselves to the zone between Mount Atlas and the Baltic Sea: who knows but that these are the limits that nature has set for them, and whether one may ever hope to see great Lapp or Negro authors.[17]

Temple subscribed to the same Hippocratic/Aristotelian scheme as did Fontenelle. It is one of the ironies of the Quarrel that "ancients" and "moderns," who professed a common contempt for medieval scholasticism, should equally and unconsciously betray the legacy of the schoolmen in this regard. Temple began "An Essay upon the Original and Nature of Government" by asserting:

> The nature of man seems to be the same in all times and places, but varied like their statures, complexions, and features, by the force and influence of the several climates where they are born and bred; which produce in them, by a different mixture of the humours, and operation of the air, a different and unequal course of imaginations and passions, and consequently of discourses and actions.[18]

His point in this particular essay was to contrast, climactically and politically, extreme to temperate forms of government:

> Thus the more northern and southern nations (extremes, as they say, still agreeing) have ever lived under single and arbitrary dominions; as all the regions of Tartary and Muscovy on one side, and of African and India on the

other: while those under the more temperate climates, especially in Europe, have ever been used to more moderate governments, running anciently much into commonwealths, and of later ages into principalities, bounded by laws, which differ less in nature than in name.[19]

The flagrant Eurocentrism of the passage might seem surprising, given Temple's reputation as a Sinophile. The essay, however, dates from 1672. Temple had resigned from public office the year before (though not yet definitively); Charles II had just allied himself with France and declared war on Holland. Temple's essay rather transparently reveals his outrage and his sympathies; the France of Louis XIV clearly constitutes for him an example of "single and arbitrary dominion," Holland a "principality bounded by laws." In his later years, Temple's views, and not only his assessment of non-Europeans, were to change significantly. His 1672 essay includes a passage that virtually seems to foreshadow Fontenelle's views, in which he questions

that which is called the authority of the ancients in matters of opinion, though by a mistaken sense: for I suppose authority may be reasonably allowed to the opinions of ancient men in the present age; but I know not why it should be to those of men in general that lived in ages long since past; nor why one area of the world should be wiser than another; or if it be, why it should not be the latter rather than the former; as having the same advantage of the general experience of the world, that an old man has of the more particular experiments of life.[20]

However, while Temple in his old age was to harbor a far more generous opinion of Asia, and a somewhat less generous one of modern Europeans, he held to his notions about climatic extremes. In a posthumously published essay, "Of Popular Discontents," he was to question the extent to which the capacity for speech distinguished all humans from other animals, on the grounds that

. . . we find so little in the common speech of some nations, especially those about the Cape of Good Hope and the northern parts of Muscovy, where they are observed to drive their trade of selling furs without the use of above twenty words, even with those that understand their language.[21]

Denizens of the far north and the far south—like Fontenelle's "Lapps and Negroes"—are depicted as possibly incomplete specimens of humanity. (The passage forcefully demonstrates the underlying archaism of the scheme. Of course the Cape of Good Hope is not particularly "torrid"; its inclusion makes sense only if one automatically associates north with cold and, south with heat, as did medieval geographers.)

The pervasiveness of this torrid/frigid/temperate scheme masks its considerable flexibility. True, Fontenelle, Temple, and their contemporaries all place Europe within the optimal, temperate zone, though even here with qualifications; northern Scandinavia and parts if not all of Russia are excluded, dis-Europeanized as it were. However, such schemes do not necessarily exclude the non-European world, at least not all of it. Fontenelle's posited geographic limits of scientific reason—Mount Atlas and the Baltic—and his doubts about the eventual emergence of "great Lapp and Negro authors" are framed in tentative language. Even were one to grant for the purposes of argument that extreme climates might not be conducive to art or reason, how extreme must "extreme" be? Are all of Asia and Africa excluded, or only the Arctic Circle and the Cape of Good Hope? In important ways, for both Fontenelle and Temple, this exclusion of non-Europeans was never total.

Fontenelle: The Modernity of Science

As the most passionate and articulate champion of the moderns, Fontenelle has long enjoyed a reputation as one of the earliest ideologues of "progress."[22] In fact, his faith in progress was remarkably restricted. His often cynical perspective on progress and its limits is already apparent in his first major work, *New Dialogues of the Dead*, which features dialogues between ancients, between moderns, and between ancients and moderns. Fontenelle's disabused cynicism finds its wittiest expression in an exchange between Socrates and Montaigne:

SOCRATES: . . . How are things in the world? Isn't it much changed?
MONTAIGNE: Extremely. You wouldn't recognize it.
SOCRATES: I am delighted. I always suspected that it would have to get better and wiser than it was in my time.
MONTAIGNE: What do you mean? It is crazier and more corrupt than it has ever been. That is the change I wanted to tell you about, and I was expecting to learn from you the history of the age which you witnessed, and in which reigned such rectitude and probity.

Eventually, the two philosophers come to the same sad conclusion that

The men of every century have the same penchants, over which reason has no power. Thus, wherever there are men, there are stupidities [*sottises*], indeed the same stupidities. . . .

For the prodigious number of relatively unreasonable men who are born every hundred years, nature provides perhaps two or three dozen reasonable ones, whom she must spread out throughout the entire globe; you can judge for yourself that there will never be a large enough quantity of them in any one place to make virtue and rectitude the fashion.[23]

Fontenelle explicitly rejects the possibility of global moral progress or, for that matter, degeneration.

Philosophy represents another endeavor where, for very different reasons, Fontenelle suggests that the moderns may not be able to outdo the ancients. His reservations are expressed in another of his dialogues, this one between Descartes and "the third false Demetrius," the last of a series of impostors who led revolts against the Russian throne by claiming to be the dead Prince Dimitri. How, asks Descartes, could he have expected that people would believe his claims, in the light of the example of his two predecessors? The cynical Demetrius retorts that the two prior attempts revealed how badly the people desired a prince. In any case, he turns the tables on Descartes. Given the thousand or more philosophers before him who attempted to explain the world, how could Descartes imagine that anyone would take his own claims seriously? Descartes, by indignantly replying that he, at least, believed his own claims, only defends his honesty at the expense of casting doubts on his lucidity. It is important to point out that Fontenelle was not an impassioned anti-Cartesian. On the contrary, he openly admired Descartes, and especially his "method" of casting doubt on received knowledge, including his willingness to question the authority of the "ancients." However, Fontenelle rejects the claims of any philosophical system, that of Descartes among others, to explain the world as a whole and consequently establish itself as "authority."

Even science, the single domain which in Fontenelle's view embodies the superiority of moderns over ancients, does not entirely escape his irony. In a dialogue between the Greek physician Erasistratus and William Harvey, Erasistratus willingly concedes that knowledge of blood's circulation in the body constitutes a real advance in learning, but retorts that it hasn't stopped anyone from dying. While Harvey optimistically asserts that his discovery will prove more useful in the future, he must concede the point. Apicius, the noted Roman gourmet, complains to Galileo that he needs to invent an instrument to amplify the sense of taste, just as the telescope has expanded the capacities of vision.

The dialogues end with a remarkable exchange between Cortez and Montezuma. Cortez disparagingly proclaims, "You were very naive [*grossiers*], you Americans, when you mistook Spaniards for men descended from the fiery sphere because they had cannons, and when their boats appeared to you as great birds flying over the sea." Montezuma retorts with comparable examples from ancient Athens, ostensibly the very model of reason and civility. Indeed, Fontenelle was later to dwell at greater length on parallels between Native American and ancient Greek mythology in his essay "The Origin of Fables." Montezuma rebuts Cortez's assertion of Mexican ignorance by citing feats of engineering that baffled the Spanish, from bridges to tall stone buildings erected without the use of machinery. Cynically, he concludes, "If only we had ships to discover your lands, and had formulated the idea that they belonged to us. We would have had as much right to conquer them as you had to conquer ours." For Fontenelle, the superiority of moderns over ancients in no way justified claims of European superiority over non-Europeans.

The ideas Fontenelle formulated in *New Dialogues of the Dead* were more systematically elaborated a few years later in the essay "A Digression on the Ancients and the Moderns," which became the rallying cry for the modern faction. It begins with a horticultural metaphor to underscore his idea of human "nature." To suggest that the ancient humans were in some sense intrinsically superior to moderns is akin to asserting that their trees were larger. Admittedly, different plants thrive in different climates, but Fontenelle retorts that "the ideas of one country are more easily transported to another than its plants." In the realm of ideas, however, Fontenelle contrasts the arts and the sciences. He concedes that in the arts, and specifically in the domains of eloquence and poetry, the ancients were effectively able to attain perfection. Even here, he characteristically asserts the superiority of the Latins, "moderns with respect to the Greeks," in all such literary endeavors, with the notable exception of tragedy. Otherwise, he finds his models of excellence in the age of Augustus—Cicero in rhetoric, Livy in history, Virgil in verse—though even these authors, he suggests, are not entirely above criticism. In any case, even if the ancients have left little if any room for improvement in these domains, there is no intrinsic reason why moderns cannot aspire to equal, if not excel, their accomplishments.

Unlike the arts, however, science is cumulative. Each successive generation builds on the achievements of its predecessors, indeed through critique. It is precisely through correcting past mistakes that science advances, according to Fontenelle. For this very reason, he can playfully imagine a time in the future when the "moderns" of his day will have become, in retrospect, ancients:

> . . . we may hope that they will admire us to excess in the centuries to come, to reimburse us for the small regard we have for ourselves in ours. . . . God knows with what contempt they will treat, comparing them to us, the superior minds [*beaux esprits*] of their own time, who may well be Americans.

Fontenelle's scenario of future American moderns may be whimsical. but its whimsy rests precisely on the fact that it is not nonsensical. By rating the knowledge of "savage" Americans, "ancient" Greeks, and "modern" Frenchmen on a single continuum, Fontenelle's scheme might appear to be a precursor of the scenarios of progress that emerged later in the eighteenth century and flourished in the nineteenth.[24] The resemblance, however, is relatively superficial. Nineteenth-century Europeans were convinced that their society as a whole was more "advanced" than that of non-Europeans; not only were they "ahead," but for all intents and purposes they were perpetually in the lead. Fontenelle, on the contrary, explicitly denied the superiority of Europeans over Americans. It was only that Europeans knew more, but this knowledge could be learned as readily by future generations of Americans as by Europeans. After all, in the siècle de Louis XIV, the true successors to the ancient Greeks lived in modern Paris, not Athens.

Fontenelle returned to this parallel between ancients and Native Americans in his essay "The Origin of Fables," which was published in 1724 but originally written much earlier.[25] By "fables," Fontenelle was referring to what we would now label mythology. He was hardly the first writer to point out supposed resemblances between Native American and classical mythology, to which he had already alluded in the dialogue between Cortez and Montezuma. However, the way in which he framed the parallel was radically different. Previously, such supposed resemblances had been conceived in religious terms. As we have seen with Mandeville, the religious universe was conceived in terms of Christians (including schismatics and heretics), Jews, and pagans. In the sixteenth and seventeenth centuries, Native American religions could be encompassed along with ancient Greek and Roman religions as "pagan." For example, the Franciscan missionary Bernardino de Sahagun, who spoke Nahautl and commanded an encyclopedic knowledge of Mexican religion, did not hesitate to identify the Aztec god Huitztilo-pochtli as another Hercules, Texccatlipoca as Jupiter, Chicomecuatl as Ceres, and so forth.[26] Admittedly, Sahagun's equivalences were intended as a way of rendering a radically unfamiliar religion more familiar, but the parallels were also meant to underscore the fundamental identity of all "pagan" religion as the work of Satan. We have seen that Lafitau's analysis, published in the same year as Fontenelle's essay on fables, was more charitable, stressing ways in which both ancient and "savage" religion incorporated residues of the original divine revelation. However, for Lafitau as much as for Sahagun, any resemblances between ancient and Native American religions was the expression of an underlying identity, the conviction that, despite apparent differences, these religions were essentially the same

For Fontenelle, ancient and Native American mythologies were analogous rather than identical. In the first place, he proposes that these myths constitute the first attempts at explanation:

> . . . there was philosophy even in these crude [*grossiers*] centuries, and it was much applied to the birth of fables. Those men gifted with a bit more genius than the rest are naturally inclined to seek the cause of what they see. From where could this river which always flows have come? must have asked a contemplator in those centuries, a strange sort of philosopher, but who might perhaps have been a Descartes in this century. After long meditation, he came to the happy conclusion that there was someone who took perpetual care to pour out that water from a jar.

To modern readers, Fontenelle's assertion that myths serve as explanations of natural phenomena seems so utterly wrong, not to mention strikingly banal, that it is easy to overlook its radical novelty. At the time, there were two prevailing approaches to understanding myth. The first was Euhemerist, derived from the lost novel of the Alexandrian Greek writer Euhemerus, suggesting that the gods were originally rulers and benefactors who had been deified post mortem. The second was a hermeneutic approach that treated myth as allegory. For Fontenelle, myth was not only philosophy but, even better, an early form of science, an attempt to explain an unknown phenomenon in terms of known and observable processes. That such explanations were wrong did not diminish from their importance, to the extent that knowledge itself develops through correcting mistaken theories.

In any case, Fontenelle did not develop this argument systematically, but instead introduced another, neo-Euhemerist perspective. In the days when "fables" were first recounted, he suggested, people understood everything in terms of the miraculous. Consequently, anyone relating real events would, in good faith, interweave miraculous elements into the narrative. This is what the audience would expect in any case, and others would add new miraculous details in the retelling, so that the original story would soon become unrecognizable. Mythology, in other words, reflected certain modes of thought as well as certain rhetorical expectations.

For Fontenelle, the problem with myths did not reside in the actual explanations or narratives themselves, but in their canonical status. "Fables" embodied ideas that, however justified they might have been at the outset, were ultimately considered beyond criticism. Of course Fontenelle was being deliberately ironic, commenting sardonically on the elevated status of classical mythological motifs in seventeenth-century French literature and the visual arts. Equating classical with Native American mythology on epistemological rather than theological grounds was a sly dig at the pretensions of the ancients, but at the same time it was a token that, for Fontenelle, Native Americans were fully human, with all the potential that this could entail.

Temple: The Ancients Strike Back

Temple's reading of Fontenelle's essay inspired him to write a retort, "An Essay upon the Ancient and Modern Learning." Fontenelle never responded to Temple's critique, and quite possibly was entirely unaware of its existence. On the other hand, it attracted far more attention in England, where it initiated a British version of the Quarrel, on somewhat different terms than in France.

Temple, a passionate gardener, begins by answering with singular literal-mindedness Fontenelle's rhetorical assertion that the trees of antiquity were no larger than those of today:

> In the growth of a tree, there is the native strength of the seed, both from the kind, and from the perfections of its ripening, and from the health and vigour of the plant that bore it: there is the degree of strength and excellence in that vein of earth where it first took root; there is a propriety of soil, suited to the kind of tree that grows in it; there is a great favour or disfavour to its growth from accidents of water and of shelter, from the kindness or unkindness of seasons, till it be past the need or the danger of them. All these, and perhaps many others joined with the propitiousness of climate to that sort of tree, and the length of age it shall stand and grow, may produce an oak, a fig, or a plane tree, that shall deserve to be renowned in story, and shall not perhaps be paralleled in other countries or times.[27]

Granted that Temple lets himself be carried away by the comparison, he makes several points that are hardly trivial. First of all, the relative uniformity of average human or arboreal nature does not necessarily apply to exceptions in "the growth and stature of souls, as well as bodies." The appearance of natural prodigies of intellect and virtue, as well as of size, is ultimately unpredictable, but there is little chance of any of them appearing in our own time. Perhaps more interesting, however, is Temple's suggestion that such naturally superior individuals must also grow in the proper soil, and be well nurtured.

The metaphor is developed most explicitly in another essay of Temple's, "Of Popular Discontents":

> . . . some ages produce many great men and few great occasions; other times, on the contrary, raise great occasions, and few or no great men: and that sometimes happens to a country, which was said by the fool of Brederode; who going about the fields with the motions of one sowing corn, was asked what he sowed; he said, I sow fools; t'other replied, why do you not sow wisemen? why, said the fool, *C'est que la terre ne les porte pas.* In some places and times, the races of men may be so decayed, by the infirmities of birth itself, from the diseases or disaffection of parents; may be so depraved by the viciousness or negligence of education, by licentious customs, and luxuries of youth, by ill example of Princes, parents and magistrates, or by lewd and corrupt principles, generally infused and received among a people, that it may be hard for the best Princes and Ministers to find subjects fit for the command of armies, or great charges of state. . . .[28]

Fontenelle the modern rested his case on the capacity for human knowledge to accumulate independently of the vicissitudes of particular societies; Temple the ancient went so far as to call the possibility of such accumulation into question:

> . . . I know not what advantages we can pretend to modern knowledge by any we receive from the ancients; nay 'tis possible, men may lose rather than gain by them; may lessen the force and growth of their own genius by constraining and forming it upon that of others; may have less knowledge of their own, for contenting themselves with that of those before them. So a man that only translates shall never be a poet, nor a painter that only copies, nor a swimmer that swims always with bladders.[29]

Temple hints here at a profoundly relativist understanding of knowledge, in opposition to Fontenelle's universalist conception. The implication is that, in different places and different times, humans have different temperaments and aptitudes, making emulation ineffective at best and counterproductive at worst. However, Temple's vision of knowledge, unlike Fontenelle's, embodies a fundamental contradiction. On one hand, as in the passage above, knowledge is depicted as the product of the particular genius of individuals and peoples, of unpredictable bursts of creativity at special times and places which by its very nature defies imitation. Subverting the hackneyed conceit that moderns are dwarfs on the shoulders of giants, Temple counters that dwarfs will forever be dwarfs, and ill-suited to heights. On the other hand, whatever skepticism Temple may express about our ability to use the knowledge of the past, his vision is nonetheless permeated by a sense of loss, a nostalgic obsession with the fragility of knowledge, and a concern for how it can be transmitted, but also for how this transmission can be interrupted.

Books, in Temple's view, are only an imperfect protection against such loss. Nothing survives, he muses, of the writings of Lycurgus, Thales, or Pythagoras, though these were "much . . . greater men" than "Hippocrates, Plato, and Xenophon . . . the first philosophers, whose works have escaped the injuries of time."[30] Indeed, it was Temple's preference for the most ancient among the ancients that got him into trouble, his assertion that "the oldest books we have are still in their kind the best."[31] Temple specifically cites Aesop's *Fables* and Phalaris's *Epistles*, even though he admits that "several learned men (or that usually pass for such, under the name of critic) have not esteemed them genuine."[32] The learned men in question were classical philologists, who predictably proceeded to lambast Temple for his pretensions. After Temple's death, his former secretary and literary executor, none other than Jonathan Swift, deployed his considerable talents to defending his patron's memory. As a result, the Quarrel, which in France, and to some extent in Temple's own essay, pitted the arts against the sciences, was transformed in England to a contest between "pedants" and "wits" (to adopt the language of the ancients)—that is to say, between learning and taste.[33]

Temple does not simply assert that books are perishable, but, more radically, that they are superfluous, that the oral transmission of knowledge may be as effective as writing: ". . . In Mexico or Peru, before the least use or mention of letter, there was remaining among them the knowledge of what had passed in those mighty nations and governments for many ages. . . ."[34] Temple, in thinly guarded language, calls into question biblical chronology in order to speculate about "what those sages or learned men were, or may have been, who were ancients to those who were ancients to us."[35] These ancients of the ancients, doubly valorized, he finds not in Greece but outside Europe. Anticipating Martin Bernal, Temple asserts. "There is nothing more agreed than that all the learning of the Greeks was deduced originally from Egypt or Phoenecia."[36] Not content to stop there, he points further east, to the "Indian Brachmans" and to China, as the wellsprings of ancient knowledge:

> For whoever observes the account already given of the ancient Indian and Chinese learning and opinions, will easily find among them the seeds of all these Grecian productions and institutions: as the transmigration of souls, and the four cardinal virtues, the long silence enjoined his scholars, and propagation of their doctrines by tradition, rather than letters, and abstinence from all meats that had animal life, introduced by Pythagoras; the eternity of matter, with perpetual changes of form, the indolence of body, and tranquility of mind by Epicurus; and among those of Lycurgus, the care of education from the birth of children, the austere temperance of diet, the patient endurance of toil and pain, the neglect or contempt of life, the use of gold and silver only in their temples, the defence of commerce with strangers, and several others by him established among the Spartans, seem all to be wholly Indian, and different from any race or vein of thought or imagination that have ever appeared in Greece, either in that age or any since.[37]

In his assertion of the superiority of the ancients over the moderns, Temple indeed suggests—far more astonishingly—the superiority of India and China over Europe.

Temple pursues a similar line of reasoning in another essay, "Of Heroic Virtue." He begins by alluding to the "four great monarchies" of the ancient world: Greece and Rome, but also Egypt and Assyria. However, if in important respects these constitute Temple's "center," he makes it quite clear that he will desert them in the essay for the periphery:

> Yet the stage of all these [ancient] empires . . . is but a limited compass of earth that leaves out many vast regions of the world, the which, though accounted barbarous and little taken notice of in story or by any celebrated authors, yet have a right to come in for their voice . . . ; and besides, in my opinion, there are some of them that, upon enquiry, will be found to have equalled or exceeded all the others in the wisdom of their constitutions, the extent of their conquests, and the duration of their empires or states.[38]

Temple circumscribes the absent center by choosing his examples east, west, north, and south: China, Peru, Scythia, and Arabia. The list is hardly random, proceeding from what Temple portrays as the most to the least heroically virtuous. More important, it is structured around two symbolic axes.

Temple identifies very different sorts of heroic virtue along the east-west axis and along the north-south axis. East and West, China and Peru, are very literally depicted as realms of utopian order:

> ... the kingdom of China seems to be framed and policed with the utmost force and reach of human wisdom, reason, and contrivance, and in practice to excel the very speculations of other men, and all those imaginary schemes of the European wits, the institutions of Xenophon, the republic of Plato, the Utopias, or Oceaneas of our modern writers. And this will perhaps be allowed by any that considers the vastness, the opulence, the populousness of this region, with the ease and facility wherewith 'tis governed, and the length of time this government has run. The last is three times longer than that of the Assyrian Monarchy, which was thirteen hundred years, and the longest period of any government we meet with in story.[39]

The virtues of order and stability along the east-west axis are contrasted with those of military courage and conquest to the north and south. Temple's Scythia is a vast and somewhat amorphous domain, the realm of barbarian hordes from the Goths to Tamerlane:

> Their bodies indeed were hard and strong, their minds rough and fierce, their numbers infinite, which was owing perhaps all to their climate: but, besides these advantages, their courage was undaunted, their business was war, their pleasures were dangers, their very sports were martial; their disputes and processes were decided by arms; they feared nothing but too long life, decays of age, and a natural or slothful death. . . .[40]

"Arabia," which for Temple includes most of the Muslim world and specifically the Turkish empire, is similarly notable for its military conquests, peculiar for "being built upon foundations wholly enthusiastic [i.e., fanatical], thereby very unaccountable to common reason, and in many points contrary even to human nature."[41] If Confucius, in Temple's description of China, emerges as the perfect sage, Muhammad, by way of contrast, is unflatteringly depicted as a clever fraud whose dominion is founded on "the practices of a subtle man, upon the simplicity of a credulous people."[42]

Temple's geographical scheme is hardly disinterested. Modern Europe is very definitely identified with the "north," its modern political institutions a legacy of a feudal order associated with the Goths, the western Scythians. The European north is favorably contrasted to the Muslim south, the realm of irrational "enthusiasm." Be this as it may, Temple concludes:

> After all that has been said of conquerors or conquests, this must be confessed to hold but the second rank in the pretensions to heroic virtue, and that the first has been allowed to the wise institution of just orders and laws, which frame safe and happy governments in the world.[43]

East and West, China and Peru, are the ultimate repositories of virtue. These, it is important to note, are precisely marked by their maximal distance from Europe. The whole of Temple's scheme serves to underscore the remoteness of "modern" Europe from idealized realms, whether in time (the "ancients") or in space (the far East or far West). No wonder that the Chinese, the ancients of the ancients, are the yardstick by which "modern" decadence is most aptly measured.

The Aesthetics of Distance

The Quarrel, at least as represented by the writings of Fontenelle and Temple, embodied a "worldview" in every sense of the word, one which self-consciously sought to encompass a reality larger than "modern" and "ancient" Europe. Such a worldview was predicated on a moralizing stance, largely shared on both sides of the Quarrel. Temple and Fontenelle are thoroughly contemptuous of the vast mass of humanity. They are equally convinced that excellence, at any time or in any place in the world, is an exceedingly rare phenomenon. It goes without saying that such an attitude was possible only for members of the elite of the day, those with access, directly (in Temple's case) or at least indirectly, to the royal courts of England or France. Fontenelle and Temple, from their olympian heights, could thus decry the sea of mediocrity which surrounded them.

"Antiquity" provided the necessary yardstick by which to measure the gap. The excellence of the ancients, for Temple, highlighted the inferiority of his contemporaries, from which there was no escape other than Epicurean moderation and (very literally) cultivating one's own garden. Fontenelle's equally non-Christian solution was to belong to that small group of men and perhaps even women who, by their contributions in the fields of science and letters, added to the global stock of knowledge first constituted by the ancients.

Strikingly, such a stance of elite contempt did not dismiss non-Europeans out of hand. Admittedly, this attitude served to distinguish the writers from their contemporaries in France or England through the use of exemplars who were "distant" either in time (classical antiquity) or space (exotic non-Europeans). Indeed, for both Temple and Fontenelle, non-Europeans constituted, in very fundamental ways, the ancients of the ancients. For Fontenelle, Native American "fables" represented the exact equivalent of classical mythology: naive explanations of natural phenomena that constituted a "bottom level" from which to evaluate knowledge, but which simultaneously signaled the universal propensity of naturally superior individuals to seek rational explanation. For Temple, India and China were the wellsprings of "ancient" learning, as embodied in the teachings of Confucius and of Indian "Brachmans" doubly removed in time and space from his neighbors and contemporaries.

Such simultaneous comparison of "modern" Europeans to classical antiquity, as well as to various non-European societies, was to remain a staple of eighteenth-century letters. As the century progressed, however, non-Europeans were increasingly cast as unambiguously inferior. Notably, the vogue of Sinophilia crested relatively early in the century, though, as we will see in the next chapter, it still had partisans such as Voltaire. Such changes in attitude were, of course, partly an epiphenomenon of the extension of Europe's political and economic hegemony over the rest of the world. At the end of the seventeenth century, such domination, especially in the Far East, certainly did not seem to Europeans to be a foregone conclusion. By the end of the eighteenth century, Europeans were confident, with good reason, that they reigned supreme.

However, I would suggest that such attitudinal shifts were also related to the gradual demise of a literary culture of elite contempt. Of course it would be a gross oversimplification, bordering on caricature, to distinguish the seventeenth from the eighteenth centuries in terms of an "aristocratic" as opposed to "bourgeois" reading public. Nevertheless, there was very definitely an extension not only of the reading public, but more broadly of what Habermas has called the "bourgeois public sphere."[44] Indeed, DeJean has suggested that the Quarrel itself was both product and symptom of the emergence of this new reading public. It was still very obviously, an elite literary culture, but a far less restricted one, consequently with far less affinity for the generalized misanthropy characteristic of both Fontenelle and Temple. Was one of the concomitants of a broader inclusiveness "at home" a need to exclude "distant" exotics, just as these exotics had served, especially for Temple, to disparage the mediocrity of contemporaries "at home"? One way or the other, it was the bourgeois idea of "progress"—an idea as fundamentally alien to the "moderns" as to the "ancients" in the Quarrel—which eventually relegated non-Europeans to a status of definitive inferiority.

EIGHT

The Specter of Despotism: Montesquieu and Voltaire

In his Latin dissertation of 1893 titled *Montesquieu's Contribution to the Rise of Social Science*, Émile Durkheim asserted: "It was he, who, in *The Spirit of Laws*, laid down the principles of the new science [of sociology]" (Durkheim 1960:1). This view, that Montesquieu was not simply a forerunner of modern sociology but literally its founder, has since been repeated time and again, notably by Louis Althusser (1959), Raymond Aron (1967), and E. E. Evans-Pritchard (1981). The sociological aspects of *The Spirit of Laws* are listed systematically by Evans-Pritchard:

> . . . the insistence on the scientific, comparative study of society, the use of the data of as many societies as possible; the inclusion of primitive societies as examples of certain types of social systems; a need to start with a classification or taxonomy of societies based on significant criteria . . . ; the idea of inter-consistency between social facts (social systems), and that any social fact can only be understood by reference to other social facts and environmental conditions, as part of a complex whole; and the idea of this interconsistency being of a functional kind (Evans-Pritchard 1981:11).

As an anthropologist, Evans-Pritchard was somewhat overeager to stress the importance of Montesquieu's inclusion of "primitive" societies or, as Montesquieu and his contemporaries called them, "savages." In fact, "savages" per se are for the most part conspicuously absent from the pages of *The Spirit of Laws*, though other examples of non-European societies figure very prominently indeed. Be this as it may, the work remains remarkable for the range of social phenomena that it attempts to analyze—law, government, marriage, economy, religion, population, warfare—as well as for the broad spectrum of societies—past and present, European and non-European—cited as examples.

The Return of Legal Relativism

Montesquieu's comparative and "sociological" approach is explicitly predicated on the principle of legal relativism, formulated at the end of book 1 in no uncertain terms:

> [Laws] should be so specific to the people for whom they are made, that it is a great coincidence if those of one nation can suit another.
>
> They should be relative to the physical qualities of the country; to its frozen, burning or temperate climate; to the quality, location, and size of the territory; to the mode of livelihood of the people, farmers, hunters, or pastoralists; they should relate to the degree of liberty which the constitution can admit, to the religion of the inhabitants, to their inclinations, to their wealth, to their numbers, to their commerce, to their mores, to their manners . . . (Montesquieu 1979: book 1, chapter 3).[1]

In fact, Montesquieu's radical relativism is itself, in the final analysis, quite relative. It is hardly a disinterested stance. On the contrary, as we shall see, comparisons are constructed with a specific political agenda in mind. This does not, of course, vitiate the very real and radical achievements of Montesquieu's demarche; rather, it puts them in their proper perspective and can also help to answer the question: Why did Montesquieu find it necessary to elaborate the kind of comparative, relativistic approach he adopted?

Of course, neither Montesquieu's broad comparative scope nor his legal relativism was entirely novel; as we have seen, both flourished among legal and historical scholars in France, especially in the sixteenth century, only to fall in relative abeyance during the seventeenth. At least three key elements of Montesquieu's *The Spirit of Laws* were directly formulated by sixteenth-century French thinkers: the doctrine of legal relativism; the historical quest for the origins of the French monarchy and its legal basis; and the comparative study of legal and social institutions, explicitly including those of non-Europeans. Montesquieu's *The Spirit of Laws* marked the decisive swing of the pendulum back in the direction of sixteenth-century thought, in sharp contrast to the style and content of his immediate predecessors. But why, all of a sudden, this return? The answer is in part that *The Spirit of Laws* is a thinly veiled critique of monarchical absolutism. Even so, while it is easy to understand the absolutist penchant for universal principles of legitimacy, it is equally true that absolutism can just as easily be challenged in the name of universal principles; Rousseau is the most obvious example of such a critique. If Montesquieu eschews such a strategy, it is because his argument is aimed at advocating what he considers the best policy for France in particular, and more generally for modern Western Europe, but decidedly not for human society in the abstract. Paradoxically, it was Montesquieu's very Gallican concern for the specificity of France that led him to return to an earlier relativist, historicist, comparative perspective which had also been staunchly Gallican, though for ideologically very different reasons and in the context of very different political controversies.

The controversies in question were those that opposed the French *parlements* to the monarchy.[2] The *parlements*, of which there were twelve in all (the largest in Paris and the others in the provinces) were in principle judicial bodies, although by the eighteenth century they played an important political role in the kingdom. Offices were either inherited or sold; indeed, Montesquieu inherited the office of *président à mortier* of the Parlement of Bordeaux in 1716, only to sell it ten years later (Shackleton 1961:15–20; 82–84). Despite the sale of offices, the overwhelming majority of magistrates in the *parlements* were, like Montesquieu, members of the aristocracy. Not surprisingly, their opposition to the monarchy tended to coincide with any measures that might be construed as an attack upon their privileges. Such measures included the monarchical proclamation of the papal bull "Unigenitus," with harsh anti-Jansenist provisions, as French law. The issue was hardly one of deep religious conviction for most magistrates, but rather one of the defense of the Gallican prerogatives of the Catholic clergy in France. In particular, the *parlements* regularly opposed attempts to abrogate aristocratic exemptions from taxation, viewing them as means to rationalize the finances of France and pay for its European wars. It would be a gross oversimplification to depict the quarrels between the *parlements* and the monarchy as pitting the interest of the "aristocracy" against that of the "bourgeoisie." Indeed, the divide between them was highly permeable, and the aristocratic magistrates themselves tended to be of relatively recently ennobled bourgeois stock. The fact that such differences were more akin to modern party politics than to class warfare did not prevent participants from adopting impassioned political stances.

Montesquieu carefully and subtly frames his defense of the *parlements* and of the aristocratic interests that they represented by comparing France and, more generally, Western Europe to other societies and forms of government, both in the European past and in the rest of the world. His first and no doubt most crucial step is to propose a typology of forms of government: republics, monarchies, and despotisms. Durkheim (1960:8–9; 24–35), among others, notes Montesquieu's debt to, but also his distance from, Aristotle's typology of constitutions in terms of rule by one (monarchy or tyranny), the few (aristocracy or oligarchy), or the many (polity or democracy).[3] Montesquieu's originality is that he bases his typology not on the number of rulers, but rather on the principle that underlies each form of government: republics are animated by "virtue," monarchies by "honor," and despotisms by "fear." This classificatory shift is animated by a set of preoccupations different from those of his predecessors in classical antiquity. Aristotle's most critical concern is whether the polis is governed for the common good or for the exclusive benefit of the ruler or ruling party. Polybius attributes the stability and military successes of Rome to its mixed constitution, with elements of monarchy, aristocracy, and democracy judiciously combined. Montesquieu's preoccupation is with the historical uniqueness of the Western European (and, a fortiori, the French) monarchical system. The central question is: What sets modern "monarchies" apart either from republics or from despotisms? The typology itself, as well as the examples Montesquieu chooses to exemplify nonmonarchical forms of government, is specifically geared to answering this question.

A "monarchy," for Montesquieu, is a regime where "one lone person governs, but by fixed and established laws" (2, 1). In this respect, it shares features with both despotism (one sole ruler) and republics (the rule of law). But what is to prevent the lone ruler from subverting the rule of law? According to Montesquieu, the answer lies in the existence of "subordinate and dependent intermediary powers" (2, 4), most notably the aristocracy. In other words, the "honor" that underpins the monarchical system is an explicitly hierarchical system of status honor, where each rank is intensely jealous of its privileges and prerogatives. By responding vigorously to any real or perceived threat to such hereditary privileges, the nobility constitutes an effective check on arbitrary royal power. This is not to say that Montesquieu paints an idealized portrait of the aristocracy. On the contrary:

> Ambition with indolence, pettiness with pride, the desire to get rich without work, the aversion for truth, flattery, treachery, perfidy, abandoning all one's commitments, the contempt for the duties of a citizen, the fear of the prince's virtues, the expectation of his weaknesses and, more than all this, the perpetual ridicule cast upon virtue form, I believe, the character of the greater number of courtiers in all places and at all times. (3, 5)

Montesquieu hastens to add, perhaps not entirely convincingly, that in this passage he does not intend to satirize monarchical government.

Montesquieu's paradoxical contention that the monarchical system works by means of, rather than in spite of, the very moral failings of its protagonists draws heavily on Bernard Mandeville's delightfully cynical *Fable of the Bees* (Mandeville 1924).[4] The motto of Mandeville's book is "Private vices, publick benefits." Its argument is that England owes its prosperity not to the moral virtues of its people, but to their failings. Mandeville's argument rests on a sort of moral psychology that, as far as intentions are concerned, equates "virtue" with "reason" and "vice" with "passion." Most human actions, he contended, are motivated by emotions—"passions"—rather than by "reason." This view was to find consistent echoes in eighteenth-century theories of morality—for example, in Adam Smith and David Hume. On one hand, Mandeville mercilessly lampoons the pretensions of the "respectable," most of whom are, he suggests, motivated by a vain desire for praise and, more generally, by a desire that others think well of them; even those few who may behave virtuously outside the public eye are more often concerned with maintaining their own good opinion of themselves than with a truly disinterested concern with public welfare. Given such a bleak assessment of human nature, it is hardly surprising that he concludes that "unhappy is the People, and their Constitution will be ever precarious, whose Welfare must depend upon the Virtues and Consciences of Ministers and Politicians" (Mandeville 1924, vol. 1:190).

As the motto of his book puts forth, however, Mandeville's paradox is that the unintended consequences of self-interested actions may be highly beneficial. Mandeville delights in arguments that egregious immorality may be in the public interest. For example, by providing an outlet for the sexual urges of rakes, prostitution may help to preserve the chastity of "proper" young women. The apparently wasteful desire for frivolous and expensive luxuries on the part of the rich provides much needed work for the masses of the poor. What is more, such wealth would hardly be available for the wasting were it not for the unscrupulous avarice of their forbears. Thrift and moderation, however virtuous in the abstract, are bad for the economy!

Montesquieu's disabused portrait of courtiers is entirely in the spirit of Mandeville. Even more important, his whole conception of "honor" as the key principle of the monarchical system is equally Mandevillian. Every individual, at least every "noble," is concerned with maintaining if not improving his rank. (It must be borne in mind that, since the sixteenth century at least, the upper strata of the bourgeoisie had been consistently ennobled; the kind of ambition that Montesquieu had in mind was hardly the monopoly of the hereditary aristocracy.) "It is true," he notes, "that, philosophically speaking, it is a false honor which directs all parties to the State: but *this false honor is as useful to the public as a true one would be to those particulars who might possess it* (3, 7; my emphasis)." One could hardly imagine a more emphatic formulation of the principle of "Private Vices, Publick Benefits."

Yet the thrust of Montesquieu's argument is ultimately very different from that of Mandeville's. For Mandeville, the principle of "Private Vices, Publick Benefits" is rooted in human nature, in the view that humans are essentially selfish and self-interested, perpetually concerned with seeking gratification of one sort or another, such that their contribution to public welfare must rest on the unintended rather than the intended consequences of their actions. Montesquieu, on the contrary, relativizes such a principle, limiting it in space and time to the monarchical systems of government characteristic of modern Western Europe. Republican as well as despotic systems are characterized by a different calculus of virtues and vices. The motto for a "republic" in Montesquieu's scheme would be "Private virtues, public benefits"; for "despotism" it would be "Private vices, public failings." In republics and despotisms alike, private morality and public welfare go hand in hand, for better or for worse. Only monarchies constitute an exception.

Romans and Despots

Not surprisingly, Montesquieu's paradigmatic examples of both republican and despotic governments are in one sense or another "distant" from modern Western Europe, either in time (Rome furnishing the principal model of republican government) or in space (examples of despotism primarily associated with Asian societies). *The Spirit of Laws* is abundantly footnoted, and it is consequently easy to determine both Montesquieu's preoccupations and his source materials. Out of a total of 667 citations, no less than 204 are from ancient Rome.[5] A few poets aside, the bulk of these citations refer to Roman historians, most notably Tacitus, Livy, and (somewhat less conventionally) Denis of Halicarnassus. Montesquieu's sources for his account of classical antiquity reflect the standard humanist education of the time, including its distinctive Latin bias. However, no less than 213 citations—a very substantial proportion—refer to the non-European world and demonstrate Montesquieu's considerable interest and familiarity with the rapidly growing corpus of travel literature. The vast bulk of these citations (165) concern Asia: 51 refer to Turkey and Persia, 22 to India and Siam, 72 to China, and 20 to Japan. (To these I would be inclined to add the 17 references to Russia and "Tartary.") By way of comparison, sources on Africa are cited only 8 times, and only 18 citations refer to the Americas. Such a strong Asiatic bias reflects, but only partly, the travel literature available to Montesquieu at the time. Out of some 805 "geographical" books on the non-European world published in France in the seventeenth century, some 218 (27 percent) are about the Americas; 127 (16 percent) about Africa; 428 (53 percent) about Asia; and 32 (4 percent) about the Pacific.[6] Clearly, Africa and the Americas are underrepresented in *The Spirit of Laws*, and are only very marginally the focus of Montesquieu's attentions.

Montesquieu's apparent lack of interest in America and his fascination with Asia reflect the structure of his argument, and not simply his personal tastes in the literature of exploration. Both American "savagery" and Asian "despotism" constitute plausible antitheses of Europe.[7] However, the contrast of American "savagery" to European "civilization" is totally unsuitable to Montesquieu's purpose. On one hand, "savagery" had served Hobbes as an example of humanity in a "state of nature," enabling him to argue that government—*any* government—was preferable to anarchy, an argument that runs absolutely counter to Montesquieu's. On the other hand, "savages" had been used to devastating effect by Montaigne (chapter 3) and, much closer to Montesquieu's time, by the Baron de Lahontan (chapter 9) as a vehicle for criticizing the moral bankruptcy of contemporary France. Such critiques were admittedly closer in tone and in spirit to Montesquieu's thought. Indeed, Montesquieu's first literary venture, the highly successful *Persian Letters*, presents a sardonic vision of French society through the eyes of two fictional Persian travelers, much as Lahontan's fictional dialogue with Adario, "un sauvage de bons sens qui a voyagé [a savage of good sense who has traveled]" mercilessly satirizes the pretensions of "civilization."[8] Lahontan, like Montaigne, extols the virtues of the "savages" as opposed to the vices of "civilized" Europe. For these authors, "savages" are "naturally" good and Europeans are "unnaturally" depraved. Montesquieu, on the contrary, maintains a greater critical distance from his Persian protagonists and, even more important, has no interest whatsoever in depicting Persia as a model society as compared to France.

In *The Spirit of Laws* even more than in the *Persian Letters*, Asiatic "despotism" constitutes an antimodel, an entirely negative vision of government as well as of society. Again, such a vision reflects, but only partly, Montesquieu's sources. If, all in all, he cites 24 different sources on Asia, the lion's share of these citations (105 out of a total of 165) derive from only four sources. Admittedly, two of these are anthologies. The *Lettres edifiantes et curieuses* (*Edifying and Curious Letters*), cited 20 times, were regularly edited by the Jesuits as part of the propaganda campaign for their overseas missions, and also constituted a major source of ethnographical and historical information. The *Recueil des voyages qui ont servi à l'établissment de la Compagnie des Indes* (Anthology of voyages which contributed to the establishment of the [Dutch] East India Company), was cited 25 times. The other two principal sources are Jean Chardin, cited 20 times, a French Huguenot jeweler whose account of his travels through Turkey and Georgia to Persia in the late seventeenth century originally inspired the *Persian Letters*; and Father Du Halde, cited 40 times, whose *Description de l'empire de la Chine* (Description of the Chinese Empire), compiled from accounts of his fellow Jesuits, "became the standard authority on matters Chinese for much of the eighteenth century" (Marshall and Williams 1982:84).

Chardin's depiction of the Persian court, though by no means invariably negative, provides ample fodder for Montesquieu's composite portrait of Asiatic "despotism." On the other hand, Jesuit depictions of China were for the most part highly adulatory, especially as compared to descriptions not only by Protestants but by representatives of rival Roman Catholic missionary orders.[9] As Vernière (1977:47) points out: "Montesquieu insists on counterbalancing the optimistic vision of the Jesuits with the hostile testimony of the Dutch [in the *Recueil des Voyages*] . . . the Englishman Anson, and the Russian ambassador Lange." Fair and equitable treatment of the Chinese is hardly the issue; in spite of the overwhelmingly favorable treatment characteristic of the sources he relies on most heavily, Montesquieu paints a bleak picture of Chinese "despotism" that corresponds to his discussions of Turkey, Persia, and India. Etiemble (1989:50–72) lays the blame on one Father Foucqet, an ex-Jesuit with an axe to grind against his erstwhile order, who was able to appeal to Montesquieu's anti-Jesuit sentiments in order to cast grave doubts about their portrayal of China. Be this as it may, in his determination to oppose a model of Asiatic "despotism" to European "monarchy," Montesquieu was quite willing to overlook the attitude of authors he cited when they suited his purpose.

The composite picture of "despotism" that Montesquieu constructs from—or against—his sources is of a society in which "one person alone, without law and without rule, decides everything according to his will or his caprices" (2,1). The portrait is unambiguously and entirely negative: ". . . despotism does frightful damage [*cause . . . des maux effoyables*] to human nature" (2, 4). The construct of "despotism" is in effect Montesquieu's answer to Hobbes, a combination of sovereign authority and a society "without law and without rule," akin to Hobbes's state of nature. Chardin's description of the Persian court is Montesquieu's paradigmatic example, though even here he exaggerates his sources for polemical effect. For instance, citing Chardin, he baldly states:

> In Persia, when the king has condemned someone, one cannot speak any-more about him, nor ask for his pardon. If he were drunk or out of his senses, the order of execution should be carried out in any case; otherwise, he would contradict himself, and the law cannot contradict itself. (3, 10)

Indeed, Chardin relates several incidents in which the Persian king loses his temper in fits of drunkenness. For example (Chardin 1988:7–8), he tells the story of how the king, in a drunken rage, annoyed that a lutenist has not played to his taste, orders the player's hands cut off. The king's favorite, expecting the king to calm down, lets the lutenist off with a reprimand. On awakening, however, the king is so furious to find the lutenist's hands intact that he orders his favorite's hands cut off as well; and when the Lord Steward attempts to intervene, the king condemns all three. But at last the king is persuaded to relent—a detail that flatly contradicts Montesquieu's assertion of the irreversibility of the despot's verdicts.

If Montesquieu uses Persia as his prototype of Asian despotism, Japan is depicted as the most extreme case, an archdespotism among despotisms, perhaps because the Japanese are symbolically the easternmost of "Eastern" peoples, but also, no doubt, because the expulsion of missionaries and re-pression of Christianity earned them the hatred of the Jesuits, while Dutch merchants, the only Europeans with any access to Japan, were unsympa-thetic to Asians of any sort. Montesquieu's vision of Japan is one of a nation where laws are so severe that they are paradoxically ineffectual:

> One punishes almost all crimes with death, because disobedience to so great an emperor as Japan's is an enormous crime. . . . These considerations are drawn from slavery [*servitude*]; and stem most of all from the fact that, since the emperor is proprietor of all goods, almost all crimes directly contravene his interests. . . .
>
> It is true that the astonishing character of this opinionated, capricious, determined, bizarre people, who brave all perils and all misfortunes, seems at first sight to absolve legislators of the atrocity of their laws. But, for people with a natural contempt for death, who rip open their stomachs on the slight-est pretext, are they corrected or stopped by the continual sight of executions? and don't they become accustomed? . . .
>
> The atrocity of the laws thus prevents their execution. When the penalty is without measure, one is often obliged to prefer impunity. (6, 13)

The play of public and private virtues and vices that characterize Mandeville's scheme applies as well to Montesquieu's depiction of "despotism." If evil in the public domain stems from the submission of the entire nation to the caprices of a single individual, a condition which Montesquieu considers equivalent to universal slavery, its private analogue is the harem, where everyone—not only wives but also the eunuchs who guard them—is similarly reduced to "domestic slavery" (the precise term Montesquieu uses in book 16 to characterize polygamy) by submitting to the caprices of the master of the household:

> As concerns polygamy in general, independent of the circumstances that can render it slightly tolerable, it is of no use to the human race, nor to either of the two sexes, that which abuses and that which is abused. (16, 6)
>
>   . . . the slavery of women is very consistent with the spirit of despotic government, which likes to abuse everything. Thus we have seen, at all times, *in Asia* [my emphasis], domestic slavery go hand in hand with despotic government. (16, 9)

If Montesquieu's characterization of "despotism" allies private and public vices, his model of republican government has "virtue" as its central governing principle. Admittedly, he repeatedly insists that he means *civic* virtue, the commitment of citizens to uphold and defend their system of government, and not "morality" per se. However, such pleas are partly disingenuous. Not only might the blanket claim of the moral superiority of republics to monarchies be considered politically seditious, but it would be doubly offensive to the Church. In the first place, it would suggest that morality depended more on the proper form of "government" than on the proper religion. Second, readers could not help but notice that in the mid-eighteenth century, the most obvious and successful examples of republican government in contemporary Europe, Holland and Switzerland, were Protestant and not Catholic. Montesquieu had good reason to avoid unnecessarily offending the religious authorities. His nomination to the French Academy in 1727 had very nearly been stymied, according to Montesquieu himself, by the objections of a Jesuit priest to the ideas expressed in the *Persian Letters* (Shackleton 1961:85–89). Montesquieu's anxieties were far from groundless. In spite of his vigorous defense against charges that the book was irreligious, it was placed on the Index of Forbidden Books in 1751 (Shackleton 1961:356–377).

Montesquieu's undisguised admiration for the "ancient" model of republican government had already been propounded in a treatise, published in 1734, called *Considerations of the Causes of the Greatness of the Romans and of Their Decadence* (Montesquieu 1968). The "decadence" in question was not so much the fall of the Roman Empire, but rather that of the Republic. In *The Spirit of Laws*, Montesquieu's assertion of the moral superiority of "ancient" republicans to "modern" monarchists is abundantly clear:

> Most ancient peoples lived in governments whose principle was virtue; and, while it remained in force, they accomplished things that we no longer see today, and which astonish our small souls. (4,4)

If monarchies are characterized by the ambitions of their subjects, republics depend on the equality of their citizens. Luxury and ostentation are central to monarchies, frugality to republics.

Nowhere does Montesquieu more forcefully expose his views on the relationship between form of government and private morality than in a short chapter (7, 9) titled "The Condition of Women, under Diverse Governments":

> Women have little restraint in monarchies; because the distinction of ranks summons them to the court, they find there the spirit of liberty which is, more or less, the only one tolerated. Each one uses her charms and her passions to further her fortune; and since their weakness permits them no pride, but only vanity, luxury reigns everywhere among them.
>
> In despotic States, women introduce no luxuries, but are themselves an object of luxury. They must be extremely enslaved . . . Their quarrels, their indiscretions, their repugnancies, their leanings, their jealousies, their outbursts, this art that small souls have of making themselves interesting to great ones, cannot be of no consequence. . . .
>
> In republics, women are freed by laws, and captive of mores [*moeurs*]; luxury is banished, and, with it, corruption and vices.
>
> In Greek cities . . . the virtue, the simplicity, the chastity of women was such that one has scarcely ever seen a people who have maintained, in this respect, better control.

Mandeville, it is true, had anticipated the argument that ancient republics were characterized by virtue, but only to satirical effect:

> I have heard People speak of the mighty Figure the Spartans made above all the Commonwealths of Greece, notwithstanding their uncommon Frugality and other exemplary Virtues. But certainly there never was a Nation whose

Greatness was more empty than theirs: The Splendor they lived in was inferior to that of a Theatre, and the only thing they could be proud of, was, that they enjoy'd nothing. (Mandeville 1924:245)

Englishmen, he sardonically retorts, would hardly wish to trade places with the Spartans. There is no trace of such irony in Montesquieu; only a sense of nostalgia that such virtues are almost beyond the comprehension of the "small souls" of the present.

In any case, Montesquieu is ultimately more preoccupied by the menace of despotism than by the ideal of a virtuous republic. The whole of book 8 is concerned with "The corruption of the principles of the three governments." The inclusiveness of the title is deceptive; "despotism" is not subject to the same risk of corruption as republics or monarchies. Rather, "the principle of despotic government is ceaselessly corrupted, because it is corrupt by its very nature" (8, 10). Monarchies and republics, on the other hand, run the real risk of turning into despotisms. Montesquieu hazards a despairing metaphor: "Rivers run into the sea; monarchies lose themselves in despotism" (8, 17)." It would seem as if monarchical absolutism was, virtually inevitably, turning France into another Persia. Indeed, Montesquieu had already (albeit obliquely) suggested as much in the *Persian Letters*. Writing of Louis XIV, Usbek the Persian suggests that "of all the governments in the world, that of the Turks or of our august sultan would please him most (letter 37)." (The *Persian Letters*, it should be noted, were published a safe six years after Louis XIV's death!) If Louis XIV represented the "arch-Orientalizing" French monarch, it hardly followed that after his reign France was safely back on the path of "moderate" government: "Most of the peoples of Europe are still governed by their mores" [*moeurs*; one might say 'customs' or even, anachronistically, 'culture']. But if, by a long abuse of power; if, by a great conquest, despotism were at one point to establish itself, neither mores nor climate would impede its establishment; and, in this fair part of the world, human nature would suffer, at least for a while, the insults in bears in the three others" ((8, 8)."

Monarchs and Aristocrats

But why, if "Asiatic" despotism constitutes the supreme political evil, is not the establishment of a "Roman" republic the antidote? Herein lies the crux of Montesquieu's argument, and its subtlety. A binary contrast of "republican" to "despotic" government would, of course, be entirely consistent with an argument from universal principles, typical of one or another seventeenth-century theorist. Precisely because Montesquieu is arguing that a republic, however ideal in the abstract, is not a workable solution to France's political ills, he needs to resort to a relativistic argument. Depending on a multiplicity of factors—climate, terrain, customs, history, size—one or another form of government is appropriate. Size is particularly critical: ". . . It is the natural property of small states to be governed as republics, middle-sized ones to be subject to a monarch, great empires dominated by a despot" (8, 20). Montesquieu, in his *Considerations*, had already attributed the demise of the Roman republic to Rome's acquisition of a great empire. Clearly, Montesquieu saw France's territorial ambitions, in Europe and abroad, as a threat to liberty.

The political point of the argument is that, *for France*, though not necessarily in the abstract, a republican government is not a plausible option. The history, customs, and size of France all militate against a republican solution, one that seemed to Montesquieu (can one blame him?) frankly unrealistic in the mid-eighteenth century. Consequently, he argues, the only *plausible* defense against the "tide" of despotism is the aristocracy, as imperfect if not morally bankrupt as it might be. This explains why Montesquieu includes such a long section at the end of the book in which he develops the thesis of the Germanic (and feudal or aristocratic) origins of France. His plea for the maintenance of aristocratic privileges cannot logically rest on an argument, like Mandeville's, from "human nature," for clearly many societies around the world maintain no such privileges; nor can it rest on the argument that this is by any stretch of the imagination an ideal form of government. Only a relativistic argument can hold: an aristocracy is the best that France can manage for the time being. It is, implicitly, more important to stave off the real threat of despotism than to attempt to institute an ideal but implausible republic.

Montesquieu's contrast of French "monarchy" to distant paradigms of "Asiatic" despotism or "ancient" republicanism is itself partly a cautionary measure. Examples existed far closer to home. Montesquieu very clearly regards Spain and Portugal as antimodels: monarchies perhaps, but monarchies that border on despotism, not least because of the size of their empires. Indeed, in his discussion of the relationship of the size of polities to the nature of government, Montesquieu very ironically cites Spain as the exception that proves the rule—"To hold on to America, it did what even despotism does not do; it destroyed its inhabitants" (8, 18)—and then proceeds to point out Spain's failure to impose despotic rule over the Netherlands. Spain and Portugal are cited as noteworthy examples of religious intolerance (e.g., 15, 13). Montesquieu's suggestion (2, 4) that the power of the clergy in Iberia constitutes the only real check on the despotic authority of the monarchy again provides a parallel between Spain and "Asiatic" despotisms, for which religion also constitutes, in his analysis, the principal moderating force. Holland, on the other hand, represents an equally appropriate example of a republic, not least by its small size. However, as eloquently as Montesquieu denounces the evils of the Spanish crown (especially in the New World), he remains curiously silent about the republicanism of Holland. Admittedly, he points out, without giving specific examples—which were no doubt unnecessary—that Catholicism is more suited to monarchies and Protestantism to republics (24, 5), not least because of "the spirit of independence and liberty" which, he suggests, characterizes the peoples of northern as opposed to southern Europe. It would certainly not have been politic of Montesquieu to idealize Holland, and would hardly have served his case for maintaining aristocratic privilege. However, the Dutch case would have made it clear to Montesquieu's contemporary readers that republican government did not in any sense contradict human nature, and was not impossible to establish in modern Europe.

In short, relativism, comparativism, and historicism served Montesquieu, as they had served his sixteenth-century predecessors, as a means of asserting the specificity of the French case in order to argue for a particular and partisan political agenda. In the sixteenth century, the argument for French legal and political particularism served as a means of asserting independence from "Roman" hegemony, not only for Huguenots but also for supporters of a French monarchy in open conflict with the ultra-Catholic party. It allowed Montesquieu to argue, along with the *parlements*, for the maintenance of aristocratic privilege, in contradistinction to the incipient despotism of Spain or the open republicanism of Holland. In other words, from its very origins, the comparative perspective has been formulated in terms of specific Western European political debates and discourses. Needless to say, this is equally true of various universalist theories, framed in terms of invariant "human nature."

Be this as it may, *The Spirit of Laws* is much more than a highly sophisticated (and, arguably, sophistical) defense of the privileges of the French aristocracy. This is no doubt because of the unresolved tension in the book between the absolute and relative senses of "best government." In absolute terms, Montesquieu's idealization of republican government, especially of Rome, is transparent and sincere. The relativist argument that different types of government are appropriate for different societies is much harder to make if one is ultimately suggesting, as does Montesquieu, that one's own society must settle for what is after all, in the abstract, only second best. It is this very tension that drives the (anachronistically speaking) sociological and functionalist tenor, not to mention the vast scope, of the work.

Paradoxically, the logical needs of Montesquieu's ideologically charged argument do not require, in and of themselves, such a broad horizon in space or time. Contemporary Western European regimes, from Spain to Holland, provided the range of examples that Montesquieu needed, and were in important respects more directly relevant instances than Asia or the ancient world. But it was precisely the spatial and temporal distance of Persia or the Roman republic that allowed Montesquieu a certain degree of latitude; their apparent irrelevance to contemporary France made them safer examples to choose. Moreover, Muslim Persia (unlike Catholic Spain) and pre-Christian Rome (unlike Protestant Holland) could safely be denigrated or idealized without antagonizing the Church too flagrantly. Not incidentally, the virtues of Rome or the vices of Asia could easily be exaggerated for polemical purposes without ruffling any feathers; we have already seen how Montesquieu systematically represented Asian regimes in a less favorable light than some of his sources. Ultimately, in Montesquieu's scheme, Asia and Rome were not necessarily important in and of themselves, but constituted ways of categorizing European politics.

Despite the systematically negative depiction of Asia in *The Spirit of Laws*, Montesquieu's representation is markedly different from more modern versions of "Orientalism" (Said 1978). Montesquieu may indeed assert the political, if not moral, superiority of Western Europe, but hardly as an invitation for domination. On the contrary, exaggerated territorial ambitions are the hallmark of "despotism." Montesquieu repeatedly insists that the Spanish conquest of America was disastrous for Spain as well as for the Americas, and he would certainly have looked askance at attempts to achieve similar dominion over Asia or Africa. In fact, in the mid-eighteenth century, European colonies in Africa and Asia were virtually all limited to coastal enclaves, geared to establishing and maintaining a monopoly over sea transport but not at all toward subjecting the populations of the interior.

Doubts about Despotism

Compared to Montesquieu, Voltaire suffers from a reputation as an intellectual lightweight, a writer better known for the ferocity of his wit than for the profundity of his ideas, a better fighter than thinker. In fact, Voltaire elaborated a thoughtful and pertinent critique of Montesquieu to which he would return again and again in his writings: in the *Essai sur les moeurs et l'esprit des nations* in 1756,[10] in a series of dialogues, *L'ABC* in 1769,[11] and finally in *Commentary on the Spirit of Laws* in 1777.[12] Not that Voltaire can resist the occasional bon mot, as when he sardonically remarks that Montesquieu's book reveals more of his wit (*esprit*) than the spirit (*esprit*) of laws.[13] This said, Voltaire much appreciated Montesquieu's wit, certainly in contrast to political theorists such as Grotius, whom he found tedious. Voltaire applauded Montesquieu's championship of liberty and his criticism of the Church. Still, Voltaire alleges with considerable justification that Montesquieu frequently plays fast and loose with his sources. (The same could be said of Voltaire, of course, but this hardly invalidates the point.) Most important, Voltaire calls into question Montesquieu's construct of despotism. He quite rightly insists that an entire system of government cannot possibly function as a response to the whims of a single individual, however powerful. Voltaire points out that the specific realms that Montesquieu singles out as despotic—China, the Islamic empires of Turkey, Persia, and Mughal India—are all characterized by elaborate legal systems that constrain the ruler as well as his subjects. Exceptional rulers, in Europe as well as in Asia, sometimes manage to circumvent the law and impose their own will. But the fact is, he insists, that such rulers remain exceptional, and can hardly be invoked to characterize the system.

China in particular constituted a positive model of government for Voltaire. For all his opposition to the Jesuits, he readily accepted, indeed relied on, their depictions of China. China occupies a prominent place in the *Essai sur les moeurs*, Voltaire's attempt to write universal history. While by contemporary standards Voltaire's history remains overwhelmingly Eurocentric, his inclusion of China and indeed of other prominent Asian empires represents a very deliberate attempt to moderate such a bias. Jesuit attempts to reconcile Chinese and biblical chronology led to China's depiction not only as the most ancient but as the most enduring state the world has ever seen, a depiction that served Voltaire's very un-Christian aims perfectly. By no stretch of the imagination did China fit Bossuet's neo-Augustinian narrative of world history, a narrative that Voltaire self-consciously sought to replace. Voltaire, again following the Jesuits' lead, uncritically accepted legendary Chinese accounts of the first emperors as great legislators and culture heroes. Such accounts, after all, did not differ so substantially from classical biographies of Solon and Lycurgus, and they fit neatly within European paradigms of great legislators as founders of political systems. Needless to say, the permanence of the Chinese empire was radically overstated, both in official Chinese and in Jesuit accounts. However, it permitted Voltaire to represent China as a model of order and good government, quite the opposite of Montesquieu's depiction of it as an exemplar of despotic rule.

Voltaire's Sinophilia, like Montesquieu's Sinophobia, was a direct reflection of his political commitments. Aside from the Church, opposed more or less stridently by both writers, Voltaire detested the aristocracy, to which he, unlike Montesquieu, did not belong. As a young man he had been mercilessly beaten by the lackeys of a nobleman he had dared to ridicule, and he quickly discovered that he had no recourse to justice other than his own caustic wit. In the political struggle between the *parlements*, which were dominated by the aristocracy, and the court, Voltaire was a staunch supporter of the monarchy.[14] For Montesquieu, the aristocracy was the only institution with the capacity to control the centralizing power of the king; for Voltaire, the monarchy was the only institution capable of holding the illegitimate authority of the aristocracy in check. For Montesquieu, Louis XIV, who had systematically attempted to marginalize the aristocracy, was the closest European equivalent to an Asiatic despot. In 1751, only a few years after the publication of *The Spirit of Laws*, Voltaire published his far more favorable account of Louis's reign, *Le Siècle de Louis XIV*.[15] Voltaire's admiration is all the more remarkable given that, near the end of his reign, Louis XIV revoked the Edict of Nantes, initiating new anti-Protestant repression and championing the cause of the Church. However profoundly Voltaire regretted Louis's religious policy, he staunchly approved his resolution to centralize state power at the aristocracy's direct expense.

The attitude of each writer to China mirrored his attitude toward Louis XIV. China was a highly centralized realm lacking a hereditary aristocracy, and it had an elaborate bureaucracy directly responsible to the emperor. If, as Voltaire contended, China was a model of stability, justice, and order, it would support his contention that an aristocracy was in no way necessary for good government. On the other hand, Montesquieu's depiction of China as a realm characterized by gross injustice and the misery of the multitude epitomized the evils of a political system ruled by a single individual unchecked by a hereditary aristocracy. Competing visions of China reflected competing visions of French politics.

Yet there was one crucial way in which Voltaire's representation of China departed drastically from that of previous Sinophiles like Temple. For Temple, the partisan of "ancient" learning, the recent accomplishments of "modern" European science and technology were of little weight. A half century later, Voltaire was far less contemptuous of "modern" learning, and this was reflected in his comparison of China to Europe: "Our character is to perfect ourselves, and that of the Chinese is, up to the present, to stay where they have arrived. . . . The Chinese, always superior in morality, have made little progress in the other sciences; no doubt nature, which gave them an

upright and wise spirit, denied them force of mind (1963, vol. 2:397–98)."
While Voltaire readily conceded that western Europe had lagged far behind
China for most of its history, he also stressed the rapidity with which Europe
had caught up with if not surpassed China, at least in certain domains that
were by no means negligible. If, on one hand, Voltaire idealized China, especially in the domains of religion and government, he also planted the seeds
of the myth, which was to become far more pervasive, of intrinsic Asian
"stasis" and European "dynamism."

Voltaire was not the only French Enlightenment figure to challenge Montesquieu's depiction of China. François Quesnay, founder of the Physiocrat
movement and arguably the forerunner of modern economic theory, wrote
a long essay in 1767, *The Despotism of China* (Quesnay 1888:562–660),
which in spite of its title is entirely laudatory and which explicitly seeks
to refute Montesquieu's claims. Quesnay was less concerned with the failings of the aristocracy than with the evils of mercantilism. In particular,
he sharply opposed the tariffs imposed on goods, especially agricultural
staples, exchanged within France between one province and another. Such
local prerogatives, he argued, discouraged the free exchange of goods and
consequently agricultural productivity. He portrayed China as a strongly
centralized government—a "despotism" in a positive sense, though the
choice of term was unquestionably infelicitous—with a remarkable degree
of agricultural productivity, which he attributed to wise economic policies,
including the absence of internal tariffs.

In short, debates about Asia in general and China in particular revolved
around political allegiances or economic policies. Even so, the inclusion of
Asia within a broad comparative perspective had implications, perhaps unintended, that went beyond purely European political controversies. Specifically, if one were to accept the functionalist logic of Montesquieu's argument
that different political regimes were suited to different times, places, and
peoples, why then should "despotism" be suited—and worse, suitable—to
Asia? *The Spirit of Laws* includes extensive discussions of the effects of various
factors—climate, geography, history, religion, custom—that may simultaneously account for, mitigate, or for that matter exaggerate the effects of one
or another form of government. Montesquieu clearly asserts that republics
and monarchies are to be found only in Europe, and that despotisms rule
the rest of the world. This is meant not at all as a complacent assertion of
European superiority, but as a cautionary statement of the despotic menace
that forever lurks beneath the surface of political life. However, it is hard
to escape Montesquieu's conclusion that there is something about non-
Europeans, especially Asia and Asians—their climate, their culture, their

character—that calls for despotic rule, or that forms of government unsuitable for "us" are perfectly adequate, perhaps even salutary, for "them." Ironically, Montesquieu's suggestion that "despotism" was in some way suited to Asia would provide the ideological justification for a European imperialism that Montesquieu never envisioned, and which he certainly would have opposed.

NINE

Savage Critics: Lahontan, Rousseau, and Diderot

"When you wish to study men, you must look close at hand; but, to study Man, you have to learn to direct your gaze afar; you have first to observe the differences to discover the common properties."

—Jean-Jacques Rousseau, *Essay on the Origin of Languages*

"Are you falling prey to the myth of Tahiti?"

—Denis Diderot, *Supplement to the Voyage of Bougainville*

In one of his many short philosophical dialogues, Voltaire pitted "a savage from Guiana who was born with much good sense, and who spoke good enough French" against a "bachelier," a student of theology.[1] Needless to say, the savage, a Socrates in the rough, easily gets the better of the theologian. The dialogue—hardly one of Voltaire's most brilliant literary efforts—is a departure from Voltaire's usual attitude towards "savages," for whom he felt few romantic inclinations as compared, for example, to the Chinese or the Turks. However, Voltaire's readers would instantly have recognized his savage as an avatar of Adario, the Huron protagonist of Baron de Lahontan's "Curious Dialogues between the Author and a Savage with Good Sense Who Has Traveled Widely"—the Enlightenment's paradigmatic eloquent savage.[2]

Unlike subsequent Enlightenment writers whose vision of "savages" was entirely literary, Lahontan had spent ten years in Canada, from 1683 to 1692, much of it in the company of Huron and Algonquin, whose language he claimed to understand. He published his account in an unusual tripartite form: an account of his journey, in the form of letters; a long section called "Memoirs of North America," in the form of (anachronistically speaking) an ethnographic account; and finally the "Curious Dialogues." The epistolary narrative of his adventures and the extended description of savage life and customs were, in fact, both typical of the genre.[3] The "Curious Dialogues," on the other hand, were a remarkable innovation—an inspiration to Voltaire, as we have seen, and to Diderot, as we will see below, among others. In this section he turns the description of the "savages" that he elaborated in the first two parts of the book into a direct critique of European society, so that the subjects are no longer the Indians but rather Lahontan's own countrymen.

Such a critique is already implicit in the "Memoirs," which begin with an extremely astute critique of earlier missionary accounts, suggesting that the images they convey of the savages are driven by their specific agendas:

> The Recollects depict them as stupid, crude, rustic peoples, incapable of thinking and reflecting on anything. The Jesuits adopt a very different language, since they argue that they have good sense, memory, and quickness of wit, mixed with sound judgment. The former say that it is useless to pass one's time preaching the Gospel to people less enlightened than animals. The latter propose that, on the contrary, the savages take great pleasure in listening to the Word of God, and that they understand scripture with ease. I know the reasons that animate the speech of one and the other; they are familiar enough to people who know that these two religious orders do not get along very well in Canada.[4]

The Recollects, who had been entrusted with the Canada missions in the early seventeenth century, were relatively quickly supplanted by the Jesuits whom they had originally invited to assist them, and were only permitted to return to Canada much later. The Jesuits, as we have seen, were particularly astute in using accounts of the missions as propaganda for the order, and were thus committed to depicting the savages as eminently convertible. The Recollects, on the contrary, were avid to emphasize the futility of the Jesuit missions.[5]

Lahontan, of course, had his own set of axes to grind, not least of which was a transparent anticlericalism with which many subsequent Enlightenment intellectuals sympathized. Like the Jesuits, he portrayed the savages as both sensible and intelligent; like the Recollects, he also suggested that they were not particularly receptive to the missionaries' teachings:

> I forgot to mention that the savages listen to everything the Jesuits preach without contradicting them, but content themselves with making fun in private of the sermons that these Fathers preach in Church, and if it happens

that a savage speak openly to any Frenchman, he must be quite persuaded of his friendship and his discretion.[6]

Indeed, according to Lahontan, as taciturn as they may be in public, in private they are "capable, in spite of their rusticity, of holding conversations which often last more than three hours, covering all sorts of subjects and in which they hold their own so well that one never regrets the time one has passed with these rustic philosophers."[7] In particular, he alludes in the course of the "Memoirs" to conversations he held with the Huron chief Kondiaronk, alias "the Rat," arguably his model for the fictional Adario of the "Dialogues."

The irony of the "Dialogues" is that Adario comes far closer than "Lahontan" to being the author's mouthpiece. It is consistently necessary to distinguish between "Lahontan" (in quotation marks), the character in the "Dialogues," and Lahontan the author. The fictional "Lahontan" serves as a straight man, consistently upholding conventional French principles so that Adario might demolish their pretensions. (In this he bears no little resemblance to Lejeune's nemesis, the "Sorcerer.") Unlike Voltaire's savage, however, "Adario" is not an entirely empty signifier, a convenient if rather lifeless double for the author. Adario's arguments are clearly informed by Lahontan's experience and understanding of his Huron (in point of fact, more often Algonquin) interlocutors, among whom he seemed to find echoes of his own skepticism and cynicism.

Like Montaigne's cannibals, Adario clearly represents a "natural" humanity in contradistinction to an artificial and corrupt Europe. Specifically, he begins with an exposition of what European contemporaries would immediately have recognized as "natural religion," as opposed to the "numerous fables" preached to the Huron by the Jesuits, and which "ils ont trop d'esprit pour les croire eux memes" (they are too intelligent to believe themselves).[8] Adario instead exposes the (supposedly) Huron credo:

1) . . . that we recognize a Creator of the Universe, under the name of the Great Spirit, or the Master of Life, which we believe is in everything without limits.

2) That we profess the immortality of the soul.

3) That the Great Spirit has provided us with reason capable of discerning right from wrong, like the sky and the earth, so that we follow exactly the true Rules of justice and wisdom.

4) That peace of spirit pleases the Great Master of Life; that on the contrary he holds a troubled mind in horror, because it makes men wicked.

5) That life is a dream, and death an awakening, after which the soul sees and knows the nature and quality of visible and invisible things.

6) That the reach of our reason being unable to extend an inch above the surface of the earth, we should not spoil or corrupt it by attempting to penetrate invisible and improbable things.[9]

This is, of course, a fairly standard manifesto of Enlightenment deism, although the first two items on the list are somewhat less far-fetched and are reminiscent of the minimalist religion Montaigne describes among the cannibals. Lahontan's description of "savage" religion in the "Memoirs" is somewhat less tidy; Lahontan is at pains to argue that the Hurons and Algonquins (like the Jesuits?) don't really believe what they seem to profess. Along with the Great Spirit, Kitchi Manitou, he alludes to an evil spirit, Matchi Manitou—who, he hastens to add, is not the devil, but rather a figure of speech used to refer to nothing more serious than fatality or bad luck. In another passage, however, Lahontan describes "Jugglers," shamans who seem to take notions of evil spirits more literally:

This Juggler comes to see the sick person, examines him thoroughly, saying, if the evil Spirit is here we will quickly expel him: After which he retires along in a little tent built on purpose, where he sings and dances, howling like a werewolf (which gave occasion to the Jesuits to say that the Devil speaks to them). After he has finished his charlatanry, he comes to suck the patient on some part of his body and tells him while pulling several small bones from his mouth "that these same bones were extracted from his body, that he should take heart, since his illness was but a trifle, and that in order to be thoroughly cured he should send his slaves and his kin to hunt elk, deer, etc. to eat these kinds of meats, on which the cure absolutely depends.[10]

In both the "Memoirs" and the "Dialogue," Lahontan suggests that the Jugglers are deluded, that the savages do not take them seriously but let them go on with their display for entertainment, and perhaps to reassure the patient. Retrospectively, Lahontan's efforts to rationalize Native American religion in terms acceptable to Enlightened Europeans and to turn it into conventional deism seem rather lame. However, the rhetorical thrust of his dialogues on religion is to suggest that the Huron are endowed with a rational form of worship, and that it is instead Christianity which is radically irrational, insisting on a benevolent deity who nonetheless condemns the greater part of humankind to hell and hinging the promise of salvation on the conviction that the Eucharist is either the literal transubstantiation of God's flesh into the communion bread (as the French Catholics assert) or merely a metaphor (if one is to believe the English Protestants in nearby New York).

Adario/Lahontan is more convincing when he hints that the French do not practice what they preach, and that the relationship between religion, law, and morality is, to say the least, twisted among Europeans as opposed to Huron. The discussion of sexual morality, first raised in the opening dialogue on religion and further developed in the last of the dialogues, is exemplary in this regard. Early on in the dialogues, "Lahontan" concedes that the Hurons "all live so morally that you only have one single difficulty to overcome to get to Heaven."[11] The rub, of course, is sex, namely the "fornication" of unmarried youth. Adario responds with a scathing denunciation of European morality: prostitution, adultery, and the double standard whereby premarital sex is tolerated for men and punished for women. Nor does the celibacy of the clergy meet with his approval. Adario, prefiguring the arguments of Montesquieu and Diderot, adopts a natalist perspective that has long dominated French arguments about demography, and castigates the clergy for failing to contribute to the reproduction of the nation and the species. His account of Huron sexual morality, duly medicalized and rationalized, actually suggests that premarital sexual experimentation is "healthy" in the most literal way, permitting young warriors to indulge in sexual activity just enough to relieve their normal urges, but not so much as to weaken them too much for the proper conduct of warfare. Marriage is only appropriate when they are older and ready to settle down in every sense of the word. Men and women are, moreover, free to marry whom they please, with the exception of relatives; and either spouse is free to divorce for any reason. As long as they are married, however, they remain strictly faithful, rendering the jealousy that characterizes European marital relations quite unnecessary. In short, the sexual life of savages is characterized not by immorality but by a different, indeed superior morality, with benefits for both individuals and society at large—one that, unlike European morality, does not conspicuously clash with everyday practice.

The hiatus between morality and practice is most clearly developed in the discussion of law. Adario wonders: "O what kind of men are Europeans; O what sort of creatures! who are forced to do good and only avoid doing wrong by fear of punishment? . . . I call a man he who has a natural inclination to do good and who never dreams of doing evil."[12] The Huron are free precisely because they have no law, in the sense of a formal and coercive legal apparatus. The law is a double sign of European decadence, first because it is needed in order to coerce people into following the dictates of their own morality; second and worse, because it can be misused by the wicked and powerful as an additional tool to punish and oppress the innocent by bearing false witness, inflicting judicial torture, or simply bribing judges. Thus law is simultaneously a token and an instrument of immorality. There is a note of personal bitterness here. Lahontan, who had been cheated out of his inheritance and his title in his childhood through legal chicanery, had personal experience of the injustice of law. However, the fictional "Lahontan" repeatedly admonishes Adario that he is unfair to judge Europeans on the basis of a few bad apples, or the legal system on the basis of its occasional and incidental errors; such caveats are hardly capable of convincing either Adario or the reader.

To the extent that the "Dialogues" can be read as satire, the "natural" morality of the Huron can be interpreted as a convenient foil for an exposition of the decadence of European society. Seen in this light, Lahontan's portrait of the Huron can seem dehumanizing, effortless, and unreflective; "natural" virtue, as Montaigne already suggested, comes perilously close to stupidity. However, the contrast between the Huron and Europeans is not just reducible to "nature" as opposed to "civil society."[13] At the heart of the matter, Adario repeatedly insists throughout the dialogues, is the invidious European insistence on "le Tien et le Mien" Thine and Mine. Lahontan is perhaps the first to identify the development of property relations as the driving force behind "civilization" (or, negatively evaluated, "corruption"), an idea that was to constitute a leitmotif of conjectural history throughout the eighteenth and indeed the nineteenth centuries. Money, for Adario, is the key symbol for this kind of society, and Adario makes it clear that the Huron actively reject a money economy, as opposed to simply ignoring its existence. Money and property generate radical social inequalities, reducing many to misery while others enjoy a surfeit of unnecessary luxuries. The clothing that money can buy serves to conceal natural distinctions between humans in favor of artificial differences. Property is equally at the heart of political distinctions, and ultimately at the heart of the subservience of an entire nation to one monarch. These inequalities are, Adario suggests, the root cause of the various vices that he painstakingly describes among Europeans.

Only by actively rejecting money and property distinctions, Adario argues, can Huron remain free. Liberty and equality (one is tempted to add fraternity) are mutually constitutive. Indeed, reciprocity—arguably another name for fraternity—is another core virtue of the Huron:

Aren't you free in any hut in the village where you can go to ask for whatever you find best to eat? Are there Huron who have ever refused anyone a share of what they have hunted or fished? Don't we pool our catch of beaver pelts throughout the Nation to permit those who haven't managed to hunt enough to purchase whatever goods they need? Don't we use our corn in the same way, to feed those whose harvest was insufficient to feed their families? If one among us wants to build a canoe or a new hut, don't we send our slaves to work for him, without being asked?[14]

Admittedly, Adario's mention of slaves, here and frequently throughout the text, seems radically to qualify his insistence on Huron liberty and equality. As far as one can gather from the text, such slaves are war captives whose status is not passed on to their progeny, and whose situation in life does not seem to differ too radically from that of their masters.

Adario's rejection of money is also a rejection of luxuries that, after all, he has had a chance to experience in his travels. Rejecting "Lahontan's" depiction of the Huron life as arduous and unpalatable, he objects:

. . . what difference is there to sleeping in a good hut or in a palace; to sleep on beaver pelts or on mattresses and between two sheets; to eat roast and boiled foods or dirty stews and pâtés prepared by filthy cooks?[15]

Ultimately, the difference between "natural" Huron and "corrupt" Europeans rests on the systematic exercise of choice, on a deliberate morality and not simply a "natural" penchant that needs no explanation.

Unnatural Vices

The first person who, fencing off a plot of land, had the idea of saying, "This is mine," and who found people simpleminded enough to believe him, was the true founder of civil society. How many crimes, wars, murders, how many miseries and horrors would the human race have been spared had someone, pulling up the stakes or filling the ditch, cried out to his equals: Don't allow yourselves to listen to this imposter; you are lost if you forget that the fruit belongs to everyone, and the earth to no one.[16]

The diatribe that opens the second part of Rousseau's *Discourse on Inequality* (1754) could easily have been written by Adario—if only Adario could write.[17] Indeed, Rousseau, more than any other Enlightenment thinker, is generally (and inaccurately) associated with the figure of the *bon sauvage* or "noble savage."[18] But, unlike Adario, Rousseau's savage does not speak for himself, nor does Rousseau have any more than a literary acquaintance with him. For that matter, Rousseau was highly skeptical of contemporary accounts of non-Europeans, complaining in a very long footnote to the *Discourse on Inequality*, "Since the three or four hundred years that the inhabitants of Europe flood the other parts of the world and incessantly publish new collections of travels, I am persuaded that we know nothing of men except for Europeans." The problem lay first of all in the categories of persons who travel—sailors, merchants, soldiers, missionaries. The first three categories he dismissed out of hand; as for missionaries, he suggested more diplomatically that "to preach the Gospel, you only need zeal and God furnishes the rest, but to study men you need talents that God does not guarantee to grant anyone in particular and which are not always the lot of saints." Rousseau did give credit to a few observers: notably Chardin (merchant though he was) in Persia, and Jesuits who described China. But he hankered, one might suggest naively, for philosophical travelers whose descriptions would finally be reliable.[19]

In any case, Rousseau avoids the fallacy of assimilating "savages" to "natural" humans. In a famous sentence at the beginning of his *Discourse*, he posits: "Let us begin by eliminating all facts, since they do not address the question." Rousseau's state of nature is decidedly antesocial, a hypothetical model of what humanity would be like in the absence of any social institutions whatsoever. Such humans live an entirely solitary existence, except that mothers care for their children until and only until they can fend for themselves, at which time they leave to become totally independent, oblivious of any bond linking them to their genitrix. They have no language. They have no tools or inventions—or, more precisely, should any one individual arrive at some discovery, she would have no means of transmitting the knowledge to others. They reproduce through chance encounters that create no lasting ties, and do so indiscriminately since they possess no standards of sexual attractiveness, such standards being preeminently social. They are animated by desires for food, sex, and sleep, and a corresponding fear of hunger and pain. In the absence of any social rules, they have neither virtues nor vices and cannot be either good or evil, although alongside their instincts for self-preservation they also feel pity for others of their own kind, a repugnance to seeing other humans suffer. If it cannot be said that such humans are happy, they are certainly not sad; after all, they are preeminently free.

Rousseau's model is in the first place a yardstick, a means of measuring the benefits and drawbacks of "society" in the abstract. It is quite explicitly meant as an answer to Hobbes's opposition of the state of nature, the war of all against all, to civil society, orderly government under sovereign authority. The very passions that drive Hobbes's state of nature are, Rousseau argues, eminently social rather than natural. Rousseau's natural man desires nothing of his neighbor's, except perhaps his lunch, which he will wrest from him—without malice!—only if it costs him less effort than returning to the forest to procure his own. Like Hobbes, and for similar reasons, Rousseau denies any assertion that all men once lived in such a hypothetical state of nature; any such assertion, by flying in the face of the biblical account of creation, could only land its author in considerable trouble.

Paradoxically, Rousseau's model, however unorthodox, is quintessentially Christian. In the state of nature, as in the Garden of Eden, humans live naked and, above all, radically innocent, without any knowledge of good and evil. But, as in the Garden of Eden, the seeds of the Fall lie within the breast of man, not in the form of free will but rather in that of "perfectibility": "It is sad that we are obliged to admit that this distinctive and almost limitless faculty is the source of all Man's ills; that it is what, given enough time, pulled him out of this original condition in which he spent tranquil and innocent days; that, through the passage of centuries, revealing its truths and its errors, its vices and its virtues, it is what makes of Man a tyrant over himself and over nature." Like the Fall, it is radically irreversible: ". . . Men similar to me whose passions have forever destroyed their original simplicity . . . can no longer nourish themselves with grass and acorns, nor do without laws and leaders."

The perfectibility in question, it must be stressed, is entirely mental. For Rousseau there is no question that men in the state of nature were physically superior:

> Let civilized man the time to assemble all his machines around him, and there is no doubt that he can easily surpass the savage; but if you wish to see an even more unequal combat, strip them naked and unarmed face-to-face, and you will quickly recognize the advantage of having all one's strength at one's disposition, of always being ready for any event, and being, so to speak, whole and at one's own disposition.

The "savages" in this case were not only meant to be hypothetical beings in the state of nature; in a footnote, Rousseau makes it clear that he is specifically referring to the likes of the "Hottentots" of the Cape of Good Hope, and of an "Indian" from Buenos Aires.

More generally, "savages" occupy an intermediate position in the *Discourse*, midway between the state of nature and "civilized" society:

> . . . it must be remarked that the beginnings of society and the establishment of relations between men required different qualities from those they had enjoyed in their primitive constitution . . . although men had become less rugged, and natural pity had already suffered some alteration, this period of development of human faculties, representing a just mean between the indolence of the primitive state and the petulant activity of our amour-propre, must have been the happiest and most durable epoch.

The proof, alleges Rousseau, lies in the many documented cases of savages who, having been "adopted" into "civilized" society, wisely bolted at the first available opportunity.

But the alleged happiness of savages comes at a price: "It would be horrible to have to praise as a benefactor the first person who suggested to the inhabitants of the banks of the Orinoco the use of those boards they apply to the foreheads of their children, and which ensure them at least a part of their imbecility and of their original happiness."

The ideal lies ostensibly in the delicate balance between imbecility and immorality. Knowledge—Rousseau specifically pinpoints the knowledge of agriculture and of iron—expands the fields of human desires and lays the foundation for inequality and injustice.

Rousseau had already condemned the corrupting potential of knowledge in his earlier *Discourse on the Sciences and the Arts* (1750). The question that the Academy of Dijon had stipulated as the subject of its competition was "Si le rétablissment des sciences et des arts a contribué à épurer les moeurs" (Whether the revival of sciences and arts has contributed to the improvement of mores). The question was clearly intended to address the moral implications of the Renaissance, an issue that Rousseau circumvented in order to examine the moral implications of knowledge in general. The grounds on which he condemns the sciences and arts are twofold. First of all, he makes a remarkable accusation:

> While government and laws ensure the safety and the well-being of the men they unite, sciences, letters, and arts, less despotic and perhaps more powerful, strew garlands of flowers over the iron chains in their care, stifling within men the sentiment of that original liberty for which they would seem to have been born, make them love their slavery and form what we call orderly peoples [*peuples policés*].

In other words, the arts and sciences sugar the pill of political despotism, encouraging subjects to accept a political "order" that ought to be morally unacceptable. Intellectuals are consequently, intentionally or not, complicit in the maintenance of despotic authority.

However, Rousseau's argument is not always consistent, as he himself later acknowledged, deploring the form if not the substance of the essay that first established his reputation as a philosopher. Elsewhere in the *Discourse* he adopts a different kind of sociological approach, in terms of the institutional mechanisms whereby societies support the sciences and arts. Such luxuries, he suggests, are possible in societies whose citizens do not devote their primary energies to their own self-government. Despotism "frees" individuals, indeed encourages them, to devote themselves to relatively frivolous pursuits; Rousseau makes it clear that arts and sciences, compared to self-government, are indeed relatively frivolous. He holds up Sparta as a model of civic virtue, as opposed to Athens, distinguished perhaps in the arts and sciences but all too prone to bad government.[20] In this respect, the sciences and arts are indexical of bad government even if they are not necessarily responsible for it.

It should be noted that for Rousseau, the sciences and arts—knowledge, in short—are not reprehensible in and of themselves. Rousseau objects to the conditions in which they are practiced and the uses to which they are put. Knowledge is not intrinsically immoral, but it is eminently prone to foster immorality. Of course, Rousseau's critics were not swayed by such subtle distinctions, and they accused him of vaunting the virtues of ignorance over knowledge. Addressing a refutation of his *Discourse* by one M. Gautier, professor of mathematics and history and member of the Académie royale de belle-lettres de Nancy, he retorts:

> M. Gautier takes the trouble to teach me that there are vicious peoples who are not learned, and I was already well aware that the Kalmuks, the Bedouin, the Kaffirs were neither prodigies of virtue nor of erudition. If M. Gautier had taken the same trouble to show me a learned people who were not vicious, I would have been more surprised.

In another similar retort, this time to M. Bordes, of the Academy of Lyons, Rousseau cites the examples from "the rusticity of ancient peoples" to show that "virtue is thus not incompatible with ignorance" while admitting that "several very ignorant peoples were very vicious. Ignorance is an obstacle neither to good not evil; it is only the natural state of mankind." Clearly, at least in his early writings, Rousseau was no unequivocal apologist of "savages." Rather than challenging the accuracy of reports alleging savage viciousness (as he would most probably have done later), he falls back on the safer argument that any association of knowledge with immorality does not, strictly speaking, imply the innocence of ignorance. "Savages," one must conclude, are always dull but only sometimes vicious.

The Political Economy of Free Love

For the first half of the eighteenth century, the paradigmatic "savages" were undoubtedly Native Americans; but with the loss of Quebec, French attention turned towards other horizons, particularly the Pacific, which was in the process of being methodically mapped out and explored by Bougainville and Cook. Diderot, returning to the playful genre of the dialogue between a clever savage and an obtuse "civilized" European, made a Tahitian his protagonist in his *Supplement to the Voyage of Bougainville*.[21] Like many of Diderot's subversive fictions—including *Rameau's Nephew* and *Jacques the Fatalist and his Master*—the *Supplement* went unpublished during his lifetime, although the manuscripts were circulated among the Parisian intelligentsia. Diderot's cautiousness was not simply paranoid. In 1749 he had published his *Lettre sur les aveugles* (Letter on the Blind), in which he detailed his comments about a much-touted experiment in Paris to restore sight to a young woman born blind. His conclusions contained a radically empiricist theory of morality. The congenitally blind, he suggested, were also in important ways morally impaired. Eighteenth-century theories of morality, including Rousseau's, as we have seen, centered on the importance of pity and sympathy, in the capacity of humans to understand the sufferings of others in terms of their own experience. This operates at least partly through sight, Diderot suggested, when we witness other's reactions to events, and specifically, as concerns morality, when we see the facial expressions of others as consequences of our own actions. He claimed that the congenitally blind, deprived of such visual cues, were consequently far more indifferent to the effects of their own actions on others. Diderot's radical materialism left no room for God in morality, as his detractors were quick to point out the royal authorities, and Diderot was consequently jailed in the fortress of Vincennes just outside of Paris. He was released after only a few days but, not unreasonably, he took this as a warning, and subsequently refrained from publishing his most controversial ideas—at least under his own name.

Indeed, the very subtitle of the *Supplement*, "Dialogue between A and B on the Inappropriateness of Attaching Moral Ideas to Certain Physical Actions That Do Not Aaccord with Them,"[22] leaves the reader little doubt that the work expounds controversial ideas about morality. If the subtitle is misleading, it is because the dialogue between A and B, two urbane Frenchmen, is only the frame for the larger part of the work, which includes an old man's diatribe on the occasion of the departure of the French expedition and, more elaborately, a long dialogue between the Tahitian Orou and his guest, the ship's chaplain. The diatribe is a ferocious (and prescient, as Tahiti was not to become a French colony until well into the nineteenth century) denunciation of colonialism. As his Tahitian compatriots say farewell to Bougainville's men, lamenting their departure, the old man laments their arrival. Some of the themes of his lament echo Lahontan if not Rousseau:

> Here, everything belongs to everyone, and you have preached I can't tell what distinction between "yours" and "mine." . . . We have no wish to exchange what you call our ignorance for your useless knowledge. Everything that we need and is good for us we already possess. Do we merit contempt because we have not learnt how to acquire superfluous needs? When we are hungry, we have enough to eat. When we are cold, we have enough to wear. . . . Do not fill our heads with factitious needs and illusory virtues. (pp. 42–43)

But the tone, at least in this part of the *Supplement*, is hardly playful. Whereas Lahotan's character Adario adamantly and apparently effortlessly resists the temptations of "civilization," Diderot's elderly Tahitian is acutely aware that such resistance is ultimately doomed, on several counts. First of all, the foreigners have laid claim to the land, inscribing "This land is ours" on a strip of metal, albeit in a language the Tahitians cannot understand and an alphabet they cannot read. Worse, they have brought with them a scourge, syphilis, which will remain to plague the Tahitians well after the expedition has left its shores. But this physical infection is symbolic of a deeper moral infection: sexual shame and covetousness.

This was not Diderot's only condemnation of the colonialism as a massive enterprise of enslavement, theft, and corruption. He collaborated extensively for the 1783 edition of the Abbé de Raynal's massive (ten-volume!) *Histoire philosophique et politique des établissments et du commerce des Europeéens dans les Deux Indes* (Philosophical and Political History of the Establishments and Commerce of Europeans in the Two [i.e., East and West] Indies).[23] Diderot the ghostwriter was fully free to vent his spleen in print, if only at the expense of sometimes contradicting the rest of the text. Indeed, passages of the *Supplement*, particularly denunciations of colonialism, were reproduced with minor modifications, if any, in Raynal's book. Yet if Diderot unequivocally condemned European colonial "establishments," his attitude to commerce, at least in certain forms, was far more sympathetic. He suggested another paradigm:

If I had commodities [they] lacked and [they] had some which would be useful to me, I can suggest exchanges. We are both free to put whatever price suits us on things we own. A needle has more real value for a people who must use a fishbone to sew up the animal skins they wear than their money would have for me. A sword or an axe will be of infinite value for the person who uses sharp stones, set in a piece of wood hardened by the fire, to act as such tools. . . . If I laugh inwardly at the stupidity of the person who gives me gold for iron, the person I regard as stupid will also laugh at me for giving iron (the use of which he knows) for gold (which is useless to him). We are both deceived or, rather, we are neither of us deceived. The exchanges should be perfectly free.[24]

Characteristically, Diderot's text is fundamentally ambivalent. At one level it is a celebration of complementarity. Each party possesses what the other desires, and unconstrained exchange is clearly a morally superior alternative to theft or coercion. Even so, Diderot suggests that the morality of exchange is also one of mutual deception. But in Diderot's examples it is far from clear that each party is equally deceived. The savage may well know the uses of needles, swords, axes, and iron, but so for that matter does the European who comes to trade. Gold may be useless to the savage, but he has no conception of its utility to his trading partner. In this act of mutual deception, the savage's cards are all on the table, while the European can keep the most vital of his cards up his sleeve, so to speak. Diderot's own ambivalence, his contradictory assertion that both parties are deceived and that neither party is deceived, betrays a somewhat unwilling awareness of the moral dubiousness of formally equal exchange. Even so, it is hardly a foregone conclusion that Diderot's praise of free trade was insincere. In this respect, his views echo those of the physiocrats. The *Encyclopédie*, in fact, was one of the first places where Quesnay exposed his economic ideas in print. While the physiocrats' opposition to mercantilism was not anticolonial per se, their condemnation of coercive and extractive economic measures as opposed to free trade must certainly have influenced Diderot's perspective.

This penchant for political economy emerges in the *Supplement* in the most unlikely of contexts: in the dialogue between the chaplain and his host, Orou, which is explicitly about sexual morality, but which takes a surprisingly utilitarian turn. Orou offers sexual hospitality to his guest, giving him the choice of his wife or any of his three daughters. The chaplain refuses at first, but finally gives in to temptation, sleeping with each of the four women in turn, but not without calling out in despair, "My religion! My orders!" In the first place, Diderot is explicitly contrasting the "natural" sexuality of the savages with the "unnatural" celibacy of the clergy, a theme he had already treated at length in another of his unpublished works, *La Religieuse* (*The Nun*), the story of a young woman cloistered in a nunnery against her will and subjected to the unwanted lesbian advances of her Mother Superior.

However, the dialogue waxes more philosophical as Orou, a faithful disciple of Adario, attempts to uncover the reasons for the chaplain's irrational if ineffectual reticence. Sexual morality—the inappropriate attachment of moral ideas to physical actions, as the subtitle of the *Supplement* indicates—is obviously the crux of the matter. When the chaplain suggests that the indissolubility of the marital bond and the mutual obligation of spouses to be faithful to one another is divinely decreed, Orou launches into a long tirade about nature and law:

> I find these strange precepts contrary to Nature, an offence against reason, certain to breed crime. . . . Such rules are contrary to the general order of things. What could seem more ridiculous that a precept which forbids any change of our affections, which commands that we show a constancy of which we're not capable, which violates the nature and liberty of male and female alike in chaining them to one another for the whole of their lives? What could be more absurd than a fidelity restricting the most capricious of our pleasures to a single individual; than a vow of immutability taken by two beings formed of flesh and blood, under a sky that doesn't remain fixed for an instant, beneath caverns poised on the edge of collapse, under a cliff crumbling into dust, at the foot of a tree shedding its bark, beneath a quivering stone? (pp. 50–51)

On the surface, the passage is fairly straightforward. The chaplain's religious precepts are contrary to nature on two counts: they unjustly limit the personal freedom of both men and women, and they run counter to the natural and eminently mutable inclinations of human beings. (The chaplain, by remaining silent here, confirms his theological ineptitude; Christian thinkers obviously concurred that religious precepts were incompatible with human nature, at least after the Fall, but they drew very different conclusions from Orou.) Were it not for the striking images of collapsing caverns and crumbling cliffs, it would be comforting to conclude that authentic nature is preferable to artificial religion; this is the kind of conclusion with which the character Adario easily triumphs over the character "Lahontan." But for Diderot, if not Orou, nature is simultaneously grander and more disquieting.

As if the conflict between nature and religion were not enough, Orou points out that the French are subject to yet a third master, the laws of the state:

And where would you be if your three masters, out of sorts with one another, took it upon themselves to permit you, command you, and forbid you the very same thing, as I suspect must happen often? . . . You'll come to despise all three of them, and you'll be neither a man, nor a citizen, nor a true believer. You'll be nothing. You'll be out of favour with each form of authority, at odds with yourself, malicious, tormented by your heart, miserable and persecuted by your senseless masters, as I saw you yesterday when I offered my daughters to you, and you cried out, 'But my religion, but my holy orders!'" (51)

The advantage of the "savage" over the "civilized" man is not that he is free, but that he has only one master to obey and the instructions are consequently less equivocal.[25]

However, Orou's moral code is far more complex than simply abandoning oneself to "natural" impulses. Rather:

Would you like to know what's good and what's bad at all times and in all places? Stick to the nature of things and of actions, to your relations with your fellow-man, to the effect of your conduct on your own well-being and on the general welfare. (52)

On the basis of this short sentence alone, one might uncharitably accuse Orou of subjecting himself to as many masters as the chaplain he derides. However, when this is specifically applied to the domain of sexual morality, it emerges that the Tahitian code (as formulated by Diderot) is based on a kind of utilitarian calculus where individual satisfaction is weighed against—or, better still, works towards the fulfillment of—collective interests. As far as sexuality is concerned, Diderot is, in the purest French tradition (and following Montesquieu's lead) unabashedly natalist:

A child is a precious thing because it will grow up to be an adult. We thus have an interest in caring for it altogether different from that shown in our plants and animals. The birth of a child brings domestic and public joy. *It will mean an increase of wealth for the hut, and the strength for the nation* [my emphasis]. It means another pair of arms and hands in Tahiti. We see in him a future farmer, fisherman, hunter, soldier, husband, father. (53)

In this way, the act of procreation simultaneously (a) satisfies individual and "natural" sexual urges, (b) serves the particular interests of the parents and their family by providing a future source of wealth and a form of old-age insurance, and (c) benefits the nation as a whole by adding to its military and economic potential. Is it that Orou knows better than the chaplain how to serve three masters? Or are his masters more congenial to one another?

It turns out that the benefits are at least partly due to Tahitian social engineering: "For [children's] maintenance and that of the aged, we set aside one part in six of all our harvests . . . So you see that the larger a Tahitian's family, the richer he is" (54). To drive home the point, in light of Orou's dialogue with the chaplain, B's comments to A include remarks about the absurdity of the demographic policies of countries where the birth of children, while a boon to the nation, impoverishes the parents. The combination of sexual freedom and a kind of social welfare program that provides for the upkeep of children is the ideal way to reconcile individual desire, personal interest, and general welfare.[26] But this marriage of free love and utilitarian natalism has its dark side, even in Diderot's Tahiti. Sterile women are obliged to wear a black veil, and menstruating women a grey veil. Sexual intercourse with such temporarily or permanently infertile women is strictly forbidden; after all, such desires have no direct utility. That both men and women who engage in such prohibited sex are subject to public censure hardly diminishes the gender imbalance. If Diderot's vision of quasi-utopian sexual freedom ostensibly gives equal weight to both male and female desire, its male bias is manifest in multiple ways. The onus of infertility lies exclusively on female shoulders; the notion that there might be infertile men who perhaps also ought to go veiled is apparently inconceivable. The "useless" sexual desires of menstruating or sterile women have no need of fulfillment; indeed, any attempts to fulfill them are deemed licentious. Men's licentiousness, on the other hand, is limited to their choice of inappropriately infertile partners. Diderot's condemnation of infertile coupling seems all the more scandalous in the light of his (or Orou's) condoning of incest—in point of real fact, a remarkably un-Tahitian expression of free love! A son may sleep with his mother if "he has so much respect for her, and feels such tenderness, that he forgets the disparity of their ages and prefers a woman of forty to a girl of nineteen," whereas a father will sleep with his daughter out of compassion if "the girl's ugly and little sought after by young men" (62). Even in this respect, the gender imbalance is flagrant: sons sleep with their mothers out of respect and tenderness, in preference to sexual partners their own age; fathers with their daughters out of pity, when they are rejected by partners their own age. Brother-sister incest is "very common" and "much approved." Even Orous's comments on the utility of children, cited above, list exclusively male occupations. Women's utility goes unmentioned, and it lies presumably in their capacity to bear children—thus explaining the opprobrium placed on sterile women. The subordination of women's desires to those of men is perhaps nowhere more obvious than in the very premise of the dialogue: Orou's offer of his wife and three daughters to the chaplain. That the four women in question should consent so enthusiastically is taken for granted.

Ultimately, Diderot's masculine sexual utopia bears intimate resemblance to physiocratic political economy, with free love a substitute for free trade. The analogy is indeed Orou's: "We have a circulation of women and children, or able-bodied persons of all ages and occupations, which is of far greater importance than the circulation of commodities, which are no more than the product of people's work." (60). Just as free trade is presumed to maximize the wealth of the nation in terms of commodities, so free love maximizes its wealth in "human capital." The implications for international sexual exchange are even more paradoxical. If the material exchange of gold for iron (to which Orou openly alludes, another link between the *Supplement* and Diderot's work for Raynal) is based on European deceit, then the exchange of women's sexual services for future progeny represents the triumph of Tahitian deceit:

> While more robust and healthy than you, we saw at once that you surpassed us in intelligence, and we immediately marked out for you some of our most beautiful women and girls to receive the seed of a race superior to ours. We tried an experiment which may still bring us success. We've drawn from you and yours the only part which we could take; and, rest assured, however savage we are, we know just how to scheme. (64)

This passage betrays the fundamental disingenuousness of the *Supplement*. How can the befuddled and ineffectual chaplain be the intellectual superior of a dialectician as subtle as Orou? Here, the putative savage's identity as the author's mouthpiece is particularly transparent, even more so than in Lahontan's dialogues. But the passage also reveals a fundamental understanding of "savages" that Diderot shares with Rousseau, whereby the savage's physical superiority over Europeans is matched by his intellectual inferiority. This physical superiority has already been emphasized in the old man's rant that precedes the dialogue between Orou and the chaplain:

> Look at these men. See how upright, healthy and robust they are. Look at these women. See how they too stand up straight, how healthy, fresh and lovely they are. Take this bow; it's mine. Call upon one, two, three, four of your comrades, and together with them try to draw it. I draw it unaided; I till the soil; I climb mountains; I go through the forest; I can run a league across the plain in less

than an hour; your young companions can hardly keep up with me, and yet I'm more than ninety years old!" (43)

As we have seen, the idea that the body develops in inverse proportion to the mind was an integral part of Bodin's system of human classification (to the detriment of Germans!). By the late eighteenth century, however, such notions were clearly incorporated into a discourse about savagery and civilization, perhaps most transparently in the form of the myth of giant Patagonians.[27] This is in sharp contrast to the views of Fontenelle, only a century earlier, for whom savages were certainly more ignorant, but not necessarily stupider, than Europeans. It is much to the merit of Lahontan—the only one of these authors who had actually known "savages" and indeed spoken with them at some length, if he is to be believed—that he never even remotely hints at the idea that the "savages" are in any sense our intellectual inferiors, or that stupidity is in some way the hidden price of physical (if not moral) superiority.

Unlike Rousseau, Diderot does not deplore the loss of innocence consequent to a sort of secular "fall." The attractiveness of Tahiti is, after all, its success in balancing natural desires with social utility—unintentional rationality, perhaps, if the Tahitians are less intelligent than we are, but rationality no less. But, asks A in the last section of the *Supplement*, "what useful consequences can be drawn from the manners and strange customs of these uncivilised people?"

> B: It seems to me that as soon as physical factors, such as the need to overcome the infertility of the soil, have brought man's ingenuity into play, the momentum drives him well beyond his immediate objective, so that when his need has elapsed he comes to be swept into the great ocean of fantasy from which he cannot pull out. May the happy Tahitian stop where he is! I can see that, except in this remote corner of the globe, there's never been any morality and perhaps never will be.

Tahitian savage society, unlike European civilized society, is essentially static, but it only takes a small push to put into play the momentum that both provides society with dynamism and at the same time prevents it from ever quite being self-consistent.

There is a deep paradox here—an aporia, to use a fancier term. Tahitian morality and society are "natural" in that they reconcile natural desire with the general good. But this is a static "naturalness," whereas nature, for Diderot, is intrinsically dynamic and unstable. From this perspective, it is

European society that is "natural" and Tahiti "unnatural." How, then, is one to choose? B suggests that, when the laws of nature, religion, and society laws seem to contradict one another—in Europe, unlike Tahiti—it is nonetheless imperative to follow the laws of society, however imperfect, rather than abandon all laws in despair:

> If the laws are good, morality is good. If the laws are bad, morality's bad. If the laws, either good or bad, are not observed, which is the worst condition possible for a society, there are no morals. (66–67)

Ultimately, B concludes, "Let's follow the good chaplain's example and be monks in France and savages in Tahiti" (74). It is, needless to say, one of Diderot's supreme ironies to turn the chaplain into an unwitting cultural relativist.

But does Diderot really want us to be monks in France? If a brief stay in the Chateau of Vincennes taught Diderot the dangers of flouting his own society's morality too openly, it hardly turned him into a conformist. Orou's devastating condemnation of the hypocrisy of Christian sexual morality is hardly meant to apply to Tahiti alone. Indeed, the entire dialogue ends on an entirely ambivalent note:

A: Perhaps we should read [to the women at dinner] the chaplain's conversation with Orou.
B: What do you suppose they might say about it?
A: I haven't a clue.
B: And what would they think of it?
A: Probably the opposite of what they say. (75)

One suspects that Diderot is implying that the women would profess horror at Tahitian sexual mores (as convention would dictate, especially for women) while they would be secretly titillated. In other words, conventions may mask sexual desires, but thay can hardly eliminate them. The frank celebration of sex in Tahiti provides welcome relief from the polished and insincere urbanity of the French salon . . . and perhaps vice versa.

Natural Savagery

Whatever real differences exist in the ways in which Lahontan, Rousseau, and Diderot portray "savages," all of them make savages into representatives of a "natural" humanity in stark opposition to Europeans. In this way, the contrast between "savages" and Europeans operates in an idiom radically different from the contrast between "Orientals" and Europeans, even if the critique of "despotism" is a central feature of both discourses. The debate over "Oriental despotism," as we have seen, revolved around the respective merits or perils of centralized monarchical authority as opposed to aristocratic privilege. In this respect, particularly in France, it was a fairly direct translation of partisan political loyalties. In writings that focus on "savages" rather than "Orientals," the Europeans instead occupy the "despotic" pole. Savages, whatever else they may be, are free. This freedom extends far beyond the political domain to embrace sexuality and indeed property relations; one thread that runs consistently from Lahontan to Rousseau to Diderot is the "savage" ignorance (and/or rejection) of "mine" and "thine."

Arguably, the "savages" in question have been reduced to the status of cardboard figures, with little or no relationship to real human beings. Frank Lestringant has eloquently argued that eighteenth-century travel literature consistently rationalizes and sentimentalizes the behaviors it describes, in contrast to Renaissance descriptions that more often leave the radical "otherness" of such behavior transparent.[28] Such rationalization is quite evident in Lahontan's descriptions of Algonquin and Huron healers—"jugglers"!— not to mention Diderot's paradoxically utilitarian exposition of Tahitian sexual morality. Does this reduce the savage to "a convenient and malleable mouthpiece . . . the herald of the imprescribable rights of Nature against the arbitrariness of established social and religious rules"?[29] Lestringant's critique raises two distinct issues. The first is the question of rationalization. In a real sense, these are attempts to make unfamiliar behavior comprehensible—an archetypical explanatory strategy in the social sciences, encompassing (for example) all varieties of functionalism. It fits quite neatly within Fontenelle's conception of science as an attempt to understand unknown phenomena in terms of known processes. Such attempts are inevitably reductionist, for better or for worse, which certainly contributes to their "cardboard" quality. Should we see them as radical misunderstandings (Diderot's Tahiti bears little if any resemblance to the real island at any point in time!) or as clumsy attempts to understand?

To understand what, or whom? Lestringant's observation that the savages are "mouthpieces" can come as no surprise to readers of Lahontan or Diderot; neither author would have wished for a reader (unless perhaps a censor) so obtuse as not to notice. "Savages" were first and foremost theoretical constructs, certainly and quite explicitly for Rousseau and Diderot, and even to some extent for Lahontan, for whom they were also real live human beings with whom he had come into contact. In effect, savages constituted a yardstick, a barometer with which to measure the extent to which European societies had departed from "nature," and with what consequences.

Unfortunately, the identification of "savages" with "Nature" does not tell us very much; Enlightenment concepts of nature were polymorphic, if not flatly contradictory.[30] Lévi-Strauss notwithstanding, it is by no means evident that Enlightenment thinkers systematically opposed nature to culture, with the possible exception of Rousseau. But Rousseau's contemporaries generally argued against his scheme by suggesting that humans are naturally social, and that his ante-social (if not ante-cultural) primitive humans were an oxymoron. Indeed, for Pufendorf, whose views remained highly influential throughout the eighteenth century, natural sociality was the very foundation of natural law. More generally, the seventeenth century had witnessed a renewal of interest in notions of natural law and natural rights, as evidenced most prominently in the work of Grotius, Pufendorf, and Locke.[31] In theory, natural law rested on principles that were universally valid and accessible to rational apprehension. Its companion construct in the theological domain was "natural religion," which also spawned a considerable (though in some states more obviously controversial) literature in the seventeenth and eighteenth centuries.[32]

In retrospect, of course, it is easy to demonstrate the patent ethnocentrism of such constructs. Be this as it may, they fundamentally underpin the irony of Lahontan's and Diderot's dialogues. If "natural law" and "natural religion" are universally valid, they must be as valid for savages as for "civilized" Europeans. If they are accessible and acceptable to any rational person, then in what better genre to expose this rationality than dialogue, a mode of argumentation where the best argument presumably gets the upper hand? The conceit, of course, is that the savages in the dialogues are both more rational and better dialecticians than Europeans, and thus are perfect vehicles for exposing the essential irrationality of European thought and behavior. Admittedly, this is incompatible with another image, that of robust but benighted savages; their coexistence in Diderot's *Supplement* in particular contributes to the dialogue's ambivalence, as contrasted with the far more consistent portrayals of Lahontan on one hand and Rousseau on the other.

In any case, it should be clear that the "natural" aspect of natural law or natural religion cannot be contrasted with the "cultural" or the "social." Of course, it is possible and consistent to argue that some features of law and religion are universally valid and that others are particular, valid only at specific places and times. (Pufendorf, for example, distinguished between the duties of "man"—universally determined by natural law— and of "citizens"—governed by the particular laws of the state.) However, the universal validity of "natural law" hardly implied its universal respect. The notion that the observation of "natural law" is the product of deliberate policy rather than as a sort of mindless reflex emerges clearly in the work of Quesnay. Quesnay definitely considered his physiocratic economic principles as part of the domain of "natural law"—that is to say, rationally demonstrable and universally applicable—but Peru and China were the realms where, in his opinion, these principles were best applied, as directed by central governments. Admittedly, only Diderot would argue playfully that Tahitian savages respected the principles of Quesnay's political economy. Not all theories of natural law are equally applicable, at least convincingly, to "savage" cases. However, for Quesnay as for Lahontan and Diderot, a respect for natural law was hardly to be found in Europe. To the extent that natural law and natural religion were hardly empty constructs, the savages who putatively respected them could not be defined in terms of pure negation, as the mere and mechanical "opposite" of Europeans. If anything, European societies were defined as negations of natural law. The irony was that the very "natural law" which Europeans negated was a product of their own creation, in reality totally alien to the savages who advocated it so eloquently in European fictions.

Reorienting the world

The constructs of "despotism" and "savagery" described in this and the previous chapters represented a crucial shift in Europe's geographical imaginary. The north-south axis derived from Hippocrates by means of Aristotle stressed the importance of the contrast between cold, temperate, and mild climates. "Savagery" and "despotism," on the other hand, corresponded broadly to the West (the Americas) or the East (Asia).[33] This is not to suggest by any means that climatic theories predicated on the north-south axis were abandoned. Montesquieu, for one, incorporated these ideas too, in *The Spirit of Laws*, admittedly a sprawling and inconsistent masterpiece.[34] As the case of Montesquieu suggests, both axes could be combined by suggesting that the climate of Asia predisposed its inhabitants to despotic temperaments.

However, "savagery" and "despotism" did not always correspond exactly to the east-west axis. For example, for Sinophiles, Peru was the New World equivalent of China, as we have already seen with Temple. The Utopian realm of El Dorado in Voltaire's (1960:137–221) *Candide*, situated in the Andes, is transparently modeled on Peru. Just before his long essay on China, Quesnay (1888:555–62) published the equally eulogistic, although far shorter, "Analysis of the Government of the Incas of Peru." As for "savages," Polynesia emerged as a focus of late-eighteenth-century fascination after the voyages of Bougainville and Cook. Diderot's Orou is, after all, the literary grandchild of Lahontan's Adario. Admittedly, Polynesia—east of China and west of the New World—did not fit very neatly into the east/west division of the world, though functionally, if not geographically, it belonged resolutely to the realm of the West.

While Asian peoples were hardly if ever classified as "savages" (with the notable exception of Siberians, peoples of the far north), nomadic pastoralists were generally categorized as "barbarians."[35] Were "barbarians," for all intents and purposes, the equivalents of "savages"? Not invariably. We have seen that Temple included Scythians and Arabs, that is to say Asian nomadic pastoralists, as the northern and southern exemplars of "heroic virtues," even if they were admittedly inferior to the Chinese and the Peruvians. On the other hand, Rousseau's (1987) "Essay on the Origin of Language," which he had originally intended to include in his *Discourse on Inequality* but never published during his lifetime, situated the birth of language among pastoral peoples. In his imaginary scenario, which foreshadows nineteenth-century theories of original savagery, he situates shepherds living in incestuous groups. When by chance a group of young men from one group happens upon a group of women from another as they are watering their flock, they fall in love immediately and break out in melody: Rousseau's vision of ur-speech. Leaving aside the radical improbability of such an operatic scene—Rousseau was himself a composer of opera and an important music critic—it should be stressed that Rousseau's young pastoralists are both incestuous and prelinguistic. Clearly, for him the distinction between pastoralists and "savages" was hardly salient. In short, Asian "barbarians" were sometimes, though hardly invariably, the functional equivalents of American and Polynesian "savages."

The difference between East and West, empires and savagery, was even reflected in the choice of literary genres where non-Europeans were granted an entirely fictional voice. As we have seen, savages were featured in dialogues, where their rhetorical virtuosity, as attested by the Jesuits as well as by Lahontan, makes them formal adversaries, especially for the caricaturally conventional Europeans whom they effortlessly flummox. Literate Asians, on the other hand, are masters of the art of letter writing. Montesquieu's (1964) *Persian Letters* are the best known examples of a popular and prolific genre, which includes Oliver Goldsmith's (1933) *The Citizen of the World*, featuring the letters of the urbane Chinese observer of London mores, Lien Chi Altangi. Françoise de Grafigny's (1983) remarkable *Letters of a Peruvian Woman* demonstrates the extent to which Peru was permutable with China or Persia. The heroine, the Peruvian princess Zilia, begins her series of letters by knotting strings, resorting to more conventional European modes of writing only once she has learned French . . . and run out of string.

American "savages" and Asian "despots" were also deployed in different kinds of arguments about different issues. "Savages" were invoked in order to contrast a "natural" order to corrupted European ideas or practices. For Lahontan, this natural order was exemplary in multiple domains: on one hand political and economic, in terms of "natural" liberty and equality; on the other hand religious, in terms of an uncomplicated "natural" theology and its accompanying sense of morality. A half century later, these domains were to go their separate ways. Rousseau focused his critique on the growth of economic and political inequality. This is hardly to imply that he was unconcerned with religion, and morality was entirely central to all of his thought. However, the Catholic Church was not a particular target of his polemic. This was hardly the case for Voltaire and Diderot, whose dialectical savages, direct descendants of Adario, expertly confounded Catholic apologists. Diderot, in particular, wanted to expose the "unnatural" sexual morality of Catholicism, ranging from the celibacy of the clergy to the prohibition of divorce and even, more scandalously, the incest taboo. For his part, Diderot was hardly unconcerned with politics and economics; he fiercely condemned imperial expansion in favor of the free exchange of goods by independent peoples. However, "savages" per se did not enter into his political and economic arguments any more than they did in Rousseau's writings on religion and morality.

In short, in the domain of political economy, the "natural" equality of savages was contrasted to the rampant and egregious inequality characteristic of European society. Arguments for or against supposedly "despotic" Asian empires were framed in terms of narrower questions about the benefits or evils of political centralization. There were important exceptions. Quesnay, for example, argued that there were "natural" laws of the economy; a strong and wise central administration, as in China, could foster the smooth operation of such laws, whereas the maintenance of aristocratic and regional privilege could get in their way. If, for Lahontan and Rousseau, economic inequality lay at the heart of European injustice, the political and legal realms certainly functioned to maintain these inequalities in place.

Even so, throughout the French Enlightenment, "savagery" and "despotism," West and East, were almost invariably invoked separately, in different contexts and to bolster or undermine different arguments. Instead, it was in Britain that the two were combined in terms of a single coherent vision, as we will see in the next chapter.

TEN

From Savagery to Decadence:
Ferguson, Millar, and Gibbon

Lewis Henry Morgan attempted in 1877 to chart the rise of humanity from "savagery" to "barbarism" and finally "civilization." By and large, progress for Morgan was an exponential curve, an ever-encompassing development of seemingly boundless human potential. His optimism was only occasionally tempered, but his scheme contained a paradox of which Morgan demonstrated a definite awareness. The *gens*, the institution that included common descendants of a single ancestor, was at the heart of pre-civilized society, but it was also anchored in the principles of "liberty, equality, and fraternity"—principles that, for Morgan as an American, were sacrosanct. For much of its recorded history, hierarchical "civilization" entailed the very negation of these fundamental principles.

Neither Morgan's particular conceptualization of "progress" nor his reservations about its consequences were entirely original. More than a hundred years before the publication of *Ancient Society*, the Scottish thinker Adam Ferguson, in his *Essay on the History of Civil Society*, published in 1767, developed very similar conclusions. Ferguson has not gone entirely unnoticed by disciplinary historians of anthropology, who in one way or another identify him as an important precursor.[1] In this light it is crucial to point out not only the similarities but also the differences between the thought of Ferguson and his contemporaries on one hand and those of nineteenth-century thinkers, notably Morgan, Marx, and Engels.[2]

Most obviously, Ferguson shares with his successors a faith in the reality of progress, which he proclaims outright from the opening paragraph of his *Essay*:

> Natural productions are generally formed by degrees. Vegetables grow from
> a tender shoot, and animals from an infant state. . . . Not only the individual

advances from infancy to manhood, but the species itself from rudeness to
civilization. (1995:7)

Of course, such a notion of progress was hardly original with Ferguson.[3]
More specifically, such notions were widely circulated in the lively intellectual milieu of mid-eighteenth-century Scotland, by a remarkable group of
thinkers of whom the most notable examples were Adam Smith and David
Hume, both friends of Ferguson. (Hume was characteristically skeptical of
such schemes of progress, but in this respect he was hardly typical of his
circle as a whole.) Adam Smith (1978:14), on the other hand, clearly expounded such notions in his unpublished lectures on jurisprudence at the
University of Glasgow in 1762–63: "There are four distinct states which
mankind pass thro:—1st, the Age of Hunters; 2dly, the Age of Shepherds; 3dly,
the Age of Agriculture; 4^{thly}, the Age of Commerce." Members of Smith's
circle published even earlier versions of this four-stage theory in the 1750s,
though Ronald Meek (1976) makes the case that Smith himself may have
been its originator, in earlier lectures that have not survived in any form.
Well before Morgan, Marx, and Engels, these Scottish thinkers had specifically measured progress in terms of "means of subsistence." While such a
scheme was not original with Ferguson, there can be no doubt that he developed it more rigorously and systematically than his predecessors.

   On the other hand, of the six parts of Ferguson's *Essay*, the final two—
which amount to a full third of the book—are discussions titled "Of the
Decline of Nations" and "Of Corruption and Political Slavery." After all,
if nations can grow "from infancy to manhood," are they not doomed to
succumb to old age? Ferguson (1995:198–99) considers and rejects this all-
too-literal analogy. Still, the preoccupation with "decline" and "corruption"
as well as with "progress" characterizes the thought not only of Ferguson,
but also of many of his contemporaries. It is important to point out that
such notions of "decline" or "corruption" referred not primarily to economic degeneration, but rather to political degeneration, and specifically
to the emergence of "despotism"—a preoccupation Ferguson shared and
indeed derived from Montesquieu. For Ferguson, the central question is:
To what extent are the very factors that lead to economic "progress" simultaneously responsible for the overcentralization of political power? How,
for better but also for worse, are "means of subsistence" related to forms of
hierarchical control? If Morgan, before Marx and Engels, attempted to write
the history of the effects of private property on the family, Ferguson much
more lucidly detailed its consequences for the state.

Whereas Morgan contrasts *societas* and *civitas*, societies rooted in kinship as opposed to those rooted in territory, Ferguson opposes "rude" to "polished" nations. Coincidentally, Ferguson's primary example, like Morgan's, is the Iroquois; specifically, he availed himself of the published accounts of the Jesuit writers Charlevoix and Lafitau. Unlike Morgan, he classed the Iroquois as "savages." For Morgan, the Iroquois reliance on horticulture clearly placed them at the more advanced stage of being "barbarians," in societies that had domesticated either animals or plants. Ferguson was by no means unacquainted with this fact, which hardly escaped the notice of the Jesuits who lived and preached among the Iroquois. Ferguson's point is that, in spite of their practice of horticulture, the Iroquois did not accumulate significant quantities of property. Ferguson argues that this economic equality has direct social and political consequences:

> . . . they admit of no distinctions of rank or condition, and . . . they have in fact no degree of subordination different from the distribution of function, which follows the differences of age, talents, and dispositions. . . . A warrior who has led the youth of his nation to the slaughter of his enemies, or who has been foremost in the chase, returns upon a level with the rest of his tribe, and when the only business is to sleep, or to feed, can enjoy no pre-eminence, for he sleeps and he feeds no better than they. . . .
>
> The character of the mind, however, in this state, is not founded on ignorance alone. Men are conscious of their equality, and are tenacious of its rights. Even when they follow a leader to the field, they cannot brook the pretensions to a formal command: they listen to no orders; and they come under no military engagements, but those of mutual fidelity, and equal ardour in the enterprise. (1995:83–4)

For Ferguson, pastoralism played a more essential role in universal history than it did for Morgan, precisely because it allowed for an accumulation of wealth:

> [Nations] having possessed themselves of herds, and depending for their provision on pasture, know what it is to be poor and rich. They know the relations of patron and client, of servant and master, and suffer themselves to be classed according to their measures of wealth. (1995:81)

Ferguson was here following the lead of Adam Smith, who had made a similar argument in his lectures on jurisprudence at Glasgow University in 1762 and 1763 (Smith 1978). In the first place, Ferguson suggests that through good luck or hard work, certain individuals come to accumulate more wealth than others. More importantly, property relations lead to the beginnings of centralized authority. Warfare becomes a strategic means of accumulating wealth. When a raiding party returns with booty, a proportionately larger share is reserved for the leader. What is more, this property is heritable, and leaders consequently leave more to their descendants, whose very wealth allows them to build up a clientele and thus to maintain their positions. The loyalty of the savage hunter/horticulturalist to his group as a whole is replaced by loyalty to the person of the chieftain, though Ferguson takes pains to point out that this incipient development of hereditary leadership is still far removed from hereditary monarchy, and that the difference between chieftain and follower remains, in many respects, minimal.[4]

At this point, Ferguson is less concerned with tracing the development of society step by step through agriculture and commerce than with contrasting these two varieties of "rude" society with "polished" nations. As might be expected, Ferguson, a member of Adam Smith's circle, associates the development of commerce with the intensification of the division of labor.[5] At first sight, this intensification would seem to be identified with "progress" itself: ". . . Every generation, compared to its predecessors, may have appeared to be ingenious; compared to its followers, may have appeared to be dull; and human ingenuity, whatever heights it may have gained in a succession of ages, continues to move with an equal pace . . ." (1995:174). On the contrary, he suggests that such specialization extracts a price:

> Many mechanical arts, indeed, require no capacity; they succeed best under a total suppression of sentiment and reason; and ignorance is the mother of industry as well as of superstition. Reflection and fancy are subject to err; but a habit of moving the hand, or the foot, is independent of either. Manufactures, accordingly, prosper most, where the mind is least consulted, and where the workshop may, without any great effort of the imagination, be considered as an engine, the parts of which are men. . . .
>
> Even in manufacture, the genius of the master, perhaps, is cultivated, while that of the inferior workman lies waste. . . . The general officer may be a great proficient in the knowledge of war, while the soldier is confined to a few motions of the hand and the foot. The former may have gained, what the latter has lost; and being occupied in the conduct of disciplined armies, may practise on a larger scale, all the arts of preservation, of deception, and of stratagem, which the savage exerts in leading a small party, or merely in defending himself. (1995:174–75)

The contrast between "civilized" and "savage" humanity here is pointed. What the general may perhaps have gained, the foot soldier has most assuredly lost.

Ferguson's critique is not simply that specialization limits the scope of individual capacities, but that its extension into the public domain is a danger to individual liberty. The professionalization of warfare, in the first place, makes defense the concern of a few rather than of the population as a whole. The same is true of a professional government bureaucracy. Paradoxically, while the "savage" has a direct stake and takes a direct part in the collective affairs of his society, the ordinary members of "polished" nations are inclined, if not obliged, to leave such affairs to specialists. Moreover, the unequal distribution of wealth clearly provides an unequal stake in the affairs of the nation as a whole. The very real risk, for Ferguson, is the monopolization of public life by a specialized army and bureaucracy for whom public order is a greater priority than individual liberty.

If, for Ferguson, the Iroquois embody the type case of the free, egalitarian "savage," China, "where pilfering, fraud, and corruption are the reigning practice" (1995:138), is the representative case of "despotism" as the outcome of overspecialization:

> They have done what we are very apt to admire; they have brought national affairs to the level of the meanest capacity; they have broke them into parts, and thrown them into separate department; they have clothed every proceeding with splendid ceremonies, and majestical forms; and where the reverence of forms cannot repress disorder, a rigorous and severe police, armed with every species of corporal punishment, is applied to the purpose. (1995:214)

It is important to insist that Ferguson's idealization of the Iroquois and disparagement of the Chinese is not just naive primitivism. It is intended, rather, as a cautionary tale about the unintended political consequences of economic and administrative specialization that are the concomitants of "progress" in the material domain. At one end of the spectrum of human society lie anarchy and material poverty, but also the liberty, equality, and fraternity—needless to say, Ferguson, writing before the French Revolution, does not use this precise language—that Morgan, too, found attractive among the Iroquois. At the other end lie wealth and order, but also the specter of despotism which only a vigilant citizenry, engaged in the affairs of the nation, could preclude.

Of the Scottish and English thinkers of his time, Ferguson was perhaps the most ambivalent about "progress." However, his contemporaries most

definitely shared his preoccupations. The relationship between the "savagery" and "barbarism" of "rude" societies, on one hand, and the risk of
"despotism" as the outcome of "civilization" on the other was the subject
of the writings of Ferguson's fellow Scot, John Millar. A student of Adam
Smith and professor of civil law at Glasgow, Millar published *Observations
Concerning the Distinction of Ranks in Society* in 1771, a few years after Ferguson's *Essay*. The work was revised in 1779 with a modified title, *The Origin
of the Distinction of Ranks* (Lehman 1960).[6] Like Smith and Ferguson before
him, Millar distinguishes between hunting, pastoral, agricultural, and commercial societies, relating mode of subsistence to increasing hierarchy. He
draws on a somewhat wider range of sources than does Ferguson. While Millar still cites Lafitau and Charlevoix extensively, for him the Iroquois cease
to be the model of "savagery" as they are for Ferguson. Millar also extends
the range of his preoccupations, beginning his work with a consideration
of the treatment of women and children, and ending with the treatment of
servants and slaves.

Millar's treatment of "the rank and condition of women in different ages"
highlights the differences between his treatment of "progress" and Ferguson's.
Millar argues that, among hunters, men were too preoccupied by the necessities of life to take too sustained an interest in women. Indeed, his portrait
of the undersexed "savage" contrasts starkly to nineteenth- and twentieth-
century fantasies about excessive "savage" sexuality. According to Millar, the
sexes were not kept separate from one another, premarital sexuality was a
matter of little concern, and husbands offered sexual hospitality to their
guests. With the advent of pastoralism and agriculture, the relations between
the sexes changed radically. Differences of wealth gave rise to a preoccupation with honor, associated not only with military prowess but also with
sexual purity and exclusive control over wives and daughters. The cultivation
of romantic passion went hand in hand with strict segregation of the sexes,
especially among the wealthy and powerful. Finally, with the development of
commerce and the advent of ever more diversified spheres of activity, women
found more opportunities for "cultivation" outside the domestic sphere,
and—as with savages—the sexes were again free to mingle, a development
that Millar very clearly approves despite the eventual risk of "dissolution," of
the efflorescence of an excessive sexuality that Millar squarely associates with
"civilization" rather than "savagery." Unlike Ferguson, Millar has little faith
in the virtues of the "savage." If for Ferguson "progress" inevitably extracts
a price, a loss as well as a gain, Millar's vision is far more sanguine. Savage
egalitarianism clearly evokes no feelings of nostalgia on his part.

By no means was Millar uncritical of his own society; this is evidenced by his treatment of slavery at the end of the book. Slavery itself, he suggests, develops along with the increase of wealth and, consequently, with the accumulation of social inequality. Savages have little use for slaves; war captives, if not put to death, are adopted into the tribe. On the other hand, "the laws and customs of the modern European nations have carried the advantages of liberty to a height which was never known in any other age or country" (1960:315). The much-celebrated liberties of ancient Greek and Roman Republics, Millar pointedly insists, did not extend to a substantial proportion of their populations who were reduced to slavery. But in commercial societies slavery is an anomaly. A faithful disciple of Adam Smith, Millar argues that slavery is not only immoral but also economically inefficient. Indeed, he ends the book with a diatribe against the pretensions of the American colonies in active revolt against Britain at the time:

> It affords a curious spectacle to observe that the same people who talk in a high strain of political liberty, and who consider the privilege of imposing their own taxes as one of the unalienable rights of mankind, should make no scruple of reducing a great proportion of their fellow-creatures into circumstances by which they are not only deprived of property, but almost of every species of right. (1960:321)

The issue of liberty, of course, raises the question of the development of centralized political authority. Millar develops in greater detail Ferguson's argument that the accumulation of wealth leads to the accumulation of power. Thus, not only are pastoralists capable of amassing more wealth than hunters, but the extent of their herds is correlated to the strength of leadership:

> ... the captain or leader of a tribe among the Hottentots, who have made but small progress in the pastoral life, and among the wild Arabs, who have seldom acquired considerable property, appears to have little more authority than among the savages of America. The great riches, on the other hand, which are frequently acquired by those numerous bands of shepherds inhabiting the vast country of Tartary, have rendered the influence of the chief proportionably extensive, and have bestowed upon him an almost unlimited power, which commonly remains in the same family, and is transmitted from father to son like a private inheritance. (1960:259)

Agriculture, by which Millar and Ferguson before him clearly mean plow agriculture as distinct from horticulture, allows for even stronger and more centralized authority. In the first place, landed property is more stable than property in animals, which can be raided, felled by disease, or wiped out by drought; secondly, property can be more easily accumulated in relatively large holdings.

Ultimately, Millar is faced with the same problem that beset Ferguson: to what extent does the development of commerce tend toward or impede the impositions of despotic authority? Here again, Millar is more optimistic than Ferguson. On one hand, he accepts Ferguson's contention that specialization in the public domain—most notably a standing army and a professional judiciary—sows the seeds for the emergence of despotic authority. On the other hand, the very circulation of commercial wealth provides, in Millar's opinion, a check on the monopolization of power. New fortunes are constantly being made and old ones frittered away, preventing the concentration of wealth—and, consequently, of political power—in the hands of a few.

The concern that "civilization" hovered between "savagery" and "barbarism" on one hand and the "corruption" of despotism on the other was hardly peculiar to the Scots. Similar preoccupations are central to Edward Gibbon's (1983) monumental *The History of the Decline and Fall of the Roman Empire*, as is implied by the very title of the book, the first volume of which was published in 1776. Gibbon was well aware of the published works, though perhaps not the unpublished lectures, of Adam Smith as well as Ferguson, both of which were to be found in his extensive library along with a vast collection of traveler's accounts, especially of Asia.[7] (Gibbon was less interested in America; he owned a copy of Charlevoix's history, but not of Lafitau.)

Could the catastrophe that befell the Roman Empire be repeated in modern Europe? In an unusual excursus at the end of chapter 38, titled "General Observations of the Fall of the Roman Empire in the West" (1983, vol. 2: 436–44), Gibbon attempts directly to answer the question: "The savage nations of the globe are the common enemies of civilized society; and we may inquire, with anxious curiosity, whether Europe is still threatened with a repetition of those calamities which formerly oppressed the arms and institutions of Rome" (Gibbon 1932, vol. 2: 440). Gibbon's answer is optimistic, and it rests primarily on his recognition that European civilization is not limited to the confines of any single state: ". . . A philosopher may be permitted . . . to consider Europe as one great republic, whose various inhabitants have attained almost the same level of politeness and cultivation" (Gibbon 1983, vol. 2: 439). The future of Europe does not depend on the fortune of any single realm, much less the abilities of any single leader.

"If a savage conqueror should issue from the deserts of Tartary, he must repeatedly vanquish the robust peasants of Russia, the numerous armies of Germany, the gallant nobles of France, and the intrepid freemen of Britain; who, perhaps, might confederate for their common defence" (Gibbon 1983, vol. 2: 441). In any case, the progress of Europe, in the arts of peace as well as the arts of war, renders any such catastrophe implausible. One of the paradoxes of Gibbon's work is that he ends his narrative in 1453 with the fall of Constantinople, the last bastion of Rome, at the very moment where, as we have noted, the idea of Europe as an "imagined community" and not just a region on maps was beginning to take shape.

The "anxious curiosity" that underpins Gibbon's question unsettles the certainty of the answer. He exorcises the specter of Europe's fall; but what of the possibility of its decline? Gibbon begins these reflections by stating baldly that "the decline of Rome was the natural and inevitable effect of immoderate greatness" (Gibbon 1983, vol. 2: 438). It is not apparent from his reflections that Europe is immune from the same malady. Is there any lesson to be learned from the decline of Rome, if not the fall, that might apply to contemporary Europe?

For Gibbon, both ancient Rome and modern Europe constitute unique islands of civilization surrounded by peoples who are, if not outright savages, at least in some profound sense uncivil. Gibbon's point of departure, before the Fall as it were, is Rome under the Antonines. As he depicts it in his opening words:

> In the second century of the Christian era, the Empire or Rome comprehended the fairest part of the earth, and the most civilised portion of mankind. . . . The gentle but powerful influence of laws and manners had gradually cemented the union of the provinces. Their peaceful inhabitants enjoyed and abused the advantages of wealth and luxury. The image of a free constitution was preserved with decent reverence: the Roman senate appeared to possess the sovereign authority, and devolved on the emperors all the executive powers of government (Gibbon 1983, vol. 1: 1).

Gibbon's choice is anything but neutral. For Montesquieu (1968), in his *Considerations sur les causes de la grandeur des Romains et de leur décadence*, (Considerations on the Causes of the Greatness of the Romans and of Their Decadence), the great catastrophe was the fall of the republic, not the empire. For Montesquieu, the republic was the embodiment of Roman "virtue," civic but also—in spite of his sometimes disingenuous protests—moral. The nature of the political order was determinant. For Gibbon, what counted was civilization, "the powerful influence of laws and manners." This is not to suggest that Gibbon considered the nature of the political order to be irrelevant. But his trenchant irony in this passage suggests that the pretense of a "free constitution," even one devoid of real substance, will suffice, provided that it allows for the preservation of civilization.

The contours of civilization in Gibbon's narrative emerge in contrast to depictions of different varieties of "uncivilized" peoples. Chapters 8 and 9 are devoted to portraying two paradigmatic examples, nemeses of Rome: Persia, the archetype of "Oriental despotism," and Germany, which typifies "savagery." He is quite explicit about the contrast: "In the more early ages of the world, whilst the forest that covered Europe afforded a retreat to a few wandering savages, the inhabitants of Asia were already collected into populous cities, and reduced under extensive empires, the seat of the arts, of luxury, and of despotism" (Gibbon 1983, vol. 1: 169). Much of chapter 8 is given over to an account of the rise and reign of Artaxerxes, founder of the Sassanid dynasty that overturned the previous rule of the Parthians. In particular, Gibbon dwells on Artaxerxes's restoration of the Zoroastrian religion, which he depicts with deep ambivalence: "The great and fundamental article of the system was the celebrated doctrine of the two principles; a bold and injudicious attempt of Eastern philosophy to reconcile the existence of moral and physical evil with the attributes of a beneficent Creator and Governor of the world (Gibbon 1983, vol. 1: 172)." Gibbon ironizes about the obscurity of Zoroastrian theology, "darkly comprehended by followers and even the far greater number of disciples" (Gibbon 1983, vol. 1: 173). Yet there are aspects of the religion that Gibbon admires, "remarkable instances, in which Zoroaster lays aside the prophet, assumes the legislator, and discovers a liberal concern for private and public happiness, seldom to be found among the groveling of visionary schemes of superstition. . . . But in that motley composition, dictated by reason and passion, by enthusiasm and by selfish motives, some useful and sublime truths were disgraced by a mixture of the most abject and dangerous superstition" (Gibbon 1983, vol. 1: 174–75).

Gibbon's characterization of Zoroastrianism as "Oriental religion," a mixture of "superstition" and "enthusiasm,"[8] foreshadows his treatment of Christianity throughout much of the book. Gibbon himself had converted to Roman Catholicism at Oxford, from which he was firmly and expeditiously packed off by his father to be properly reeducated by a Calvinist minister in Lausanne.[9] In his maturity, Gibbon maintained both his Christian faith and his deep mistrust of the Roman Church—its theology, its pomp, and not least of all its monks. Anticlerical rather than anti-Christian, he nonetheless considered the adoption of Christianity as the religion of the

Roman Empire as an important contributing factor to its decline, if not its fall. Gibbon's distaste for Oriental despotism and for Oriental religion are reflected in his portrait of the aging Constantine, the emperor responsible both for the transfer of the seat of empire to the East and for the adoption of Christianity as its official faith. In the person of Constantine, the decay of the empire is assimilated to its Orientalization:

> A secret but universal decay was felt in every part of the public administration, and the emperor himself, though he still retained the obedience, gradually lost the esteem, of his subjects. The dress and manners which, towards the decline of life, he chose to effect, served only to degrade him in the eyes of mankind. The Asiatic pomp which had been adopted by the pride of Diocletian assumed an air of softness and effeminacy in the person of Constantine. He is represented with false hair of various colours, laboriously arranged by the skillful artists of the times; a diadem of a new and more expensive fashion; a profusion of gems and pearls, of collars and bracelets; and a variegated flowing robe of silk, most curiously embroidered with flowers of gold. (Gibbon 1983, vol. 1: 562–63)

Gibbon's depiction of the barbaric Germans is no more flattering than his portrayal of Oriental corruption. He relies for all intents and purposes on Tacitus's (1948) account, but entirely subverts its tone. Where Tacitus frequently betrays his admiration of many of the Germans' qualities, Gibbon displays contempt: "They passed their lives in a state of ignorance and poverty, which it has pleased some declaimers to dignify with the appellation of virtuous simplicity" (Gibbon 1983, vol. 1: 191). First and perhaps foremost, he stresses the absence of writing among the Germans: ". . . The use of letters is the principal circumstance that distinguishes a civilised people from a herd of savages incapable of knowledge or reflection." Gibbon compares such a gulf to "the immense distance between the man of learning and the *illiterate* [emphasis in original] peasant" whose existence consequently "surpasses, but very little, his fellow-labourer the ox in the exercise of his mental faculties" (Gibbon 1983, vol. 1: 190).

Even the relative absence of economic inequality is interpreted by Gibbon as a brake on civilization. Commenting on the absence of money among the Germans and the little value they place in silver and gold, he concludes: "The value of money has been settled by general consent to express our wants and our property, as letters were invented to express our ideals; and both these institutions, by giving a more active energy to the powers and passions of human nature, have contributed to multiply the objects they were designed to represent" (Gibbon 1983, vol. 1: 191). The Germans' annual redistribution of land by leaders to followers is, for Gibbon, a token not of equality butr of a lack of interest in property and possessions. The counterpart of that lack of interest is inveterate indolence: "The care of the house and family, the management of the land and cattle, were delegated to the old and the infirm, to women and slaves. The lazy warrior, destitute of every art that might employ his leisure hours, consumed his days and nights in the animal gratifications of sleep and food" (Gibbon 1983, vol. 1: 192). It should be noted that, among animal gratifications, sex is conspicuous here by its absence. Even the German virtue of chastity, noted with great approval by Tacitus, falls victim to Gibbon's irony. Civilization, by furnishing women with "elegance of dress, of motion, and of manners gives a lustre to beauty, and inflames the senses through the imagination" (Gibbon 1983, vol. 1: 198). German women, on the other hand, "were most assuredly neither lovely, nor very susceptible of love. While they affected to emulate the stern virtues of *man*, they must have resigned that attractive softness in which principally consists the charm of *woman*" (Gibbon 1983, vol. 1: 199).

Significantly, in Gibbon's scheme, both Oriental despotism and German savagery are guilty of fundamental, fatal, but opposite violations of gender distinction. Oriental despotism gives rise to masculine effeminacy, in sharp contrast to what Gibbon identifies as the spirit of martial virility. The German savages are unimpeachably, perhaps even excessively, virile—women as well as men. Civilization consists, among other things, in the production of properly masculine men and feminine women. On the other hand, civilization generates difference whereas savagery is characterized by uniformity:

> The different characters that mark the civilised nations of the globe may be ascribed to the use and the abuse of reason, which so variously shapes and so artificially composes the manners and opinions of an European or a Chinese. . . . The savage tribes of mankind, as they approach nearer to the condition of animals, preserve a stronger resemblance to themselves and to each other. The uniform stability of their manners is the natural consequence of the imperfections of their faculties. (Gibbon 1983, vol. 1: 901)

Civilization, in other words, is a process of simultaneous differentiation and humanization. Savages (and also, as we have seen, peasants!) are closer to animals than are civilized humans, and consequently they are more alike. Such likenesses constitute a leitmotif in Gibbon's overall narrative, as one group of pastoralists after another—Huns, Alani, and Mongols, among hordes of others—erupts into Europe with devastating regularity, each new group generally resembling the last.

The single positive facet of German society that Gibbon identifies, and which the Germans share with each successive wave of barbarian invaders, is their fierce attachment to personal liberty. Herein lies the central paradox at the heart of Gibbon's worldview. Civilization is the key to most of what Gibbon cherishes: learning, the arts, material prosperity. But it also carries with it the seeds of unfreedom. In his first-prize essay on the arts and sciences, Rousseau (1971) had addressed the question of the contribution of the arts and sciences to the well-being of humanity, and had answered pessimistically that, however worthwhile they might be in themselves, they had usually served to foster the interests of privilege if not despotic rule. Gibbon was certainly not prepared to go so far; for him, the benefits of civilization, including of course the arts and sciences, outweighed the possible costs. Yet the decline, if not the fall, of the Roman Empire lay bare the risks of "corruption," involving not only the loss of liberty but also the decline of the moral fabric of society, as embodied in gendered terms as virility. Savagery entailed the aggressive masculinity not only of men but of women. Only civilization could render women fully feminine. The crux, however, was to avoid the production of effeminate men. Gibbon's excursus in chapter 38 may have reassured his readers that Europe, unlike the Western Roman Empire, was hardly likely to fall. But Gibbon's reassurances provided no clear remedy for sparing Europe from the kind of "corruption" represented by Oriental despotism.

Why, we might ask, this overpowering preoccupation with "corruption" and "despotism" alongside narratives of progress? In the first place, one can point to the influence of Montesquieu's thought on Ferguson, Millar, and Gibbon, all of whom cite him, discuss his conclusions, and clearly take his ideas most seriously even when they criticize him. The idea of "despotism" is, as we have seen, central to *The Spirit of Laws*. "Despotism" is quintessentially localized in the East, in Persia and in China; Montesquieu's central concern is to forestall the "corruption" of European political institutions through the increasing centralization of political power in the hands of the ruler, thus transforming European "monarchies" into Oriental-style "despotisms."

However, the ideological place of "despotism" played a different role in eighteenth-century France than in Britain, largely because power struggles took somewhat different forms. In France, the aristocratically controlled *parlements*, staunch defenders of aristocratic fiscal and other privileges (including the right to buy and sell judicial offices), were pitted against a monarchy whose efforts and administrative centralization it often managed to frustrate. In Britain, the conflict was between factions that came to be known as "court" and "country."[10] The "court" faction was associated with the Whig party, or at least that part of it which managed to monopolize power in Parliament for much of the century; the "country" faction was essentially an opposition, consisting not only of the Tory party but also of dissatisfied Whigs. The threat of "despotism" was a rallying cry for this "country" opposition. Indeed, Montesquieu himself, who visited England and was very much an anglophile, clearly derived some of his concept of "despotism" from the British ideologues. However, where Montesquieu was concerned with taxation, and specifically with aristocratic exemptions, the British "country" ideologues were concerned with borrowing and the national debt. Whereas the French crown was desperate to generate revenues in order to free itself from crippling debt and thus acquire more room for maneuver, the British "court" Whigs were in a much better position to obtain credit and use it to entrench themselves in power. Specifically, funds could be used to create bureaucratic "offices" whose occupants were entirely beholden to the party in power. By the same token, they could be used to fund a professional standing army, again under the control of the "court." The adherents of the "country" faction consequently railed against the evils of deficit spending and its direct consequences: the creation of a specialized and professionalized bureaucracy, not to mention an army and, hardly incidentally, the bureaucracy's simultaneous clientelization. Instead, they envisaged a nation of mostly small-scale proprietors directly engaged in civic affairs, including participation in citizen militias, the alternative to a standing army.

To one extent or another, Ferguson, Millar, and Gibbon all drew on the ideological rhetoric associated with the "country" opposition, even if their specific political involvements (and all three were politically involved in one way or another) were noticeably different. Yet their writings are not just political propaganda but a grand synthesis of the literature on the "savage" horticulturalists of North America, the "barbarian" pastoralists of the Asian steppes, and the "despotic" civilizations of the Islamic world and the Far East. At the center is a paradox: the opposition between a state of "savagery" that embodies liberty without order and a state of "despotism" that embodies order without liberty. It is a narrative at once triumphal—to the extent that modern Europe and especially Britain embodies both liberty and order—and anxious, envisaging the possibility that this is a delicate balance indeed. Well before Marx, the British writers of the late eighteenth century were acutely aware, each in his own way, of the contradictions brought about by the spectacular development of commerce and the division of labor.

In any case, these late British writers were the first to develop a sophisticated, sociologically acute, and developmental account of the emergence of hierarchy in world-historical terms. Indeed, they were the first to suggest to what extent this history of hierarchy was also a history of means of subsistence and, consequently, forms of property. Yet these exercises were hardly disinterested, particularly among the Scots. Ferguson's and Millar's works were intended to convey specific political messages, and Ferguson in particular was not averse to overt political moralizing. Ferguson and Millar's understanding of hierarchy and property was, first and foremost, rooted at home. They sought to understand the world, not just to change it, but above all to keep it from changing in the wrong direction.

ELEVEN

Cultural Critique: Herder

"People who are ignorant of history and know only their own age believe that the present taste is the only one, and so necessary that nothing else besides it is even thinkable. . . . This ignorance is also joined by pride (a brother-and-sister pair as inseparable as envy and stupidity), their age is the best of ages, because they dwell within it and other epochs did not have the honor of their acquaintance."

—Johann Gottfried Herder, "Of the Changes in the Taste of Nations in the Course of the Ages"

"Civilization," the essence of everything Gibbon cherished in ancient Rome and modern Europe, was actually a radically new concept in his time. The *Oxford English Dictionary* cites its first usage, at least in this sense of the word, to 1760, only sixteen years before Gibbon published the first volumes of *The Decline and Fall*, and only seven before Ferguson's *Essay on the History of Civil Society*. Norbert Elias (2000) has attempted to trace the genesis of this paradigm of "civilization" to the rise of court society in early modern Europe. He argues that the advent of modern statecraft and warfare rendered the aristocracy obsolete as a military force and transformed it into a court bureaucracy. If the distinguishing attributes of the medieval aristocracy had been its military paraphernalia—a war horse, weapons, armor—the courtly aristocracy required a new idiom of distinction. In these new circumstances, social differences centered on behavior, especially manners. This ideology has left traces in the English language: "good breeding," referring to socially acceptable behavior, literally seems to suggest that this is a product of one's pedigree rather than of one's upbringing. The problem with maintaining such a distinction was that the manners of the aristocracy could always be emulated, especially by those who were directly below them in the social hierarchy, the upper levels of the bourgeoisie. As a result, manners, like fashion—another important marker of social distinction—were perpetually in a state of flux; yesterday's manners, like yesterday's fashion, were never quite up to snuff. The system was never entirely rigid, especially not in Britain and France. There were ways of buying into the aristocracy (though sometimes it took a few generations), and positions at court were open to capable individuals from the bourgeoisie, provided that they could behave in an appropriately "civilized" manner.

According to Elias, the situation was quite different in Germany, which was fragmented into many often miniscule courts. There were relatively few positions at court, and they were effectively monopolized by the hereditary nobility, no matter how appropriately the bourgeoisie might behave. Confronted by such a glass ceiling, the German bourgeoisie elaborated an ideal of "culture" as opposed to "civilization."[1] If "civilization" resided in behaviors and institutions—"the gentle but powerful influence of laws and manners," to use Gibbon's phrase—"culture" denoted the more intangible realms of thought and sensibilities. A well-mannered aristocratic imbecile might avoid snoring too loudly during a Haydn symphony, and might know the right moments to applaud. Such superficial skills hardly required any appreciation, much less understanding, of the music, the real qualities that constituted "culture."

This opposition between "civilization" and "culture" was central to the thought of Johann Gottfried Herder, whose vision of history was explicitly formulated as an alternative to the "civilizational" schemes of French and British Enlightenment thinkers. From 1762 to 1764, Herder studied under Immanuel Kant in Königsberg,[2] though the relationship between them soured after Herder left to assume a post at Riga. Kant did not publish any writings exposing his own vision of universal history until the 1780s, when he also published an unfavorable review of Herder's work (Kant 1991:201–20). A decade earlier, he began giving lectures on anthropology—lectures he only published at the very end of his life, in 1798 (Kant 1978) —and on physical geography. He also published a short article on racial typology (Eze 1997:38–48), insisting that humans constituted a single species divided into four races; this typology was included in his course on physical geography rather than in one on anthropology.[3] It is conceivable that Herder, who was initially quite close to Kant, was aware of many of these ideas well before their publication. Kant's book on anthropology, for example, was published more than two decades after his ideas on the subject were formulated. One way or another, although Kant's ideas were published after Herder had first published his philosophy of history, they furnish a useful point of contrast to Herder's far more radical scheme.

Kant's vision of universal history was first elaborated, relatively definitively, in an article published in 1784, "Idea for a Universal History with a Cosmopolitan Purpose" (Kant 1991:41–53). The essay is not "history" in the conventional sense of the word. There is very little in it about the past, and no reference whatsoever to concrete events or empirical data. Rather, it is a history that is prospective, indeed teleological—a history of the future. Its central protagonists are nature on one hand, and humanity as a species on the other. The central premise is that nature operates in such a way as to realize, over time, the full development of the inherent capacities of any species. Since the distinguishing capacity of humans is "reason," it follows that the end of nature is to develop human reason as fully as possible.

There is a paradox here. Reason can only develop through the deliberate actions of human free will; but humans very rarely, if ever, act with such an aim in mind. Kant uses an interesting and perceptive analogy to demonstrate the unintended collective consequences of individual human actions. Demographic facts—births, marriages, and deaths—are the outcomes of seemingly capricious and unpredictable acts of free will. On the other hand, national statistics demonstrate that their aggregate effects are stable and predictable, even if individual decisions (one might cite Kant's own decision never to marry!) seem radically indeterminate.

> Individual men and even entire nations little imagine that, while they are pursuing their own ends, each in his own way and often in opposition to others, they are unwittingly guided in their advance along a course intended by nature. They are unconsciously promoting an end which, even if they knew what it was, would scarcely arouse their interest. (Kant 1991:41)

The mechanism that "naturally" drives this development is "the *unsocial sociability* of men" (Kant 1991:44; emphasis in original).[4] In Kant's scheme, humans are subject to contrary if not contradictory impulses: social on one hand, individualistic on the other. Social by nature, they are also driven by the determination to impose their individual will on others, meeting the resistance of others who seek to do likewise. "It is this very resistance which awakens all man's powers and induces him to overcome his tendency to laziness. Through the desire for honour, power or property, it drives him to seek status among his fellows, who he cannot *bear* yet cannot *bear to leave*" (ibid.; emphasis in original). Selfish desires, intrinsically immoral in and of themselves, are a necessary natural counterbalance to physical, moral, and intellectual indolence—to a state of contentment where humans would live like sheep (the simile is Kant's) rather than be obliged to develop their natural potential. "All the culture and art which adorn mankind and the finest social order man creates are fruits of his unsociability" (Kant 1991:46)."

War is the ultimate expression of this unsociability and drive to domination. In a limited sense, Kant accepts the Hobbesian paradigm of war leading to the establishment of civil society:

> While the purposeless state of savagery did hold up the development of all
> the natural capacities of human beings, it nonetheless finally forced them,
> through the evils in which it involved them, to leave this state and enter into
> a civil constitution in which all their dormant capacities could be developed.
> (Kant 1991:49)[5]

For Kant, however, conflict was not only a perpetual threat but also a perpetual spur, driving humanity towards a more perfect social order. For Hobbes, international relations, along with savagery, constituted evidence of the state of nature as the war of every man against every man. What for Hobbes constituted a limit became a horizon for Kant. The resolution, for Kant, was to be a cosmopolitan social contract, a global federal order that would keep the peace between sovereign states, an order whose features he later developed systematically in his essay "Perpetual Peace" (Kant 1991:93–130). Such states would guarantee individuals the maximum amount of freedom while at the same time preventing them from infringing on the freedom of others. Perpetual peace, in other words, was the unintended outcome of all but perpetual war. Kant was not so naive as to expect such a resolution in the immediate future:

> We are *cultivated* to a high degree by art and science. We are *civilized* to the
> point of excess in all kinds of social courtesies and proprieties. But we are still
> a long way from the point where we could consider ourselves *morally* mature.
> (Kant 1991:49; emphases in original).

In Kant's thought, moral maturity is intrinsically linked to the concept of "enlightenment." Indeed, only a month after his essay on universal history, Kant published another essay in the same journal, titled "An Answer to the Question: What Is Enlightenment?" (Kant 1991:54–60). In the very first sentence of the essay, Kant answers his own question by categorizing enlightenment as "*man's emergence from his self-incurred immaturity*" (Kant 1991:54, emphasis in original). In this context, the immaturity in question is, strictly speaking, not moral but intellectual. "Enlightened maturity" refers to one's independent exercise of one's own understanding, and immaturity is self-incurred to the extent that people willingly abdicate this responsibility by accepting the intellectual authority of others. Maturity has a political precondition, which is the freedom to express ideas, and especially to publish them. Such freedom generates a "public sphere"[6] in which ideas, including religious and political ideas, are debated. Kant explicitly praises Frederick the Great for allowing such intellectual freedom in exchange for allegiance: "*Argue* as much as you like and about whatever you like, *but obey!*" (Kant 1991:55, emphasis in original)." In the long term, such debate in the intellectual arena is the equivalent of war in the domain of politics. The individualistic, antisocial desire to excel, to impose one's own opinion, raises the collective public level of debate, and ultimately the collective (though not necessarily the individual) exercise of "reason." It is important to note that for Kant, reason is also, and perhaps first and foremost, moral reasoning. This is precisely why "enlightenment," the free exercise of ideas, is also a recipe for moral maturity, which in turn is a precondition for perpetual peace.

Kant's theory of universal history is predicated on a vision of human nature, of "unsocial sociability," which he elaborated in far greater detail in his lectures on anthropology, *Anthropology from a Pragmatic Point of View* (Kant 1978). The qualification "pragmatic" refers to the distinction between "anthropology" as the study of the human anatomy and as the investigation of the human character. In terms of modern disciplines, Kant's anthropology is arguably closer to psychology than to anthropology as currently practiced. In its subject matter and organization it resembles, and was arguably modeled after, Hume's (1888) *A Treatise of Human Nature*, with half of the book devoted to cognition and reason and the other half to pleasure, desire, and individual, gendered, national, and racial characterization. In fact, the very concept of "human nature" was an Enlightenment construct, deriving in large measure from Locke's empiricist epistemology (Smith 1995; Zammito 2002:221–53.) At issue were the relationship of thought to sensations, of reason to emotions, and of all of these factors to moral ideas and behavior. These questions were all of central importance to Kant for his political philosophy as well as for his metaphysics.

Kant's lectures on anthropology at the University of Königsberg did not directly lead to the institution of the subject as a modern academic discipline. Admittedly, Kant's subject matter was related to that of modern anthropology, even if the methods were entirely distinct. Indeed, Zammito

(2002) has forcefully argued that Kant's and Herder's philosophical anthropology was a foundation for the modern discipline. Vermuelen (2015), on the other hand, dismisses such claims, stressing instead the importance of German ethnography and ethnology—terms coined in Germany in the eighteenth century, which were only adopted in France and Britain in the nineteenth century. These other disciplines, associated in particular with scientific expeditions in Siberia, were preoccupied with an entirely different set of issues: the description and classification of different peoples on the basis of historical origins as indicated by language. (Such concerns, as we shall see below, were closer to Herder's anthropology than to Kant's.) Arguably, both intellectual currents contributed to the constitution of the modern discipline, if in very different ways; but they were concerned with answering questions that were very different, not only from one another but from anthropology as we now know it.

Kant's anthropology, in general and in relation to his teleological vision of human history, represented an attempt to reconcile the claims of "culture" and of "civilization." Admittedly, in the passage cited above, "culture," characterized by the development of "art and science," takes pride of place over civilization, the "social courtesies and proprieties" that Kant seems to regard with mild exasperation. At first sight, Kant's idea of history—the growth and ultimately the triumph of reason and "enlightenment"—might seem to be preeminently cultural, a question of thoughts and sensibilities rather than behaviors and institutions. But while culture, very definitely conceptualized in the singular, is clearly the "end" of history, the means by which it is achieved fall directly within the purview of "civilization."

The effects of civilization on culture are reflected in the interplay of individualism and sociability in the domain of thought and reasoning. Kant's analysis of "logical egoism" in his lectures on anthropology is symptomatic:

> . . . It is a risk to hold a view which conflicts with public opinion, even if it is deemed to be reasonable. Such a display of egoism is called paradoxical. . . . Preference for the paradoxical is logical obstinacy in which a man does not want to be an imitator of others, but rather prefers to appear as an unusual human being. Instead of accomplishing his purpose, such a man frequently succeeds only in being odd. . . . Opposite to the paradoxical is the commonplace, which sides with the general opinion. But with the commonplace, there is as little safety, if not less, because it lulls the mind to sleep, whereas the paradoxical awakens the mind to attention and investigation, which often leads to discoveries. (Kant 1978:11–12)

While Kant clearly has more sympathy for the overly individualistic paradoxical thinker than for the overly conformist commonplace one, he calls
for a balance between the two extremes. Public opinion can serve to effect
such a balance, not in the form of an example but as a corrective. By this,
Kant has in mind an informed public, especially of experts in a particular
domain—a sort of peer review avant la lettre. The precondition for the
emergence of a meaningful public opinion is freedom of expression. Such
freedom depends of course on political institutions, specifically within the
framework of the state. Only civilization, in the form of state institutions
that permit and protect free expression, fosters the development of culture
in the form of collective—though not always individual—reason.

A decade before Kant had begun publishing his vision of universal history, his erstwhile pupil Herder (2004) had already written a short book in
1774, *Another Philosophy of History for the Education of Mankind: One among
Many Contributions of the Century*. The title ironically references works of
philosophical history from the French and Scottish Enlightenment. Herder
specifically mentions Montesquieu, Voltaire, Hume, and Robertson.[7] Two
years earlier he had written a negative review of Millar's *Observations* (Zammito 2002:333); elsewhere he expressed his contempt for Fontenelle (Flaherty 1992:133). Indeed, Isaiah Berlin (1976:145) characterized him as
"one of the leaders of the romantic revolt against classicism, rationalism,
and faith in the omnipotence of scientific method." More recently, scholars (e.g. Zammito 1992; Muthu 2003; Sikka 2011) have insisted on including him within the confines of the Enlightenment, within which, after all,
there was considerable room for sometimes acrimonious debate. Be this as it
may, Herder's critique involved a formulation of human history and human
purpose very different from those of the French and Scottish thinkers and
historians he excoriated.

Herder begins his sketch of a historical narrative with a sharp critique
of Montesquieu's paradigm of Oriental despotism: "We have construed for
ourselves an *Oriental Despotism* by singling out the most extreme and violent
occurrences from what are usually decaying empires, which resort to it only
in their final throes and thus reveal their very fear of death!" (Herder 2004:
7)[8] In another part of the book, Herder lambastes *The Spirit of Laws* for what
he considers its reductionism: "[Everything] torn from its spot and place and
spilled out upon *three* or *four marketplaces* beneath the banner of *three miserable platitudes*—[mere] *words!*—and *empty, useless, indefinite, all-confusing
esprit-words* at that!" (Herder 2004:78)

Herder proposes instead a different and far more positive paradigm, a
pastoral patriarchy that corresponds to the infancy of humanity. Small chil-

dren need firm guidance and stable authority during this phase of their lives. It is not only unreasonable but sometimes positively harmful to expect them to be capable of exercising independent judgment. Herder pursues this metaphor throughout the book, identifying different historical epochs, associated with different peoples, with different phases of human life: infancy, childhood, youth, maturity, old age. The metaphor is hardly new, of course. Montaigne (see chapter 3) had already contrasted the "childhood" of the cannibals with the senescence of sixteenth-century Europe. Herder does not entirely reject such a cyclical vision but, rather than applying it to humanity as a whole. he applies it to particular historical epochs whose florescence is inevitably followed by decline. Nor was the analogy intended to be patronizing, a retrospective evaluation of previous peoples and epochs from an alleged position of superiority. On the contrary, this was precisely the attitude Herder vituperated in French and Scottish philosophies of history. For him, no particular "age" (either in the human life cycle or among historical epochs) was in any definitive sense superior. Each had its own fundamental contribution to make. The contribution of Oriental patriarchal pastoralism was a deep sense of religiosity:

> The *delicate sensitivity* of these regions, with the quick, soaring imagination that so readily clothes everything in divine splendor; *reverence* for everything that is might, esteem, wisdom, strength, God's footstep, and right along with this, a childlike *submission* that is combined—naturally for [the Orientals], incomprehensibly for us Europeans—with the feeling of reverence; the defenseless, scattered, tranquility-loving, *herd-like condition* of the shepherd's life that *wants to live itself out* gently and without exertion on a plain of God . . . and just because we are so incapable of *understanding* this anymore, of *feeling* it, let alone *taking delight* in it—we *mock*, we *deny*, we *misconstrue*! (Herder 2004:9)

Herder's association of Oriental despotism with pastoral societies seems curious, to say the least. For Montesquieu and others, the paradigm was associated with large-scale Asian empires, notably China, Persia, and Turkey, none of which qualify as pastoral societies by any stretch of the imagination. However, none of these empires directly serves Herder's purpose, which is to examine the foundations of modern European society. The association of patriarchal pastoralists with profound religiosity suggests that he really had the Bible, specifically the ancient Hebrews, in mind, even if they were not specifically mentioned. The publication of Niebuhr's account of his expedition to the Arabian peninsula, just two years before Herder's text, plausibly reinforced such associations (Carhart 2007:27–44; Vermuelen 2015:219–67).

Even so, Herder's suggestion that Montesquieu's categorization of Oriental despotism is only a depiction of "decaying empires," a degeneration of a once-flourishing way of life, is problematic to say the least. For example, nineteenth-century Britons in India were simultaneously capable of admiring ancient Hindu civilization and despising modern Indians as their degenerate descendants (Trautmann 1997).[9] From the patriarchal pastoralism of the Near East, Herder moves on to elaboration of a very different kind of order in Egypt, based on agriculture: ". . . *Man was placed under the bondage of the law*: the inclinations that had once been merely paternal, child-like, shepherd-like, patriarchal now became *civil, village-like, city-like*. The child had outgrown his dresses and ribbons: the boy now sat on the school bench and learned *order, diligence, customs of civility*" (Herder 2004:12). The two ways of life were incompatible and, in important respects, antithetical. Pastoralists despised a settled existence and its accompanying values, just as village and city dwellers heaped scorn on pastoral nomads. These Egyptian core values were expressed in particular by art. Herder perceptively criticizes the judgment of Winckelmann, the great German art historian of ancient Greece, who disparaged the art of ancient Egypt from the vantage point of classical Greek aesthetics. The qualities of movement and action characteristic of Greek sculpture were absent from Egyptian art, not by default but by design. For Egyptians, such qualities were beside the point, indeed undesirable, in sculpture whose very essence was to memorialize the dead. Indeed, for Herder, the arts more generally—not only painting, sculpture, and architecture but also music, song and poetry—were fundamental expressions of the core values, the spirit, of a nation or a historical epoch. As a result, they cannot be judged, perhaps not even understood, from another vantage point. The relativism that Herder proposes is in the first place aesthetic.

The Phoenicians, more or less contemporary to the Egyptians, constituted in Herder's scheme an alternative national character centered on commerce as opposed to agriculture, and with an entirely different aesthetic: "After the Egyptians' sculptures and their big and intimidating works, one began to play so advantageously with *glass*, with pieces of decorated *metal, purple fabric,* and *canvas,* with Lebanese *utensils, jewelry, pottery, ornamentations* . . ." (Herder 2004:17). The stage is set for the emergence of Greece, the epoch and nation for which Herder betrays the most affection—certainly more than for the preceding Orientals and Egyptians, much less the "swindling, avaricious" Phoenicians. He also prefers them to their successors, the martial Romans, the Gothic Middle Ages, and least of all his "Enlightened" contemporaries: "Greece became the cradle of *humaneness,* of *friendship between peoples, of fine legislation,* of all that is *most agreeable,* in *religion, customs, prose, poetry, common practices,* and *arts"* (Herder 2004:19).

The aesthetic dimension was not the only facet of ancient Greece that appealed to Herder. Paradoxically, its political fragmentation was in itself a source of inspiration: ". . . the *strange occasions* of the *division* and *unification* from the earliest times onward, their *separation* into peoples, *republics, colonies;* and yet their *spirit of community* [persisted], *the feeling of one nation, one fatherland, one language"* (ibid.). The parallel with eighteenth-century Germany is striking: a nation divided into a myriad of states while sharing a more or less common language and a sense of national identity. For Herder the nation, rather than the state, is the fundamental unit; the distinction was even more evident in Germany than in Britain or France. Herder's deep mistrust of the state is yet another factor that clearly separates him from his former teacher.

Despite his transparent preference for Greece, Herder maintained a consciousness that the very qualities he found so endearing came at a cost. The cost in this case was a certain superficiality, even a frivolousness, especially in the religious domain: "The religion of the Orient was deprived of its *holy veil,* and naturally, since everything was *put on display* in the *theater* and the *market* and the *dancing-square,* is soon became 'a *fable,* nicely drawn out, gossiped about, composed and composed anew—a *dream of youths* and a *myth of maids!'* The Oriental wisdom, removed from behind the screen of mysteries, [became] *pretty chatter, a teaching-construct* and *the squabbling of the Greek schools and markets"* (Herder 2004:20). Such a combination of linked virtues and weaknesses characterized all epochs and nations. The military valor of the Romans at its best embodied stern rectitude, and at its worst implacable cruelty. For Herder, the Middle Ages were an amalgam of the sublime and the unspeakable.

However much Herder might admire Greece, he is entirely dismissive of any attempts to revive classical antiquity. Historical epochs are sui generis, their character permeating every aspect of life and art. For example, "the same Gothic spirit permeated the *interior* and *exterior* of the Church, shaping *governments* and *ceremonies, doctrines* and *temples;* sharpening the *bishop's crozier* into a *sword* because everyone was carrying a sword; and creating *church benefices, fiefs,* and *serfs* because that was how things were everywhere" (Herder 2004:39). For this very reason, any attempt to return to or to replicate the past is impossible. For this very reason, Herder's vision of history is neither cyclical nor teleological. It does not, and indeed cannot, repeat itself; but it does not progress in a predictable direction either. Rather, for Herder, history is simultaneously cumulative and transformative. Each historical era builds in fundamental ways upon the contributions of its predecessors. Herder constantly harps on the idea that ancient Greece could never have emerged without building on the accomplishments of Orientals, Egyptians, and Phoenicians, the very peoples whom the Greeks despised and whose capital importance, in terms of their own history, they failed to recognize. For Herder, such misrecognition is, if anything, typical. The spirit of any age is self-consciously elaborated in contrast to those of its predecessors or its contemporary alternatives. But even the deliberate adoption of elements from past epochs does not escape a similar reformulation:

> . . . No nation *following upon another*, even if it had *all the same accessories*, ever *became* what the other had *been*. Let all their *means of culture* be identical; *the culture* (itself) *can never be the same*, because it is now devoid of the various *influences* that shaped the older, now *altered* nature. The *Greek sciences* that the Romans appropriated became *Roman*; *Aristotle* became and *Arab* and a *scholastic*. And the *Greeks and Romans* of modern times:[10] what a *wretched affair!* (Herder 2004:77)

It is important to point out that neither in this passage nor elsewhere does Herder refer to "culture" in the plural (Muthu 2003:318). Indeed, well into the late nineteenth century, "culture" was always conceived as a singular entity, and the notion that there existed different "cultures" seemed an oxymoron (Stocking 1968:69–90). Even so, Herder's contention that Greek thought or Greek art radically changed its significance in the process of appropriation by Romans, medieval scholastics, or modern neoclassicists opened up a conceptual space that eventually led to the conception that "culture" was a plural rather than a unitary phenomenon.

Herder contends that every historical epoch has its own character that entails a distinct set of values, aesthetic sensibilities, and criteria for evaluating what constitutes "happiness."[11] On this basis, he rejects other Enlightenment philosophies of history, which are formulated in terms of putatively universal values that are at best particular to modern Europe, and at worst profoundly hollow. For example, he constantly berates his contemporaries' derision of Oriental despotism and medieval Catholicism, not least for their smug contempt of the spiritual realm. He broadly characterizes such philosophies, and the historical explanations they generate, as "mechanical." Such a term of derision encompasses many styles of explanation, all of which Herder rejects. They include faith in a universal yardstick of human reason, such as "science," as in the case of Fontenelle. They encompass approaches that Herder finds overly formulaic, such as Montesquieu's scheme for classifying all societies as republican, monarchical, or despotic. Last but not least, Herder rejects explanations of history in terms of unintended outcomes of individual human calculations, specifically in the domains of economics and politics. Herder mercilessly disparages the explanations typical of Scottish political economists:

> In Europe slavery has been abolished because it has been calculated how much more these slaves cost, and how much less they yielded, than free men. There is only one thing we continue to permit ourselves: to *use* and *trade three continents as slaves*, to *banish* them to silver mines and sugar mills. But these are not Europeans, not Christians, and in return we receive silver, gems, spices, sugar—and [venereal] disease. All this for the sake of trade and for the *mutual fraternal assistance* and *community* among countries. (Herder 2004:62–64)

He heaps equal scorn on theories that emphasize political calculation, specifically in terms of a hypothetical balance of power—a notion he considers hypocritical claptrap justifying the cynical machinations of rulers, among whom he singles out Frederic the Great and Louis XIV as especially contemptible. The state, for Herder, perpetrates violence, with colonial domination perhaps its most egregious manifestation.

In spite of his vehement anticolonialism, his empathy for the plight of non-Europeans in the face of European rapacity, Herder pays relatively little attention to non-Europeans in their own right, at least in *Another Philosophy of History*. Of course Egypt and the Near East receive extensive treatment as embodiments of "infancy" and "boyhood" (the gendering is Herder's, not mine) in a historical account that ends with Enlightenment Europe. Herder insists that the analogy is not meant to be dismissive or disparaging; he argues that all ages are necessary in the development of any human, and that each age has its advantages and drawbacks. However, to the extent that history is cumulative and each epoch builds upon the contributions of its predecessors even as it transforms them into an integral part of a new synthesis, we are left with the impression that the histories of Egypt and the Near East are arrested—and that, unlike the history of Europe, they have not been subject to continual transformation. In Herder's later work, as we shall see, he maintains this vision of an ahistorical Orient. But the aim of Herder's philosophy of history is to situate the contemporary predicament of Europe in general, and Germany in particular, so as to stress the priority of the nation as opposed to the state, and of expressive culture over "mechanical" reason. He is tracing a certain genealogy of Europe, and non-Europeans are only critical when they figure in this genealogy, particularly at the beginning.

Curiously enough, despite Herder's emphatic rejection of the French and Scottish view of the world in terms of institutions and political economy, his treatment of Oriental patriarchs, Egyptians, and Phoenicians parallels three of the four stages of human progress theorized by the Scots: pastoralism, agriculture, and commerce. Similarly, though Herder alleges the critical importance of climate and geography in the formation of national character, the only instances he provides are exclusively among non-Europeans. Egypt's location along the Nile, he insists, is suited to agriculture but not to a pastoral existence, while Phoenicia's location along the Mediterranean coast predisposes it to sailing and overseas commerce. Climate, geography, and modes of livelihood are never invoked to explain the emergence of Greece and Rome, much less the Middle Ages and modern Europe. Such "mechanical" influences, it might seem, are more determinant in establishing the character of non-Europeans as opposed to Europeans—though it must be stressed that Herder only makes such a distinction implicitly, and conceivably unintentionally.

Strikingly, Herder's book omits almost all reference to the stock figures of French and Scottish thought: "savages" and China. This can in no way be attributed to lack of knowledge or lack of interest on Herder's part. On the contrary, in 1774, the very same year in which he published *Another Philosophy of History*, he published a collection titled *Alte Volkslieder*, which "included songs by peoples all over the world, from Madagascar to Lapland and from Kamchatka to Greenland . . . gleaned from explorers' reports and manuscripts as well as other publications" (Flaherty 1992:137). However, while "savages" occupied a strategic place in the conjectural histories of French and Scottish thinkers, they simply did not fit into the kind of European genealogical history that Herder was elaborating. Nor, apparently, did the Chinese. French and Scottish thinkers might have established significant parallels between the Chinese and the Egyptians, which were both conservative, authoritarian, agricultural regimes with a deep reverence for the ancestral dead. These were precisely the kind of parallels to which Herder vociferously objected in Montesquieu's writings.

A decade later, when Herder decided to revisit and expand his philosophy of history in *Ideas for the Philosophy of the History of Mankind* (Herder 1966), he certainly corrected these omissions, including a section on China as well as one on peoples whom others classed as "savages." In the preface he called into question the pertinence of his analogy between historical epochs and the ages of human development in his earlier writing: "It had never entered into my mind, by employing the few figurative expression, the *childhood, infancy, manhood,* and *old age* of our species, the chain of which was applied, as it was applicable, only to a few nations, to point out a highway on which the *history of cultivation*, to say nothing of the *philosophy of history at large*, could be traced with certainty" (Herder 1996:v). In the preface, at least, Herder insists that the history of Europe is not the history of humanity as a whole.

If *Another Philosophy of History* is concise and polemical, *Ideas* is a sprawling though less overtly controversial work. It appeared in four separate volumes, each consisting of five books, published from 1784 to 1791. Each volume has its own nearly self-contained focus. The first volume sets the stage, beginning with a discussion of the earth as a planet and of its specific geography, continuing with a discussion of the natural realm of plants and animals, and ending with a consideration of the general properties of humanity as a whole. The second volume focuses on humans as a single species (both Herder and Kant rejected polygenetic theories of human origin) as well as on the causes of natural and cultural human variation. Only in the third volume does Herder take up a historical narrative per se, beginning with Asia (China, Tibet, India, and southeast Asia) and ending with Greece and Rome. The fourth volume treats the origins of modern Europe.

"Savages" occupy a prominent place in the second volume, though they disappear almost entirely from the second half of *Ideas*. The second volume begins in book 6 by reviewing the different types of humans throughout the globe, in terms of their physical as well as their intellectual and moral dispositions. The organization of Herder's treatment of human diversity mirrors the familiar schema of cardinal directions: Arctic dwellers to the north, nations who dwell on the "Asiatic ridge" to the east, Africans and Pacific islanders to the south, and native Americans to the west, with "well-formed nations" in the center. Climate plays an important role in determining human variation. For example, because of the extreme cold, peoples living near the North Pole are invariably short. The "well-formed" zone is admittedly a wide band, stretching from Kashmir through Europe. Indeed, Kashmir is described in lyrical terms: Herder goes so far as to suggest it as a possible location for the Garden of Eden, the paradiselike birthplace of humanity (Herder 1966:284). Ancient Greece embodied the pinnacle of perfection: ". . . The perfect human form found a site on the coast of the Mediterranean, where it was capable of uniting with the intellect, and displaying all the charms of terrestrial and celestial beauty to the mind, as well as to the eye. . . . Time and circumstances assisted in exalting its juices, and crowning it with that perfection, which still excites the admiration of every one in the models of Grecian art and wisdom" (Herder 1966:144). Europe constitutes a standard, in terms of physical and intellectual if not moral terms, from which all others deviate only to their detriment. "From the region of wellformed people we have derived our religion, our arts, our sciences; the whole frame of our cultivation and humanity, be it much or little. In this tract has been invented, imagined, and executed, at least in its rudiments, every thing that can form and improve man" (Herder 1996:145). Admittedly, Herder's tableau of human variation, even as it promulgates a European norm, never indulges in grotesque descriptions of non-Europeans, as does the French naturalist Buffon (1835) in his influential book on variations in the human species.

Indeed, there is a constant tension, especially in the second volume, between Herder's assertion of European superiority and his equally firm faith in the shared humanity of all peoples, that *all mankind are only one and the same species* (Herder 1996:164; emphasis in original). Herder goes so far as to reject the very notion of "race": "There are neither four or five races, nor exclusive varieties, on this Earth. Complexions run into each other: forms follow the genetic character: and upon the whole, all are at last but shades of the same great picture, extending through all ages, and over all parts of the Earth" (Herder 1966:166). In his discussion of Africa, Herder radically relativizes the importance of skin color: "Since whiteness is a mark of degeneracy in many animals near the pole, the negro has a much a right to term his savage robbers albinoes and white devils, degenerated through the weakness of nature, as we have to deem him the emblem of evil, a descendant of Ham, branded by his father's curse" (Herder 1966:146). Admittedly, for Herder, differences in climate account for differences in bodily form and in temperament—differences which, once established, are not readily subject to change even when peoples move from one region of the world to another, as they often do. This explains why, according to Herder, native Americans, who all descend from the same immigrant group from Asia, are so homogeneous. On the other hand, interbreeding, another by-product of migration, at least in the Old World, has far more rapid consequences, breaking down the differences that climate initially establishes. Herder unambiguously considers such intermixture as productive and beneficial. The horror of miscegenation that haunted so many nineteenth-century European thinkers was totally alien to his ideals. On the contrary, Germany itself, descended from migrants originating in Asia, was a critical counterexample: "We northern inhabitants of Europe should have been still barbarians, had not the kind breath of fate wafted us at least some flowers from those climes [Greece and Rome], to impregnate our wild blossoms, and thus in time ennoble our flock" (Herder 1966:143).

Herder argues that "cultivation" and "enlightenment"—which are, as he points out, different metaphors, of soil and sun respectively, for a virtually identical concept—are universal to all humans:

> Even the inhabitant of California or Tierra del Fuego learns to make and use the bow and arrow: he has language and ideas, practices and arts, which he learned, as we learn them: so far, therefore, he is actually cultivated and enlightened, though in the lowest order. Thus the difference between enlightened and unenlightened, cultivated and uncultivated nations, is not specific, it is only in degree. (Herder 1966:228)

This notion of the unequal distribution of universal human dispositions combines Herder's commitment to respect all human beings with his firm conviction of the superiority of European achievements, though not necessarily of Europeans themselves. Aside from "cultivation" or "enlightenment" in general, he identifies three specific features as "the common property and excellence of our [human] fraternity . . . the disposition to *reason, humanity*, and *religion*" (Herder 1966:251). The universality of "religion" is no doubt self-explanatory, and he adduces numerous examples from travelers' account for good measure. Reason, Herder argues, is implicit in language, which involves the capacity to formulate and use abstract categories as well as to manipulate symbols. If all nations have language, then they also possess "reason"—if, again, in varying degrees. The notion of "humanity" is not quite so clear, nor quite so consistent throughout the text.[12] It refers to the human capacity for empathy, for fellow-feeling, and more broadly to contextually and historically varied notions of justice and morality. The family as a "natural" unit (only Rousseau, it would seem, was perceptive enough to conceive of the family as a social rather than a natural phenomenon) was the original locus of "humanity," as evidenced by love of family members. In the last book (15) of the third volume, Herder later proposes that the development of "humanity" and "reason," in the form of a just society free from violence, is the "end" of history. This teleological slant comes as something of a surprise in light of Herder's critique of the hollowness of European "mechanical" reason, especially in *Another Philosophy of History*, but also in many other passages of the *Ideas*.

Indeed, passages from the *Ideas*—especially in the second volume, where Herder contrasts non-Europeans, and especially "savages," with Europeans—are by no means unequivocal assertions of European superiority: "Vain, therefore, is the boast of so many Europeans, when they set themselves above the people of all the other quarters of the Globe, in what they call arts, sciences, and cultivation" (Herder 1966:241). Paradoxically, the very fact that Europeans are the heirs to the accumulated knowledge of their predecessors frequently leaves them inferior as human beings to savages: "Steer thy frigate to Otaheite [Tahiti], bid thy cannon roar along the shores of the New Hebrides, still thou art not superior in skill or ability to the inhabitant of the South-Sea islands, who guides with art the boat, which he has constructed with his own hand" (ibid.). To a greater extent than the European, the savage must rely on his own knowledge and abilities. The use of borrowed knowledge does not render anyone superior. Herder uses the example of books written in "delicate and modest" language. The readers of such books, not to mention speakers of the language, are not necessarily "delicate and modest" by any stretch of the imagination.

> No one will deny Europe to be the repository of art, and of the inventive un-
> derstanding of man: the destiny of ages has deposited its treasures there: they
> are augmented and employed in it. But every one, who makes use of them has
> not therefore the understanding of the inventors: nay, this very use tends to
> render the understanding inactive; for while I have the instrument of another
> for my purpose, I shall scarcely take the trouble, to invent one for myself."
> (Herder 1966:242)

The superior enlightenment or cultivation of Europe does not in any way make the European a superior person, and in some respects it may actually be limiting.

In a similar vein, a European is by no means necessarily happier than the savage. It is important to note that for Herder, happiness is an important human value. He is not, it is important to insist, contrasting a stereotypically happy savage, content with the little he possesses, with a restless Faustian European forever driven to greater accomplishments. For Herder, however, European standards of happiness are not universal, or even necessarily ideal: "It would be the most stupid vanity to imagine, that all the inhabitants of the World must be Europeans to live happily" (Herder 1966:219). But standards of happiness are not morally neutral, and the concrete happiness of savages can be more compelling than the abstract happiness of Europeans:

> The savage, who loves, himself, his wife, and child, with quiet joy, and glows
> with limited activity for his tribe, as for his own life, is, in my opinion, a more
> real being, than that cultivated shadow, who is enraptured with the love of the
> shades of his whole species, that is of a name. The savage has room in his poor
> hut for every stranger, whom he receives as his brother with calm benevolence,

and asks not once whence he comes. The deluged heart of the idle cosmopo-
lite is a hut for no one. (Herder 1966:222–23)

Once again, in the contrast between the savage and the European as a moral
human being, the savage turns out to be superior.

Herder's suggestion that savages may not only be happier than but morally superior to his European contemporaries clearly echoes Rousseau. Following Rousseau, he posits a direct link between the adoption of agriculture
and the origins of social inequality:

> Even where agriculture has been introduced, it has cost some pains, to limit
> men to separate field, and establish the distinction of mine and thine. . . .
> Generally speaking, no mode of life has effected so much alteration in the
> minds of men, as agriculture, combined with the enclosure of land. While
> it produced arts and trades, villages and towns, and, in consequence, gov-
> ernment and laws; it necessarily paved the way for that frightful despotism,
> which, from confining every man to his field, gradually proceeded to prescribe
> to him, what alone he should do on it, what alone he should be. (Herder
> 1966:207)

If Herder hesitates to condemn agriculture outright, it is at least in part because, as he admits, "I myself eat the bread which it has produced" (Herder
1966:208). Even so, he insists that "justice be done to other ways of life,
which, from the constitution of our Earth, have been defined, equally with
agriculture, to contribute to the education of mankind" (ibid.). Herder
means foragers and pastoralists, but also horticulturalists who till the soil
without enclosing it. In this passage, at least, he celebrates the variety of
human modes of livelihood, problematizing rather than privileging European ways.

In spite of his blanket reservations about agriculture, Herder still recoils
from treating different modes of livelihood as uniform categories. In different parts of the world, hunters or pastoralists may pursue superficially
similar kinds of activities in very different ways. "The merchants of England
differ not more from those of China, than the husbandmen of Whidah
[Ouidah on the West African coast, in modern Benin] from the husbandmen of Japan" (Herder 1966:202). National character, what we would label
"culture," is at least as significant for Herder as modes of livelihood, clearly
distinguishing his thought from that of his French and British contemporaries.

Herder's reservations about agriculture pale in comparison to his condemnation of the state as an institution: "If nothing else in the history of the World indicated the inferiority of the human species, the history of governments would demonstrate it' (Herder 1966:247). Savages are definitely better off without the state: "How many people upon Earth are entirely ignorant of all government, and yet are happier than many, who have sacrificed themselves for the good of the state?" (Herder 1966:223) Herder contrasts "natural" relationships—father and mother, husband and wife, son and brother—to the "artificial" nature of the state: "The state gives us nothing but instruments of art, and these, alas! may rob us of something far more essential, may rob us of ourselves" (Herder 1966:224). If the notion that the family constituted a "natural" unit was hardly original, Herder's extension of naturalness, by extension, to the nation is a radical departure with specific political implications:

> . . . A nation is as much a natural plant as a family, only with more branches. Nothing therefore appears so directly opposite to the end of government as the unnatural enlargement of states, the wild mixture of various races and nations under one scepter. (Herder 1966:249)

Empires are hybrid monsters, and in the ancient world Herder singles out Persia and Rome for particular opprobrium. Modern European imperialism is not simply immoral in the suffering it callously imposes on others, but intrinsically unnatural, a horrible project in and of itself. If the state in any form is an evil—though perhaps a necessary evil—its proper form is one that corresponds to a single nation and not to a composite.

In short, if savages lack agriculture and the state, this may leave them happier than us, and it may be a blessing rather than a curse. Compared to Europeans, they rely more on their own capacities and less on the kinds of historically inherited knowledge and skills that Europeans are deluded into believing are tokens of their own worth. They fully acknowledge the importance of "natural" relationships that more fully realize their essential humanity than the "artificial" relationships so valued by modern Europeans. Granted, they are physically and perhaps even mentally (though perhaps not morally) outside the orbit of "well-formed" humanity but, all told, that does not seem to be such a disadvantage. In any case, as humans, they are by no means devoid of "cultivation" and "enlightenment." Unlike Europeans, however, they seem to be "people without history" (cf. Wolf 1982). If savages appear prominently in the second volume, which treats of humanity in more general terms, they disappear from the third and fourth volumes, which chronicle the sweep of human history as Herder understands it, beginning with its earliest manifestations in Asia and culminating in Europe.

At the very end of the second volume Herder speculates that humans originated in Asia—specifically East Asia—the site of the earliest recorded civilizations, as far as Herder knew. The third volume begins with China, the other notable absence in *Another Philosophy of History*. Herder's description of China is remarkably pejorative.[13] Unlike that of Montesquieu and other French and Scottish thinkers, however, his disapproval is not principally political. By beginning with China, Herder largely precludes his previous theoretical gambit of locating "Oriental despotism" in the realm of pastoral patriarchy. This is not to say that he renounces his previous point of view. By positing the Chinese as descendants of pastoral Mongols, he manages to retain his theory of the origins of "Oriental despotism," locating it here in the ideological prominence of filial piety in China. Such a stress on filial piety, Herder suggests, while an entirely fitting practice among pastoralists, is an entirely inappropriate basis for a realm such as China, and Chinese conservatism in this domain is an index for its general refusal to accept change.

Yet Herder's rejection of China and almost anything Chinese, including the "millions of pounds of enervating tea" (Herder 1966:298) imported by Europe, is largely motivated on aesthetic rather than political grounds. He even objects to the Chinese language, whose tonal structure, foreign to European ears, makes it difficult for Europeans to understand and distinguish different words:

All accounts of the language of the chinese [uncapitalized in the text] agree, that it has contributed unspeakably to the form of this people in their artificial mode of thinking: for is not the language of every country the medium, in which the ideas if its inhabitants are formed, preserved, and imparted? particularly when a nation is so firmly attached to its language as this, and deduces all civilization from it. . . . Every thing in it turns of systematic niceties: it expresses much with a few sounds, while it depicts one sound with many lines, and says one and the same thing in a multiplicity of books. What a waste of industry is employed in penciling and printing their works! but this is their chief art and delight; for fine writing is to them more beautiful than the most enchanting picture, and the uniform jingle of their maxims and compliments is prized by them as the sum of elegance and wisdom. (Herder 1966:296–97).

Herder's suggestion that the nature of different languages conditions the character and values of different people is tempered by his conviction that some are superior to others, and that he is qualified to judge this superiority.

In India, for example, "the order of bramins [sic] has preserved its artfully constructed and beautiful language" (Herder 1966:308). A footnote suggests that the language in question is Bengali and not Hindi or Sanskrit, though perhaps this hardly matters. Unsurprisingly, Herder waxes eloquent about the merits of the Greek language:

> They [sic] were no hieroglyphic patchwork, no series of singly ejected syllables, like the language beyond the mungal [sic] mountains [presumably he is thinking particularly of Chinese]. . . . The words were more smoothly connected, the tone modulated into rhythm: the language flowed in a fuller steam; its images, in pleasing harmony: it raised itself to the melody of the dance. And thus the peculiar character of the greek language, not constrained by mute laws, arose as a living image of nature, from music and the dance, from history and song, and from the talkative free intercourse of many tribes and colonies. (Herder 1966:359)

Interestingly, German actually pales by comparison:

> The northern nations of Europe were not thus fortunate in their formation. . . . The german, for example, has unquestionably lost much of its intrinsic flexibility, of its more precise expression in the inflection of words, and still more of that energetic tone, which it formerly possessed in a more favourable climate. Once it was a near sister of the greek; but how far from this is it now degenerated! (ibid.)

Not only in its character, art, and literature, but even very literally in its language, Greek remains the gold standard for Herder—one from which China is far removed.

Herder's distaste for the Chinese language is matched by his dismissal of their forms of expression:

> Their pictures of monsters and dragons, their minute care in the drawing of figures without regularity, the pleasure afforded their eyes by the disorderly assemblages of their gardens, the naked greatness of minute nicety in their buildings, the vain pomp of their dress, equipage, and amusements, their lantern feasts and fire-works, their long nails and cramped feet, their barbarous train of attendants, bowings, ceremonies, distinctions, and courtesies, require a mungal [i.e., Mongol] organization. So little taste for true nature, so little feeling of internal satisfaction, beauty, and worth, prevail through all these,

that a neglected mind alone could arrive at this train of political cultivation, and allow itself to be thoroughly modelled by it. (Herder 1966:293)

Even though Herder concedes that the Chinese have invented silk and porcelain, gunpowder, printing, bridge building, and navigation—an impressive list!—he reproaches them for lacking the European "spirit of improvement."

Quite uncharacteristically, Herder even suggests a quasi-racial (if not racist) explanation for the Chinese character: ". . . This race of men, in this region, could never become greeks or romans. Chinese they were, and will remain: a people endowed by nature with small eyes, a short nose, a flat forehead, little beard, large ears, and a protuberant belly: what their organization could produce, it has produced; nothing else could be required of it" (ibid.). Interestingly, Herder ascribes such alleged inferiority from Chinese isolation, from the physical separation of China from much of the rest of the world combined with a refusal to intermingle with others either biologically or culturally. China's dogmatic conservatism, he suggests, is a product of isolationism as much as of isolation. As a result, "this nation, like many others on the globe, has stood still in its education, as in the age of infancy" (Herder 1966:298). If, in the preface to the *Ideas*, written several years before this passage, he had eschewed the metaphor of the ages of man to categorize universal history, he had apparently returned to it by the time he undertook to write about China.

Herder's vision of Tibet is, if less elaborate, equally unflattering: "The lama account of the creation of the World abounds with monstrous fables: the threatened punishments and penitences for sin are severe: and the state, after which their sanctity thrives, in highly unnatural, consisting in monastic continence, superstitious absence of thought, and the perfect repose of nonentity" (Herder 1966:301). It is important to point out that Herder's aversion is specifically to Tibetan Buddhism, rather than to Buddhism in general. On the contrary, he points out that Buddhism "has had very different effects on the countries, in which it has flourished. In Siam, Hindostan, Tonquin, and some others, it lulls the minds of men and renders them compassionate and unwarlike, patient, gentle, and indolent" (Herder 1966:302). Admittedly, this is hardly enthusiastic praise, but it is not a blanket condemnation either. More important, Herder is suggesting that religions such as Buddhism are not unitary phenomena but are experienced very differently in different environments and by different peoples, inflected by climate and national character. It is the fact that Tibet is a theocracy which most offends Herder's sensibilities: "The tibetan religion is a species of the papal, such as it prevailed in Europe itself in the dark ages" (Herder 1966:304). The Protestant pastor here betrays his reticence about Roman Catholicism, in Tibetan garb.

Herder's account proceeds systematically from east to west, from the Far East to the Near East, from Asia to Europe, and last but not least from southern Europe to northern Europe. As in *Another Philosophy of History*, his aim is to demonstrate that history is cumulative, that each historical epoch, situated in a particular locus, incorporates elements of the past just as it transforms them and often appears to reject them. Consequently, northern Europe, and in particular Germany, benefits from the accumulated "cultivation" of its predecessors. In this respect Asia has been left behind, stuck in the infancy or at best the childhood of history, while, as we have seen, the "savages" of the Americas, the polar regions, Africa, and Oceania lie entirely outside the sweep of history. This is in large measure a consequence of Europe's climate and location: "Had Europe been rich as India, unintersected as Tartar, hot as Africa, isolated as America, what has appeared in it would never have been produced" (Herder 1966:632). Even so, the course of history has placed Germany at the summit of accumulated human knowledge.

This is not to suggest that Herder's work is univocally Eurocentric. Rather, it reflects core principles that, if not flatly contradictory, at the very least exist in a tension that is difficult, perhaps impossible, to resolve. The first principle asserts the fundamental worth of all humans, the conviction that all nations are, if in different degrees, "cultivated" and "enlightened," and that they share a capacity for religion, for reason, and for what Herder labels "humanity." The second principle is that such cultivation is most fully embodied in the expressive arts: language, music, dance, song, poetry, architecture, painting, sculpture. "The music of a nation, in its most imperfect form, and favourite tunes, displays the internal character of the people, that is to say, the proper tone of their sensations, much more truly and profoundly than the most copious description of external contingencies" (Herder 1966:194). The "external contingencies" in question here are the modes of livelihood and political institutions so central to the analyses of most French and British Enlightenment thinkers. The third principle is that such modes of expression are unique to each nation, and express its fundamental character in ways that are conceivably incomprehensible to others: "If the Voluspa of the Icelander were read and expounded to a bramin, he would scarcely be able to form a single idea from it; and to the Icelander the Vedam would be equally unintelligible. Their own mode of representing things is the more deeply imprinted on every nation, because it is adapted to themselves, is suitable to their own earth and sky, springs from their mode of living, and has been handed down to them from father to son" (Herder 1966:197). If these modes of representation are particular to specific nations, this is because nations, like families, are profoundly "natural" units in Herder's scheme. Taken together, these principles would seem to constitute a sort of "national" if not "cultural" relativism.

Such apparent relativism exists in tension with a vision of history that is not only cumulative but unitary and even, at times, surprisingly teleological, positing "humanity"—peace and justice—as the "end" of the historical process. Such a conclusion is all the more startling in that, unlike Kant, Herder does not spell out a mechanism—however implausible—by which such an end is to be attained. Be this as it may, this accumulation of "cultivation" is only realized in the fullest sense in Europe, and northern Europe at that. But such an assertion is saved from smugness by Herder's deep distrust of the very European values and institutions that might seem to embody European superiority. Even the very accumulation of knowledge and techniques may diminish the worth of the individual, especially for those who mistake their inherited capacities for tokens of their personal worth, as if they were themselves responsible for the inventions on which they rely. More crucially, Herder contrasts the "artificial" institutions of Europe to the "natural" units of family and nation. The state, in particular, embodies everything that is artificial in Herder's eyes. Its intellectual counterpart is a "mechanical" philosophy that classifies people in sweeping terms of political economy—as "despots" or "republicans," "hunters" or "agriculturalists"—rather than stressing the particularities of their language, their music, their visual arts.

Ultimately, Herder's is a peculiar nationalism, one that celebrates the nation as it distrusts if not entirely rejects the state. Such tensions explain why Herder is often depicted as the ancestor both of German nationalism and of cultural relativism, at the expense of stressing one component of his thought to the neglect of another.

TWELVE

"Others" Are Good to Think

In a famous remark on totemism, Claude Lévi-Strauss (1963:89) quipped that "natural species are chosen not because they are 'good to eat' but because they are 'good to think.'" The same might be said of many of the writings considered in this volume: other peoples are not only "good to dominate" but also "good to think." I want to insist that I do not want to write revisionist history, to suggest that what Europeans wrote about non-Europeans was generally innocuous if not well-intentioned. Needless to say, some writings were very definitely justifications of European domination; indeed, Lévi-Strauss, whose writings on myth often centered on issues of food and cooking, never denied that some natural species were indeed good to eat—even delicious. Hernan Cortes's (1971) *Letters from Mexico* are only the most egregious example of how representations of others are intended as justification for imperial dominion. Nevertheless, in the wake of Edward Said's (1978) *Orientalism*, it has been the prevalent assumption that European domination was, implicitly if not explicitly, at the core of all such work. By the beginning of the nineteenth century this was unquestionably an accurate characterization. To project such attitudes back in time, at least uncritically, is not only to fall prey to anachronism, but, worse, to essentialize Western European attitudes as irrevocably tainted—forgetting that "Western Europe" itself is a historical entity and not a taken–for-granted place.

Throughout this book I have attempted to show how characterizations of non-Europeans have figured, sometimes centrally and sometimes peripherally, in polemical arguments of concern primarily—sometimes exclusively—to Europeans: arguments about politics, religion, history, even art and literature. In some cases such characterizations are so superficial as to border on caricature. Diderot's Tahitians, to take one example, are largely figures of his own fertile imagination, bearing little resemblance to any populations alive or dead. Others have attempted more systematically to incorporate relatively reliable information. Be this as it may, in most cases the information has taken a back seat to the polemics, ranging from the deadly serious (the French Wars of Religion) to the comparatively frivolous (the Quarrel of the Ancients and the Moderns). But the stakes have been the domination not necessarily of Europeans over non-Europeans, but of the claims of one group of Europeans—a religious community, a political faction, an intellectual clique—over another. Representations of non-Europeans (and sometimes, it is important to add, more-or-less sincere attempts at understanding) have been mobilized as tools for thinking and arguing about purely European issues.[1]

In sixteenth-century France, the most urgent of these issues were related to the Wars of Religion pitting partisans of the monarchy not only against Protestants but against the hardline Catholic League. Montaigne's idealized depiction of the Tupi of Brazil, who were untroubled by any such theological controversies, self-consciously insisted that the behavior of his compatriots, Catholics and Protestants alike, was far more barbaric than that of the "cannibals." At the same time but in a different vein, Jean Bodin was proposing (in an unpublished and unpublishable manuscript) a vision in which partisans of different religions, not only Catholics and Protestants but also Jews and Muslims, could worship in harmony. In print, Bodin mustered the Hippocratic and Aristotelian theory of climates to bolster the arguments of French monarchist and Protestant legal thinkers that different laws were appropriate to different times and places—arguments that directly challenged the hegemony of Roman law, and indirectly the hegemony of the Roman Church.

In the seventeenth century, representations of non-European peoples were mobilized in a very different struggle in the religious domain: turf wars between the Jesuits and other religious orders. The race for non-European converts was in the first place an attempt to outnumber and outflank Protestantism globally. It was related to European imperial ambitions, particularly in the New World, but more often to attempts by different European powers to procure favorable terms of trade with foreign nations. Jesuit rivalry with Dominicans and Franciscans in China was initially inflamed by competition for trade with China between the Portuguese, operating out of Goa and backing the Jesuits, and the Spanish, based in Manila and backing rival orders. Precisely because they were a new order, the Jesuits used more aggressive strategies, adapting missionary tactics and messages to the societies they were attempting to convert, as well as systematically publishing their results along with descriptions of these societies. The Quarrel of the Chinese Rites pitted the Jesuits against their rivals within the Church, who accused them of compromising doctrine in an attempt to win converts at any price. In New France, controversies between the Jesuits and the Recollect friars were more muted, if only because the Jesuits were able to sideline their less powerful and politically connected rivals. Even so, Lahontan was astute enough to point out that the divergent interests of Jesuits and Recollects generated equally but oppositely distorted representations of Native Americans. The Jesuits depicted the Native Americans as intelligent but also well-disposed to conversion, thus suggesting that their own missionary efforts were yielding fruit. The Recollects, on the other hand, portrayed them as stupid, ignorant and recalcitrant savages, thus suggesting that Jesuit methods were bound to be ineffective. Of course, Lahontan's own portrait of Adario in particular, and Native Americans in general, as both intelligent and highly critical of Catholic doctrine reflected his own anticlerical bias.

At the turn of the eighteenth century, in the Quarrel of the Ancients and the Moderns (in which the stakes were no higher than the opinion of the reading public), non-Europeans were marshalled on both sides of the dispute. Fontenelle puckishly imagined a future world of Native American "moderns" for whom Frenchmen in the age of Louis XIV would, in their own turn, be idealized as "ancients." Temple's preference for "ancients" also led him to suggest that the roots of "ancient" learning lay not in Greece and Rome, but in India and China. China and Peru, as distant as possible from Europe, were exemplars of the most heroic of heroic virtues: that of good government.

Indeed, throughout much of the eighteenth century, political debates, especially in France, centered on the question of whether China represented the epitome or the antithesis of good government. Montesquieu's image of China as abominably despotic was embedded in his support of the aristocratic *parlements* in their opposition to the French monarchy. Voltaire's anti-aristocratic stance led him both to back a more centralized French monarchy and to call into question the very paradigm of "despotism" while suggesting that China's very lack of a hereditary aristocracy was perfectly consistent with good government. British political factions of "court" and "country," with significant analogies to French partisan politics, were slower to incorporate putatively "Oriental" despotism into their polemical arsenal, but ultimately Montesquieu's influence made itself felt.

Whatever the literary and intellectual merits of Lahontan's writings, he was definitely responsible for linking representations of "savagery" with the concept of "nature," and most especially "natural religion" and "natural equality." Granted, the identification of "savages" with the realm of nature was not original with Lahontan; Hobbes, to cite but one example, used "savagery" as evidence for his paradigm of the state of nature as the war of every man against every man. Far closer to Lahontan's perspective, Montaigne, by playing on the meanings of *sauvage* ("wild"), had suggested that the Tupi "savages" were, if not entirely "natural" humans, certainly closer to the natural realm than were his own compatriots. Even so, Montaigne placed far more emphasis on savage "simplicity" than on "naturalness." In any case, Lahontan's depiction of the natural religion of savages was, unlike Montaigne's, deliberately formulated as a critique of Christianity in general and Roman Catholicism in particular. The critique was echoed by Voltaire and Diderot, who also employed Lahontan's adoption of the dialogue as a literary form, pitting clever savages against obtuse clerics. (The dialogue form also allowed the authors to suggest disingenuously that any unorthodox opinions expressed were not their own.) However, as enthusiastic as they may have been about Lahontan's lampooning of Catholicism, Diderot and Voltaire were not quick to echo his views on economic, political, and social inequality. Rousseau, on the other hand, insisted on the natural equality of humans and the corrupting effects of private property. Scottish thinkers—Adam Smith, Adam Ferguson, John Millar—who were quite unconcerned with deflating the pretensions of the Catholic Church, were far more interested in using savagery as a baseline for evaluating the perils and benefits of civilization and its inevitable inequalities.

The Germans were latecomers to these debates, not least due to the terrible consequences and aftereffects of the Thirty Years War. By the mid-eighteenth century, however, German intellectuals were fully aware of the writings of their counterparts in France and Britain, staking out their own positions and engaging in their own controversies—notably Kant's and Herder's very different visions of the past, present, and future world order. Kant's ideal was explicitly more cosmopolitan and implicitly more parochial: an international federation of independent states guided by enlightened reason, cradled in a specifically male, European, bourgeois public sphere. Herder contested the putative universality of such Enlightenment values, arguing instead for the incommensurability of the values of different nations and different historical epochs. This vision included, to greater or lesser extent, non-European peoples: he was sharply critical of Montesquieu's construct of "Oriental despotism," and reproached Winckelmann for depreciating the aesthetics of ancient Egypt from a classical Greek perspective.

Many—hardly all—of these authors incorporated a stance in their work that might be categorized as "relativism," though relativistic in very different ways and to different purposes. To the extent that "cultural relativism" is a position that has often been identified with modern anthropology, one might be tempted to seek its antecedents in some of these writers. Such an identification is in important respects anachronistic: there can be no concept of "cultural relativism" before the invention of the concept of "culture." Of all these authors, Herder is the only one who might plausibly be labeled a cultural relativist.

In any case, precisely because all of these works were in a profound way polemical, relativism of one sort or another was invariably employed as a rhetorical tactic in defense of positions that were anything but relativist. Montaigne might point out that we are as strange to strange peoples as they are to us—a textbook formulation of relativism—only to conclude that, in the absence of any rational criteria for judging, we should stick to established custom. This was explicitly a defense of Roman Catholicism; the cost of religious change was horrible violence and civil war. The Church accepted his argument at the time. During his trip to Rome, he submitted the *Essays* to the Vatican for approval. Later, the Church emphatically rejected such a stance, which could after all be used to justify the refusal of the Chinese, the Indians, the Abyssinians, and Native Americans—all explicit targets of proselytization by the seventeenth century—to convert.

Montaigne's contemporaries, French legal historians like Bodin, proposed a very different kind of relativism: the notion that different laws were appropriate in different times and places. Unlike Montaigne's version, such relativism was explicitly deployed to argue against the hegemony of the Catholic Church, not always as a wholesale rejection of Catholic doctrine but as a means of giving the monarchy more room to maneuver, to steer (not always successfully) between Protestant and hardline Catholic factions. This argument for legal relativism was resurrected by Montesquieu on behalf of an entirely different cause: as a plea for the values of status, honor, and aristocratic privilege as the only plausible defense against monarchical centralization under the circumstances. The very kind of argument that Bodin framed in defense of a fragile French monarchy was used by Montesquieu to oppose what he considered its excessive claims.

In the *Supplement to the Voyage of Bougainville*, Diderot formulates yet another version of relativism. One of the two unnamed participants in the dialogue that frames the text tentatively draws as its moral that one should perhaps behave like a Tahitian in Tahiti and like a Frenchman in France. Diderot, having learned his lesson after a short imprisonment in the Chateau de Vincennes, was careful to remain as tentative as possible, and in any case circulated the dialogue only in private and not in print. Even so, such moral relativism was transparently an attack on the Church's pretensions to dictate a universally valid code of moral behavior—one that Diderot was content to ridicule, at least in private.

Herder's relativism revolved around his notion of *Volksgeist*, the spirit of the people, as reflected in song, literature, art, and mythology—in other words, in a term that Herder would have accepted, in "culture." Such forms of expression incarnated incommensurable sets of values associated with very different kinds of virtues and accompanied by different failings. This is not quite the cultural relativism of modern anthropology. Herder is quite prepared to identify the defects of other epochs and peoples, though on balance he is even more critical of his own era. But his philosophy of history culminates with Germany, not as an assertion of German superiority but as an assertion of its independent worth. If German worth was to be expressed in cultural terms, this was because it was anything but a unified state. As a nation it was, in Benedict Anderson's (1991) terms, an imagined—and only an imagined!—community. Indeed, Herder's contribution was seminal to the process of this imagination. But German nationalism is hardly a "relativist" project, even if it was justified in relativist terms.

In short, non-European peoples (or, more properly, their representations) were integral features of attempts to understand and even construct European religion, European law, European politics, even European culture. However, their significance depended on their place (and Europe's) in European representations of the world as a whole. The early modern period saw the demise of the medieval map centered on Jerusalem. The Mercator projection was, after all, a sixteenth-century invention. Even so, Bodin's conceptualization of the world in terms of a north/south, cold/hot axis was by no means entirely Eurocentric. In the first place, the division into cold, temperate, and hot zones divided Europe, with Germany and Scandinavia classified as "cold," France as "temperate," and Spain, Italy, and Greece as "hot." Asian empires—Turkey, Persia, and China—were also "temperate," whereas the hot climate of African countries, specifically Morocco and Abyssinia, explained their remarkable religiosity, a positive quality for Bodin. To the extent that, in Bodin's humoral scheme, "cold" and "hot" explained the relative predominance of body over mind or vice versa, a hot climate was superior to cold as mind was to body. Bodin was explicitly dismissive of the pretensions of Germany and of the Holy Roman Empire, as compared specifically to China and Abyssinia. This was hardly a vision of the world that either advocated for or reflected European hegemony.

By the eighteenth century, this north/south axis, while it was never entirely replaced, ceded terrain to an alternative view of the world in terms of east and west (Launay 2010b). This division was embodied in the Mercator map that placed Europe and Africa in the center, with Asia to the east and America to the west. Symbolically, Asia to the east was the heartland of empires, often (not invariably) disparaged as despotic. America, to the west, harbored savages. The distinction was not absolute. To the West, Peru was more or less equivalent to China, especially for writers who lauded China as an exemplar of good government: Temple, Quesnay, even Voltaire. To the east, nomadic pastoralists—"barbarians"—were in many respects the functional equivalent of American savages. Eighteenth-century voyages of discovery expanded the realm of savagery: the maritime explorations of Bougainville and Cook in the Pacific, but also Russian expeditions, often staffed by Germans, to newly annexed regions of Siberia.

The east/west axis was more flagrantly and arbitrarily Eurocentric than the north/south axis. North and south are, after all, determined by the earth's axis of rotation, whereas east and west are intrinsically relative. Even so, if the directions "north" and "south" are constrained by reality, they have no intrinsic significance until they are invested with symbolic meanings that are hardly determined by the "facts" of geography. Eighteenth-century authors were able to incorporate the north/south axis into schemas that reinforced notions of European exceptionalism and superiority. Montesquieu, for one, subscribed to theories of climactic determinism, but he did so in order to suggest that "republics" and "monarchies" were uniquely suited to Europe while the rest of the globe was relegated to "despotism," if not savagery. Buffon, the preeminent French naturalist, explained the variation of human types in terms of climactic determinism, taking the European "type" as the norm from which deviation needed to be explained (Duchet 1971; Glacken 1967). It is important to stress that such an ideology of European exceptionalism was not necessarily a call for domination. Montesquieu, for example, was convinced that the scale of a regime was a fundamental determinant of its nature: only small polities could function effectively as republics, whereas great empires were inevitably despotic. French imperial expansion was, in Montesquieu's terms, a recipe for disaster. Even so, arguments promulgating European exceptionalism, whatever their intentions, were easily incorporated into ideologies of European imperial expansion.

From the late sixteenth century through most of the eighteenth, these debates involving sometimes peripherally, sometimes central representations of non-Europeans tended to be the product of French thinkers. Of course these were never exclusively French preoccupations, but the prevalence of this early version of "French theory" calls for explanation. I am afraid I can only provide tentative and provisional suggestions, in terms of conjunctures of French political and religious controversies at different moments in history. The most obvious contrast is between France and Britain. In the sixteenth century, both France and Britain experienced violent clashes between Protestants and Catholics. However, Henry VIII broke with the Catholic Church, whereas Francis I, who had toyed with the idea of following suit, ultimately remained loyal to Rome while asserting the qualified independence of the French monarchy. When the Wars of Religion erupted in France, the monarchy found itself caught between Protestant and hardline Catholic factions. Legal relativism, as proposed by Bodin but also by many of his contemporaries (Huppert 1971, 1999), was a stance that allowed the monarchy to maintain its distance from the Church without necessarily breaking from allegiance to it—a position that would have been entirely unnecessary for the British crown. The notion that different regimes were appropriate in different places (and perhaps different epochs) opened a theoretical space for the scrutiny of other nations, both within and outside Europe.

In any case, religious strife was even more acute in Britain in the seventeenth century than in the sixteenth. In this case, however, allegiance to the Catholic Church was hardly germane. The critical British contributions to political theory at the time—Hobbes, Locke—were deductive rather than empirical, centering on the extent and conditions in which individuals surrendered some of their liberty to central authority. For neither Hobbes nor Locke did time or place make much difference. Paradoxically, while the seventeenth century saw a proliferation of travel literature in Britain and France, as well as throughout the rest of Europe, it was primarily in the eighteenth century that this literature entered into the content of political and religious debates.

In France, factional contests between partisans of the monarchy and of the *parlements* opened up a space for the revival of legal relativism and an even more central theoretical role for understanding non-European societies. Montesquieu, arguing for the *parlements*, and Voltaire, partisan of the monarchy, debated the relationship between the absence of a hereditary aristocracy in Asian empires—China, the Mughal empire, Persia, Turkey—and the quality of government, whether despotic or just. The factional quarrels between "court" and "country" factions in Britain were not entirely analogous. The *parlements* were regional bodies dominated by the aristocracy, and whose responsibilities were primarily judicial. "Court" and "country" were factions within a national parliament, a legislative rather than a judicial body. Neither faction was in any meaningful way identified with the aristocracy, whose members, allied with nonaristocrats, were found in both parties. The central issue debated by Montesquieu, Voltaire, and their partisans—

whether the absence of a hereditary aristocracy in Asian empires such as China was compatible with good government or was a major contributing cause of egregious despotism—was quite irrelevant in the British context. In its polemics, the "country" party appealed to the republican values of ancient Rome against the alleged tyranny of the partisans of the "court" faction.[2]

The French recourse to "savages" as exemplars of "natural religion" was equally inappropriate in the British context. This is hardly to suggest that the idea of "natural religion" was foreign to Britain. On the contrary, "natural religion" was a central feature of the British Enlightenment (Manuel 1959). However, if in Britain the concept was the object of philosophical speculation, in France it was explicitly a polemical tool aimed at the Catholic Church. The Church actively monitored public debate in France. Montesquieu's candidacy to the French Academy was originally rejected, explicitly because of religious objections to passages of the *Persian Letters*, and he took great, if ultimately unsuccessful, pains to ensure that *The Spirit of Laws* would not be placed on the Index of Forbidden Books. Diderot was even, if only briefly, imprisoned for publishing ideas that the Church deemed beyond the pale of acceptability, and he subsequently circulated his more controversial writings in manuscript form. The "natural religion" espoused by literary "savages" in France was intended to demolish the pretensions of the Church rather than to be part of an attempt to construct a serious theological alternative. The deliberate irony of the philosophes was that they based their portraits of "savages" on the writing of Jesuit missionaries, and that they almost invariably kept copies of the *Edifying and Curious Letters* in their libraries (Duchet 1971). By and large, British missionary attempts among the "savages" were far more desultory and unsystematic, and were a far smaller component of British representations of savagery (Sayre 1997). Dialectical "savages" did not thrive on British soil, at least not as far as religion was concerned.

On the other hand, "savagery"—as exemplary of political liberty and economic equality, and indeed as a tool for thinking about the relationship between the two phenomena—ultimately found an echo, particularly among the Scots: Adam Smith, Ferguson, and Millar. The Scots were particularly concerned with the negative and positive consequences of the growth of the division of labor, a central feature of their critique (especially Smith's, of course) of mercantilism. The French, too, had their critique of mercantilism, particularly the physiocrats, led by François Quesnay. However, Quesnay was particularly concerned with boosting agricultural productivity, particularly that of staple grains, which he saw as being hampered by barriers to free trade within French borders. Goods exchanged across provincial borders in France were subject to tariffs. He saw local privileges, as elaborated and defended by the regional *parlements*, as brakes on prosperity, and instead idealized Chinese "despotism" (as he termed it), whereby centralized monarchical power might guarantee free trade within the boundaries of the realm (Quesnay 1888). The Scots were more concerned with manufacture than with agriculture. As partisans of the "country" faction, they saw centralized authority as an impediment to free trade rather than as a guarantor of it.

French discourses about "savagery" on one hand and "despotism" on the other had been elaborated separately to address different debates. Montesquieu, for example, was quite uninterested in savagery, whereas the struggles between the *parlements* and the monarchy were of little concern to Rousseau. Even writers like Voltaire and Diderot, who touched on both savagery and despotism in one way or another, did so in different contexts without relating one set of issues to the other. Paradoxically, it remained for the British, especially the Scots, to build on these separate discourses elaborated largely in France by synthesizing them into a single scheme. To accomplish this, they needed to strip both "savages" and "despots" of certain dimensions that had been central to French debates. The religious and specifically anti-Catholic dimension of the "savage" disappeared entirely, as did both the pro- and antiaristocratic focus of debates about China and Persia. "Savages" and "despots" stood at two poles: equality and liberty for the first, inequality and subjection for the second. At the heart of the dilemma was the idea that the price of "progress"—not only economic but intellectual—was inequality, a necessary consequence of the division of labor. Reconciling progress and liberty was at best a delicate balance.

The end of the eighteenth century saw not only the synthesis of French ideas by the British, but their rejection by the Germans in terms of a very different vision of the world. In particular, German thinkers had little interest in economic realities, including the thorny question of inequality. Despite Kant and Herder's acknowledged debt to Rousseau, this was an aspect of his thought that seems to have escaped their attention. Kant's ideal of the free exchange of ideas, guaranteed by the central authority of the state if not the monarch, oddly resembles an intellectual equivalent of Quesnay's model for the free market for grain. Herder gave more explicit recognition to economic arguments, if only to reject them outright. He had no more patience with the Scots than with the French. He rejected Kant's universal standard of reason in favor of the multiplicity of aesthetic values. Different historical epochs, and indeed different peoples, had incommensurable appreciations of what was good and beautiful. There was no single standard by which to judge everything. History was not teleological; there existed no real progress (even, as in Ferguson's thought, a highly ambivalent one), nor for that matter a real deterioration. Even so, history was cumulative. Particular peoples were marked by their past—even, or perhaps particularly, if they explicitly rejected the values of past epochs.

The British and the Germans, synthesizing or rejecting elements of a centuries-long trajectory of French speculation about the importance of "others," formulated two competing global visions of human history that encompassed Europeans as well as non-Europeans. On one hand, human societies past and present could be situated on a single trajectory of progress, although this was conceivably a cyclical trajectory that also included corruption and decay. Underlying such a trajectory were economic and political forces. On the other hand, human cultures were depicted as expressions of incompatible systems of moral and aesthetic values, in a vision of history where development could not be equated with "progress" and the real qualities of each people or epoch were offset by necessary failings. In the nineteenth century these visions gave rise to very different traditions. One was broadly geological and archaeological, an understanding of a universal schema of human history that corresponded to different layers under the earth's surface. The second was modeled after comparative philology: the classification of different cultures into multiple families who spoke, and by implication thought and felt, literally in different terms. These differences were echoed in the late nineteenth century by the divergent ways in which anthropology was institutionalized in Britain and in Germany. These influences were real. Scottish Enlightenment writers figured prominently in the personal library of Lewis Henry Morgan (Trautman and Kabelac 1994), while Herder had a profound influence on the thought of Adolf Bastian (Koepping 1983). Ultimately, French attempts to make sense of the realities of French religious, political, and economic disputes ultimately gave rise to British, German, and later American attempts to understand human diversity. One could, I suppose, call them "roots" of anthropology as a discipline, or more broadly of modern Western representations of others. (To identify them as *the* roots is simply presumptuous.) I prefer to focus on the differences between these attempts to understand ourselves in terms of the world and the place of ourselves and others within it—attempts that have always been tentative, contested, and thoroughly interested. If I have ended with divergent rather than convergent views, it is in the hope that I have resisted the temptations of a teleological vision, of the idea that we (whoever "we" may be) have a single history. In any case, these histories are never exclusively ours. To understand ourselves, we must understand others, however imperfectly. They are not only "good to think"; they are necessary.

ACKNOWLEDGMENTS

This book has been more than twenty years in the making. I began to work seriously on this project thanks to a fellowship from the Alice Kaplan Institute for the Humanities at Northwestern University in 1994–95, which gave me a year's leave to begin to find my bearings. With gracious assistance from the director, Timothy Breen, and the assistant director, Elzbieta Foeller-Pituch, I managed in the course of the year to sketch out the directions I intended this book to take, arriving at a rough outline that has been constantly modified over the years.

Parker Shipton, who edits the marvelous series of Blackwell Anthologies in Social and Cultural Anthropology, generously invited me to contribute a volume of readings, *Foundations of Anthropological Theory: From Classical Antiquity to Early Modern Europe* (Launay 20101a). Compiling this anthology. I was better able to see my way through the organization of this book. What is more, the set of readings is an almost perfect companion to this volume for readers who would like a more sustained sample of the work of the authors discussed here.

Part of chapter 6 has previously been published as "Lafitau Revisited: American 'Savages' and Universal History," *Anthropologica* 52, no. 2 (2010): 337–43, reprinted with permission from University of Toronto Press (www .utpjournals.com), copyrighted by the Canadian Anthropology Society / Société canadienne d'anthropologie. An earlier version of chapter 8 appeared as "Montesquieu: The Specter of Despotism and the Origins of Comparative Law" in Annelise Riles, ed., *Rethinking the Masters of Comparative Law* (Oxford and Portland, OR: Hart Publishing, 2001), pp. 22–38, used by permission of Bloomsbury Publishing.

Over the years, I have shown individual chapters to some of my colleagues, who have generously provided comments and advice. Special thanks go to Micaela di Leonardo, Katherine Hoffman, Karen Hansen, Caroline Bledsoe, Bill Murphy, Mary Weismantel, Matthew Johnson, Mark Hauser, James Brown, Sylvie Romanowski, Jane Winston, Robert Lerner, Richard Kieckhefer, David Joravsky, Ken Alder, George Huppert, Andrew Lyons, Harriet Lyons, Annelise Riles, Dmitri Bondarenko, Larry Rosen, and Dale Eickelman. More recently, I have shared parts of the manuscript with some of my students, and have certainly benefited from their suggestions as well: Nurhaizatul Jamil, Bilal Nasir, Vanessa Watters, and Foroogh Farhang. I must confess with considerable embarrassment that I have lost track of all those who kindly provided me with guidance in this enterprise, and I ask forgiveness of any and all individuals whom I may have neglected to thank. Your comments have been invaluable, and your encouragement even more so. In spite of such noteworthy assistance, it goes without saying (but I will say it anyway) that any errors or misconceptions in the book are all mine.

It has been an unmitigated pleasure working with the University of Chicago Press. Years ago, David Brent expressed great interest in this book, and continually encouraged me to submit it to the Press without expressing undue impatience with the pace of my progress. Since then, Priya Nelson has taken over the editorship and shown the same patience and dedication that have made this all possible. Dylan Montanari has lent his support as well, in shepherding me through the process of publication.

Last and most important, I want to thank my wife Catherine, who has suffered through this project from beginning to end. Long ago, she came to the conclusion that I would finish this book after my retirement . . . if ever! For once, I am genuinely happy to have proven her wrong.

NOTES

CHAPTER ONE

1. The term "erratick manners" refers to the pastoral nomadism of Central Asians and of Bedouin, and is not meant to suggest temperamental instability.
2. On the ambivalent place of Africa in early modern accounts, see Launay 2010b.
3. See Burrow 1966 and Stocking 1987 for accounts of Victorian anthropology, particularly in Britain.
4. In fact, Morgan's earlier work, as late as the 1860s, did not yet reflect this radical shift in conceptualizaions of time (Trautmann 1987).
5. The word "prehistory" was coined by the Scottish antiquarian Daniel Wilson in 1851 (Trigger 1989:83), and popularized by John Lubbock, president of the Ethnological Society of London, in his book *Pre-Historic Times, as Illustrated by Ancient Remains and the Manners and Customs of Modern Savages* in 1865.
6. Fabian (1983) has argued that anthropology emerged out of the "denial of coevalness."
7. See Hartog 1980.
8. Examples include Harris 1968; Voget 1975; Evans-Pritchard 1981; Erickson 1998; and Barnard 2000.
9. For example, Aron 1967.
10. See, for example, Métraux 1963; Fazioli 2013; Mason 2015.
11. For a critical review of Said and the debates his work has launched, see Varisco 2007.
12. White (1978), in a book that is exactly contemporary to Said's, makes a related point: that narratives, specifically historical narratives, are structured in terms of given rhetorical tropes.
13. On non-European authors, see Khair et al. 2005 and Euben 2006.
14. In a related vein, the Jesuits adopted models of sixteenth-century public French schooling to their own ends in the seventeenth century (Huppert 1984, 1999).

CHAPTER TWO

1. See, for example, Duby 1968:289–357.
2. Larner (1999) dicusses the relationship of Marco Polo to Rustichello, and the composition as well as the content of the book in detail.
3. References in the text are to *The Travels of Sir John Mandeville*, translated by C. W. R. D. Moseley (1983). There are several monographs on Mandeville: Letts 1949; Bennett

1954; and Deluz 1988. There has been a recent revival of interest in Mandeville: Howard 1971; Zacher 1976:130–57; Campbell 1988:122–61; and Greenblatt 1991: 26–51.

4. The extent to which Mandeville used (or did not use) Marco Polo as a source is discussed in Bennett 1954:31 and Deluz 1988:51; but compare Letts 1949:52.

5. Manuscript and printed editions of Mandeville are listed in detail in Bennett 1954:263–385; see also Deluz 1988:370–82.

6. Rubiés 2000a (46–49) has more recently provided a far more nuanced comparison, contrasting their personas (Rubiés identifies the author of Mandeville as a cleric) as well as their presumed authorial intentions.

7. Campbell 1988; for Mandeville, see also Greenblatt 1991.

8. Since the seminal contributions of Letts 1949 and Bennett 1954, there have been several recent monographs exclusively devoted to Mandeville (Deluz 1988), the composition (and reworking) of the book in its different manuscript versions (Higgins 1997), and his contemporary audiences (Tzanaki 2003). Zacher 1976, Campbell 1988, Greenblatt 1991, and O'Doherty 2013 all include chapters on Mandeville. See also Rubiés 2000b; Sobecki 2002;, Castro Hernandez 2013; and Moseley 2015.

9. I am here treating the book and its author as unitary. However, Higgins (1997) has conclusively examined the ways in which the manuscript has itself been reworked several times to conform to very different agendas. Even so, I am hardly alone in writing about "Mandeville" rather than "Mandevilles." The differences between the texts are quite beyond the purview of my analysis.

10. Citations are all from C. R. W. D Moseley's translation (Mandeville 1983).

11. Presumably, one might situate the kingdom in Southeast Asia, since its description follows shortly after an account of the kingdom of Java. However, it is impossible to locate with any precision many of the people and places described by Mandeville.

12. Helms (1988:211–60) admirably traces the cosmological dimensions of premodern and early modern European depictions of distant "others." Arguably, however, she exoticizes such cosmologies a bit too conveniently, comparing them to non-Western conceptualiztions of "distant" places rather than to the contemporary practice of anthropology as a discipline.

13. On the legend of Gregory and Trajan and its theological implications, see Whatley 1986. Grady (2005) specifically links the legend to Mandeville's writings.

14. Howard (1971:14–15) argues unconvincingly that this depiction is ironic, and consequently that Mandeville "rejects extremes of self-abnegation and self-destruction, placing value on civilization, government, learning" (p. 17).

15. See Kieckhefer 1974, especially pp. 162–63.

16. With the notable exception of Greenblatt (1991), modern commentators have simply ignored Mandeville's attitude towards the Jews. Even Greenblatt treats the phenomenon as a "the most significant exception to the tolerance that is so impressively articulated elsewhere in Mandeville's travels" (p.50) rather than questioning the salience of the very categorization of "tolerance."

CHAPTER THREE

1. Montaigne, *Essays* II, 29. The translations from the French are my own. Since there are so many editions of the work in French, and so many translations into English, I have simply indicated the book and chapter numbers of the individual essays.

2. See Weiss 1969 for a comprehensive account of the achievements of the Italian humanists of the fourteenth and fifteenth centuries.

3. Nakam 1984:411–12.
4. On the origins of the modern concept of Europe, see Hay 1957; Pagden 2002.
5. *Essays* I, 50.
6. *Essays* II, 10.
7. *Essays* II, 36.
8. *Essays* I, 23. For the dating of individual essays, I have relied on Frame 1965:324–26. With the exception of book III, the essays were not published in the order in which they were composed. Conveniently, "Of Custom" is both the earliest in date and the first in order of publication of the essays dealing extensively with the intellectual impact of the New World.
9. *Essays* I, 26, "On the Education of Children."
10. Hodgen 1964:131–54.
11. *Essays* II, 12.
12. Michel de Montaigne, *Journal de Voyage*. In the earlier parts of the journal, Montaigne had a secretary write his notes. Thus, the passage above refers to him in the third person. In the course of the journey, he dismissed the secretary and wrote the journal entries himself.
13. Peter Burke (1981:48) somewhat playfully categorizes Montaigne as an "ethnographer" and his Italian journey as "fieldwork."
14. Nakame (1982) discusses in great detail the ways in which contemporary events, particularly the Wars of Religion, were reflected in the *Essays*.
15. Frame 1954:235, 246, 270.
16. Frame 1954:141.
17. *Essays* I, 31. For particularly insightful discussions of the essay, see de Certeau 1986:67–79 and Lestringant 1997:52–55, 94–111. See also Lévi-Strauss 1991:277–97.
18. Lestringant 1997:41–42.
19. Hodgen 1964:377–78.
20. Lestringant, 1997:44–49; see also Lestringant 1994, his intellectual biography of Thévet.
21. *Essays* II, 11.
22. *Essays* II, 36.
23. See Norbert Elias's (1983) penetrating analysis.
24. On Montaigne's early career, see Frame 1964:46–62. Chapter 8 below discusses the French system of provincial parliaments, whose functions were more judicial than legislative.
25. *Essays* I, 26; II, 10.
26. *Essays* I, 49.
27. *Essays* I, 43.
28. *Essays* I, 42.
29. *Essays* I, 36.
30. *Essays* I, 54.
31. Montaigne's informant is sometimes identified as a "sailor" (e.g., Nakam 1982:164), but a sailor would hardly have spent ten or more years in Brazil. The French colony under Villegaignon only lasted for about five years, so one must assume that the man in question was not a colonist either.
32. *Essays* II, 17.
33. Lestringant 1997:4–55; see also de Certeau 1988:209–43; Lestringant 1990, 1994a.
34. *Essays* I, 54.
35. *Essays* II, 10.

36. *Essays* III, 6.
37. *Essays* I, 54.
38. *Essays* III, 9.
39. *Essays* II, 17.

CHAPTER FOUR

1. For accounts of the development of the comparative approach in sixteenth-century French law and history, see Franklin 1963; Huppert 1970; and Kelley 1970.
2. Lach 1965, vol. 1, book 1: 204–8.
3. On Bodin, see Franklin 1963; Hodgen 1971:2766–83; Lestringant 1993a:253–290; and Couzinet 1996.
4. On Thévet, see Lestringant 1994.
5. For a discussion of Leo Africanus's impact on Bodin, see Zhiri 1995:47–92.
6. See Glacken 1967:434–47.

CHAPTER FIVE

1. Huppert 1970:73.
2. From his *Discourse on Method* in Descartes 1950:9; my translation.
3. Hobbes 1968; Locke 1947; Spinoza 2007.
4. Lach 1965:204–17.
5. Todorov (1982) provides an interesting and passionate discussion of these sources (especially Duran and Sahagun), among others.
6. See Clendinnen 1987.
7. On Acosta's supposed plagiarism, see O'Gorman 1972:123–30. See also Pagden 1986.
8. O'Gorman 1972:180.
9. On the *Edifying and Curious Letters* and their reception in the Enlightenment, see Duchet 1971:76–79.
10. Acosta 2002:329–30.
11. There is a wealth of studies on the early Jesuit missions in China. See Pinot 1932; Dunne 1962; Spence 1984; Rule 1986; and Brockey 2007. There is a wealth of information on the Jesuit and other seventeenth-century writings on China in Lach and Van Kley 1993, especially books 1 and 3.
12. On the implications of the clothing of the Jesuit mission, see Person 1994.
13. The Jesuits had already pioneered a similar—and similarly controversial—approach in south India, identifying themselves in dress and manner with Brahmans rather than with pariahs; see Zupanov 1999.
14. Spence 1984.
15. On the Jesuit interpretation of Confucianism, see Rule 1986.
16. Rule 1986:27–28.
17. Lach and Van Kley 1993:512–13.
18. The question of the extent and the ways in which Trigault's text departs from Ricci's is beyond the scope of this discussion, not to mention the author's competence.
19. Cited in Lobo 1984:xxxii.
20. Subsequent discussion is based on the first book of Trigault's compendium; I will refer to the author as Trigault for purposes of convenience.
21. Trigault 1942:11.
22. Trigault 1942:13.
23. This insistence of similarity is in marked contrast to the writings of the Portuguese

Jesuit Luis Frois (*Traité de Luís Fróis sur les contradictions de moeurs entre Européens et Japonais*, trans. by Xavier de Castro, revised edition [Paris: Editions Chandeigne, 1994]), who in 1585 depicted all the ways in which Japanese ways were the polar opposite of European ways; see Launay 2003.

24. C.f., for example, Jean and John Comaroff, *Of Revelation and Revolution: Christianity, Colonialism, and Consciousness in South Africa*, vol. 1 (Chicago and London: University of Chicago Press, 1991).

25. On European Sinophilia and Sinophobia, see Etiemble 1988–89.

26. Navarrete 1962. For a sympathetic account of Navarrete's life and work, see Cummins 1993.

27. The most famous critique of such Jesuit practices is Blaise Pascal's *Lettres Écrites à un Provincial*.

28. Gottfried Wilhelm Leibniz, *Writings on China*, trans. Daniel J. Cook and Henry Rosemont, Jr. (Chicago and La Salle, IL: Open Court, 1994). For an excellent account of the impact of the Rites Controversy on seventeenth- and eighteenth-century thought, see Pinot 1932.

29. Lecomte 1990.

30. Lach and Van Kley 1993:1679.

31. Lecomte 1990:247–48. All translations from Lecomte are my own.

32. Lecomte 1990:364.

33. Lecomte 1990:359.

34. Lecomte 1990:164. For a detailed account of the Jesuit account of Chinese chronology and its impact on the Enlightenment, see Virgile Pinot, *La Chine et la formation de l'esprit philosphique en France (1640–1740)* (Paris: Paul Geuthner, 1932), pp. 189–279.

35. Lecomte 1990:98–114.

36. Lecomte 1990:298.

37. Lecomte 1990:299.

38. Lecomte 1990:303.

39. Lecomte 1990:306.

40. Lecomte 1990:320–38.

41. Lecomte 1990:316–17.

42. Lecomte 1990:322.

43. Lecomte 1990:325.

44. Ibid. This is just the first of seven paragraphs describing such a banquet.

45. Lecomte 1990:327–28.

46. The Jesuits, like later Enlightenment thinkers, uncritically accepted Chinese accounts of the earliest mythical emperors, great legislators, and benefactors of humanity. In all fairness, such accounts did not differ greatly from classical accounts of mythical legislators, notably Numa Pompilius and Lycurgus, as portrayed by Plutarch among others.

47. Lecomte 1990:279.

48. See below, chapter 7.

CHAPTER SIX

1. The Jesuits in New France are the unlikely heroes in the second volume of Francis Parkman's (1983) *France and England in North America: The Jesuits in North America in the Seventeenth Century* (vol. 1: 331–712). For a comparison of the Jesuit missions to China and to New France, see Li 2001.

2. The complete texts of the Jesuit relations, along with a number of other important travel narratives, are to be found in *The Jesuit Relations and Allied Documents: Travels and Explorations of the Jesuit Missionaries in New France, 1610–1791*, 1896–1901. Biard's relation is found in vols. 3 and 4.

3. Sagard 1990.

4. *Jesuit Relations*, vol. 5.

5. Le Jeune describes how small hunting bands would construct small temporary huts in which everyone (dogs included) would sleep to conserve warmth; for this reason, he uses the term "huts" to refer to the hunting bands themselves and not just their lodgings.

6. De Certeau 2000.

7. This comment is from Le Jeune's earlier relation of 1633; all other passages are from the relation of 1634.

8. See White 2012, especially chapter 5.

9. Chapter 4 below.

10. The fact that the so-called Hottentots lived south of the equator, where the climatic effects of the north/south distinction were reversed, frequently escaped the attention of such commentators, who simply assumed that extreme south and extreme heat were coterminous.

11. Compare Jean and John Comaroff's (1991:210–11) discussion of the dialogue between Livingstone, the "medical doctor," and the Tswana "rain doctor."

12. See chapter 9 below.

13. Lafitau 1974.

14. Vol. 1:259–61. Nevertheless Harris (1968:17) laments that Lafitau's "view of American Indian cultural processes was completely trammeled by belief in the fall and the Biblical version of the dispersal of the tribes of Israel."

15. Page numbers for Lafitau all refer to Fenton and Moore's translation.

16. Mandeville 1983:125–26.

17. Acosta 2002:282.

18. Acosta 2002:287.

19. Vol. 1, p. 188.

20. Vol. 1, p. 189.

21. Vol. 1, p. 217.

22. See chapter 8 below.

23. See chapter 9 below.

24. See chapter 10 below.

CHAPTER SEVEN

1. Standard accounts of the Quarrel are Rigault 1856 and Gillot 1914. Recent reinterpretations include Levine 1991 and DeJean 1997.

2. "An Essay upon the Ancient and Modern Learning," *The Works of Sir William Temple*, vol. 2 (Edinburgh, 1754), p. 175. Subsequent references to works of Temple are from the same volume.

3. The point is made, rather too mechanistically, in Bernal 1987. While the argument suffers from polemical overstatement, his conclusion that Western scholarly constructions of the ancient world became much more narrowly Eurocentric in the late eighteenth century is unquestionably correct.

4. "Cette nation grave et sérieuse connut d'abord la vraie fin de la politique, qui est de rendre la vie commode et les peuples heureux. . . . Comme la vertu est le fondement

de toute la société, ils l'ont soigneusement cultivée. . . . Leurs lois étaient simples, pleines d'équité, et propres à unir entre eux les citoyens" (This solemn and serious nation first realized the true goal of politics, which is to make life practical and peoples happy. . . . Since virtue is the foundation of all society, they cultivated it scrupulously. Their laws were simple, full of equity, and suited to unite the citizenry). Bossuet 1966:357–58, my translation).

5. Frank Manuel (1959:40–46), in his survey of eighteenth-century theories of mythology and religion, gives prominent place to Fontenelle's comparison of ancient Greek and American Indian myths.
6. Temple 1963:30.
7. See, e.g., Appleton 1951:42–46.
8. For a biography of Fontenelle, see Niderst 1972.
9. Samuel Holt Monk, introduction to Temple 1963:vii–xlii.
10. Cited in Marburg 1932:18.
11. Cited in Marburg 1932:34.
12. Niderst 1972:298–99.
13. Cited in Niderst 1972:327.
14. Bernard de Fontenelle, "Digression sur les Anciens et les Modernes," in Fontenelle 1818, vol 2:355–65. Subsequent references to works of Fontenelle are from the same volume.
15. Fontenelle 1818, vol. 2: 354.
16. Ibid.
17. Ibid.
18. From "An Essay upon the Origin and Nature of Government," in Temple 1754:29.
19. Temple 1754:30.
20. Temple 1754:42.
21. From "Of Popular Discontents," Temple 1754: 357–58.
22. See, e.g., Bury 1920; Nisbet 1969.
23. Fontenelle, "Dialogues des morts anciens et modernes," p. 188–91.
24. The most thorough study of the emergence of a "stage" theory of progress in the eighteenth century is Meek 1976. For the nineteenth century, see notably Burrow 1966; Stocking 1987; and Adam Kuper 1988.
25. I have translated this essay into English in Launay 2010a:207–13.
26. Sahagun 1950–82.
27. Temple 1963:52.
28. Temple 1754:368.
29. Temple 1963:50.
30. Temple 1963:48.
31. Temple 1963:64.
32. Ibid.
33. For an account of the English avatars of the Quarrel, see Levine 1991.
34. Temple 1963:39.
35. Ibid.
36. Temple 1963:42.
37. Temple 1963:47.
38. Temple 1963:105.
39. Temple 1963:121–22.
40. Temple 1963:145.
41. Temple 1963:151.

42. Temple 1963:164.
43. Temple 1963:172.
44. Habermas 1991.

CHAPTER EIGHT

1. Unless otherwise identified, all citations in this chapter are my translations of passages from Montesquieu 1979, identified by book and chapter.
2. See Egret 1970 for a detailed account of the struggles of the French monarchy and the *parlements* in Montesquieu's era.
3. This tripartite division derives from Aristotle's *Politics*, book 2 (Aristotle 1962:101–48), but it was also adopted by Polybius (1979:302–52), whose importance for Machiavelli (who in turn heavily influenced Montesquieu's thought) has been amply discussed by Pocock (1975).
4. Montesquieu cites *The Fable of the Bees* in a footnote to book 7, chapter 1, so there can be no doubt that he had not only read the book but kept it in mind while writing *The Spirit of Laws*.
5. Montesquieu's sources are carefully analyzed in Vernière 1977:40–48, on which I have based the following discussion.
6. These figures are taken from Cohen 1980:7. I have omitted from the calculation those works that deal with Europe or are classed as "general." Incidentally, Cohen's tabulations demonstrate that proportionally fewer books were published about Asia in the eighteenth century; to the extent that most of Montesquieu's sources are drawn from the late seventeenth and early eighteenth centuries, the seventeenth-century figures are perhaps more representative.
7. By Montesquieu's time, there was an extensive literature in French on American savages, given the extent of French colonial interests in North America as well as missionary enterprises, especially on the part of the Jesuits; see Sayre 1997.
8. Montesquieu 1964 (first published 1721); Lahontan 1931 (first published 1703).
9. On Jesuit descriptions of China, see Etiemble 1988, vol. 1:241–307; and Lach and Van Kley 1993:168–200, 222–69, and 1564–71.
10. Voltaire 1963.
11. Voltaire 1966:253–345, especially 256–66.
12. Voltaire 1785.
13. Voltaire 1966:263.
14. For Voltaire's involvement in the controversy between the monarchy and the *parlements*, see Gay 1959:87–143 and 309–33.
15. Voltaire 1922.

CHAPTER NINE

1. Voltaire 1966:95–103.
2. Lahontan 1931. Chinard's introduction is a thorough, if not very sympathetic, account of Lahontan's unusual life. Other recent discussions of Lahontan include Pagden 1993:120–40; Sayre 1997:31–48 and 106–8; Ellingson 2001:65–76; and Muthu 2003:24–31.
3. Sayre 1997 extensively discusses the relationship between these two forms.
4. Lahontan 1931:92.
5. This was not, strictly speaking, true of Sagard, a Recollect and the first missionary to write an account of the Huron, but an apt characterization of Hennepin, who ac-

companied La Salle on his travels and whose depictions of "savages" was anything but flattering.

6. Lahontan 1931:105.
7. Lahontan 1931.
8. Lahontan 1931:159.
9. Lahontan 1931:160.
10. Lahontan 1931:126.
11. Lahontan 1931:174. As mentioned above, Lahontan had more extensive contact with Algonquin than with Huron. However, since he identifies Adario as "Huron," I will use the term as a convenient label, not to be taken literally.
12. Lahontan 1931:183–84.
13. I have deliberately avoided using Lévi-Strauss's opposition between "nature" and "culture." The modern concept of "culture" was never part of the repertoire of the French Enlightenment, and certainly not of Lahontan.
14. Lahontan 1931:209.
15. Lahontan 1931:202.
16. Rousseau 1971, *Discours sur l'origine et les fondements de l'inégalité parmi les hommes,* part 2.
17. Indeed, the written word is very much a part of European "corruption" that Adario explicitly rejects, as Pagden (1993:134–40) has elegantly argued.
18. Ellingson (2001) has persuasively argued that this is a deliberate and reactionary misrepresentation of Rousseau and other Enlightenment thinkers. However, Ellingson dwells too much on the English word "noble," which can also refer to explicitly aristocratic values. This said, the phrase *"le bon sauvage"* is entirely absent from Rousseau, Lahontan, Diderot, and others.
19. On Rousseau's familiarity with contemporary travel accounts, see Pire 1956 and Morel 1909; see also Duchet 1971.
20. Rousseau's preference for Sparta over Athens was in fact quite conventional in his day, and certainly not one of the philosopher's many idiosyncracies.
21. Pagden (1993:141–81) is a particularly insightful discussion of the *Supplement,* and more generally of Diderot's views on "savages." See also Duchet 1971:407–68.
22. Didreot 1992:35. Page numbers in the text refer to this translation.
23. The definitive study of Diderot's contribution to Raynal's œuvre is Michèle Duchet, *Diderot et l'Histoire des deux Indes ; ou, L'écriture fragmentaire,* (Paris: A.-G. Nizet, 1978).
24. Raynal, book 8, ch. I; IV, in Diderot 1992:43.
25. A century before Diderot, Samuel Pufendorf (1991:7) had already suggested this division of law into natural, civic, and religious domains, all the while stipulating that "it would be very ignorant to set these disciplines against each other or to imagine any contradiction between them."
26. Sankar Muthu (2003:46–71) argues that by stressing the existence of such social engineering, Diderot portrays the Tahitians as essentially "cultural" beings endowed with agency, as opposed to Montaigne's, Lahontan's, and Rousseau's "natural" savages, whose uncivilized virtues are more by default than by design. Actually, these policies are more the product of Diderot's imagination than of real Tahitians, and in any case his portrayal of "savages" (Tahitians included) are far more ambivalent than Muthu suggests.
27. See Duvernay-Bolens 1995. Diderot, however, is skeptical about the reported size of the Patagonians (p. 39).

28. Lestringant 1993b:127–38.
29. Lestringant 1993b:136.
30. Thomas (1983) elegantly demonstrates the extent to which conceptions of and attitudes towards nature were in fluctuation during the early modern period.
31. See Tuck 1979.
32. See Manuel 1959.
33. Launay (2010b) explores the consequences of this shift in early modern depictions of Africa.
34. See Glacken 1967:551–622 for an extensive discussion of enlightenment varieties of climactic determinism, including Montesquieu but also subsequent thinkers.
35. For a comprehensive discussion of Enlightenment ideas about "barbarians," see Pocock 2005.

CHAPTER TEN

1. For example, Harris 1968; Evans-Pritchard 1981.
2. Quite apart from any indirect influence of Ferguson on Marx and Engels via Morgan, Marx was familiar with Ferguson's work, which he cited approvingly and at length in *Capital*, vol. 1, ch. 14. On Ferguson's influence not only on Marx but on Schiller and John Stuart Mill, see Kettler (1965: 3–11) and Oz-Salzburger (1995:xxv). On Ferguson, see also Pocock 1999:330–45 and Gellner 1994:61–80.
3. For historical accounts of the notion of progress, see Bury 1932 and Nisbet 1969.
4. All told, Ferguson placed far less emphasis on the importance of pastoralism in introducing economic inequality than did Adam Smith or, slightly later, John Millar (1960). See also Pocock 1981, 2009.
5. Ferguson's *Essay*, it is important to emphasize, was published nine years before *An Inquiry into the Nature and Causes of the Wealth of Nations* (Smith 1976).
6. Millar's book, like Ferguson's, received high praise from both Marvin Harris (1968:48–52) and Evans-Pritchard (30–34).
7. Gibbon's entire library has been catalogued by Keynes (1980).
8. Gibbon explicitly derives this terminology from Hume's (1992) *The Natural History of Religion*.
9. Gibbon (1984) relates the incident at length in his memoirs.
10. On the ideology of "court" and "country" in Britain, see Dickinson 1977 and Pocock 1989:104–47.

CHAPTER ELEVEN

1. For the concept of "culture," specifically in the context of the German Enlightenment, see Carhart 2007.
2. See Zammito 2002 (also Muthu 2003) for a detailed account of the relationship between the thought of Kant and of Herder.
3. Vermuelen (2015:374) notes that Kant pioneered this sort of typology.
4. The gendering of this phrase is, if not fully intentional, at least symptomatic of Kant's ideas about the roles of men as opposed to women as social actors and thinkers.
5. Ten years later, in his essay "Perpetual Peace" (Kant 1991:93–130), he suggested that such savage warfare was responsible for inducing humans to settle throughout the entire globe—another unintended benefit of "natural" unsociability.
6. The term is not Kant's, but is rather central to the argument of Habermas (1991), who attempted to contextualize Kant's paradigm, conceding that it was highly gendered

(male) and classed (bourgeois). That it was also European and white went perhaps without saying.

7. In an earlier fragment (Herder 1992:66), he had demonstrated far more appreciation of Hume, and had even conceded merit to Voltaire at his best.

8. Italics in citations from *Another Philosophy of History* are from the translation, and are not my own.

9. Similar attitudes prevailed towards other modern peoples—for example, Greeks and Egyptians—as compared to their ancient predecessors (Launay 2015:84).

10. Herder is referring here to the classical revival in Europe from the Renaissance to the Enlightenment, and is not at all attempting to disparage modern Greeks or Italians.

11. See Sikka 2011:44–83 for an extended discussion of the importance of "happiness" for Herder's relativism.

12. For discussions of Herder's use of the term, see Berlin 1976 and Sikka 2011.

13. For a discussion of Herder's view of China, see Sikka 2011:106–16.

CHAPTER TWELVE

1. Such practices were hardly unique to early modern Europeans; we can easily find analogies in ancient Greece (Hartog 1980) or the contemporary United States (di Leonardo 1998).

2. *Cato's Letters* (Trenchard 1723–24) are an obvious example of the use of models from classical antiquity in eighteenth-century British political polemics.

BIBLIOGRAPHY

Acosta, José de. 2002. *Natural and Moral History of the Indies*. Translated by Frances López-Morillas. Durham and London: Duke University Press.

Adams, William Y. 1998. *The Philosophical Roots of Anthropology*. Stanford, CA: CSLI Publications.

Althusser, Louis. 1959. *Montesquieu: La politique et l'histoire*. Paris: Presses universitaires de France.

Anderson, Benedict. 1991. *Imagined Communities; Reflections on the Origins and Spread of Nationalism*, 2nd edition. London and New York: Verso.

Appleton, William W. 1951. *A Cycle of Cathay: The Chinese Vogue in England during the Seventeenth and Eighteenth Centuries*. New York: Columbia University Press.

Arens, William. 1979. *The Man-Eating Myth: Anthropology and Anthropophagy*. New York: Oxford University Press.

Aristotle. 1962. *The Politics*. Translated by T. A. Sinclair. Harmondsworth: Penguin Books.

Aron, Raymond. 1967. *Les Etapes de la pensée sociologique*. Paris: Editions Gallimard.

Barnard, Alan. 2000. *History and Theory in Anthropology*. Cambridge: Cambridge University Press.

Bennett, Josephine Waters. 1954. *The Rediscovery of Sir John Mandeville*. New York: Modern Languages Association of America.

Berlin, Isaiah. 1976. *Vico and Herder: Two Studies in the History of Ideas*. London: Hogarth.

Bernal, Martin. 1987. *Black Athena: The Afroasiatic Roots of Classical Civilization*. 2 vols. New Brunswick, NJ: Rutgers University Press.

Bodin, Jean. 1945. *Method for the Easy Comprehension of History*. Translated by Beatrice Reynolds. New York: Columbia University Press.

———. 1975. *Colloquium of the Seven about Secrets of the Sublime*. Translated by Marion Leathers Daniels Kuntz. Princeton and London: Princeton University Press.

———. 1993. *Les Six Livres de la République*. Edited and abridged by Gérard Mairet. Paris: Livre de Poche.

———. 1995. *On the Demon-Mania of Witches*. Translated by Randy Scott. Toronto: Centre for Reformation and Renaissance Studies.

Boon, James A. 1982. *Other Tribes, Other Scribes: Symbolic Anthropology in the Comparative Study of Cultures, Histories, Religions, and Texts*. Cambridge: Cambridge University Press.

Borges, Jorge Luis. 1964. *Labyrinths: Selected Stories and Other Writings*. Augmented edition. Edited by Donald A. Yates and James E. Irby. New York: New Directions.

Bossuet, Jacques-Bénigne. 1966. *Discours sur l'Histoire Universelle*. Paris: Garnier-Flammarion.

Brockey, Liam Matthew. 2007. *Journey to the East: The Jesuit Mission to China, 1579–1724*. Cambridge, MA, and London: Harvard University Press.

Buffon, Georges-Louis Leclerc, Comte de. 1835, *Variations dans l'espèce humaine*. In *Oeuvres Complètes*, Vol. 9, Paris: Pourrat Frères, pp. 168–373.

Burke, Edmund. 1984. *Selected Letters of Edmund Burke*. Edited by Harvey C. Mansfield, Jr. Chicago and London, University of Chicago Press.

Burke, Peter. 1981. *Montaigne*. New York: Hill and Wang.

Burrow, J. W. 1966. *Evolution and Society: A Study in Victorian Social Theory*. Cambridge: Cambridge University Press.

Bury, J. B. 1920. *The Idea of Progress: An Inquiry into Its Origin and Growth*. London: Macmillan.

Campbell, Mary B. 1988. *The Witness and the Other World: Exotic European Travel Writing, 400–1600*. Ithaca, NY, and London: Cornell University Press.

Carhart, Michael C. 2007. *The Science of Culture in Enlightenment Germany*. Cambridge, MA and London: Harvard University Press.

Castro Hernandez, Pablo. 2013. "El libro de viajes como enciclopedia: Un catálogo de monstruos y maravillas en los viajes de Sir John Mandeville." *Revista Sans Soleil-Estudios de la Imagen* 5, no. 2: 188–204.

Certeau, Michel de. 1985. "Histoire et anthropologie chez Lafitau." In *Naissance de l'ethnologie? Anthropologie et missions en Amérique XVIè–XVIIè siècle*, edited by Claude Blankaert, 62–89. Paris: Éditions du Cerf.

———. 1986. *Heterologies: Discourse on the Other*. Translated by Brian Massumi. Minneapolis: University of Minnesota Press.

———. 1988. *The Writing of History*. Translated by Tom Conley. New York: Columbia University Press.

———. 2000. *The Possession at Loudun*. Translated by Michael B. Smith. Chicago and London: University of Chicago Press.

Chardin, Sir John (Jean). 1988. *Travels in Persia 1673–1677*. New York: Dover Publications. Reprint of English translation published in 1720.

Clendinnen, Inga. 1987. *Ambivalent Conquests: Maya and Spaniard in Yucatan, 1517–1570*. Cambridge: Cambridge University Press.

Clifford, James. 1988. *The Predicament of Culture: Twentieth-Century Ethnography, Literature and Art*. Cambridge, MA, and London: Harvard University Press.

Coetzee, J. M. 1988. *White Writing: On the Culture of Letters in South Africa*. New Haven and London: Yale University Press.

Cohen, William B. 1980. *The French Encounter with Africans: White Response to Blacks, 1530–1880*. Bloomington: Indiana University Press.

Comaroff, John, and Jean Comaroff. 1991. *Of Revelation and Revolution: Christianity, Colonialism, and Consciousness in South Africa*, vol 1, Chicago and London: University of Chicago Press.

Cortes, Hernan. 1971. *Letters from Mexico*. Translated and edited by Anthony Pagden. New Haven and London: Yale University Press.

Couzinet, Marie-Dominique. 1996. *Histoire et Méthode à la Renaissance: Une lecture de la Methodus de Jean Bodin*. Paris: Librairie Philosophique J. Vrin.

Cummins, J. S. 1993. *A Question of Rites: Friar Domingo Navarrete and the Jesuits in China*. Cambridge: Scholar Press.

Dampier, William. 1906. *The Voyages of Captain William Dampier*, 2 vols. Edited by John Masefield. London: E. Grant Richards.

DeJean, Joan. 1997. *Ancients against Moderns: Culture Wars and the Making of a Fin de Siècle.* Chicago and London: University of Chicago Press.

Deluz, Christiane. 1988. *Le Livre de Jehan de Mandeville: Une "géographie" au XIVè siècle.* Louvain-La Neuve: Publications de l'Institut d'etudes médiévales, Université Catholique de Louvain.

Descartes, René. 1943. *Oeuvres choisies,* vol 1. Paris: Garnier Frères.

Deschamps, Eustache. 1832. *Poésies morales et historiques d'Eustache Deschamps.* Paris: Imprimerie de Crapelet.

Dickinson, H. T. 1977. *Liberty and Property: Political Ideology in Eighteenth-Century Britain.* London: Weidenfeld and Nicolson.

Diderot, Denis. 1992. *Political Writings.* Edited by John Hope Mason and Robert Wokler. Cambridge: Cambridge University Press.

Di Leonardo, Micaela. 1998. *Exotics at Home: Anthropologists, Others, American Modernity.* Chicago and London: University of Chicago Press.

Duby, Georges. 1968. *Rural Economy and Country Life in the Medieval West.* Columbia: University of South Carolina Press.

Duchet, Michèle. 1971. *Anthropologie et histoire au siècle des Lumières.* Paris: Maspéro.

———. 1978. *Diderot et l'histoire des deux Indes: ou, L'écriture fragmentaire.* Paris : A.-G. Nizet.

———. 1985. *Le Partage des savoirs: Discours historique, discours ethnologique.* Paris: Editions la Découverte.

Dunne, George H., S.J. 1962. *Generation of Giants: The Story of the Jesuits in China in the Last Decades of the Ming Dynasty.* South Bend, IN: University of Notre Dame Press.

Durkheim, Émile. 1960. *Montesquieu and Rousseau: Forerunners of Sociology.* Ann Arbor: University of Michigan Press.

———. 1995. *The Elementary Forms of Religious Life.* Translated by Karen E. Fields. New York: The Free Press.

Duvernay-Bolens, Jacqueline. 1995. *Les Géants Patagons: Voyage aux origines de l'homme.* Paris : Editions Michalon.

Egret, Jean. 1970. *Louis XV et l'opposition parlementaire 1715–1774.* Paris: Librairie Armand Colin.

Elias, Norbert. 1983. *The Court Society.* Translated by Edmund Jephcott. Oxford: Basil Blackwell; New York: Pantheon Books.

———. 2000. *The Civilizing Process.* Revised edition. Translated by Edmund Jephcott. Oxford and Malden, MA: Blackwell Publishers.

Ellingson, Ter. 2001. *The Myth of the Noble Savage.* Berkeley, Los Angeles, and London: University of California Press.

Engels, Friedrich. 1986. *The Origin of the Family, Private Property, and the State.* Harmondsworth, UK: Penguin Books.

Erickson, Paul A. 1998. *A History of Anthropological Theory.* With Liam B. Murphy. Toronto: Broadview Press.

Etiemble. 1988–1989. *L'Europe Chinoise.* 2 vols. Paris: Gallimard.

Euben, Roxanne L. 2006. *Journeys to the Other Shore: Muslim and Western Travelers in Search of Knowledge.* Princeton, NJ, and Oxford: Princeton University Press.

Evans-Pritchard, E. E. 1981. *A History of Anthropological Thought.* Edited by André Singer. London and Boston: Faber and Faber.

Eze, Emmanuel Chukwudi. 1997. *Race and the Enlightenment: A Reader.* Cambridge, MA: Blackwell.

Fabian, Johannes. 1983. *Time and the Other: How Anthropology Constructs Its Object.* New York: Columbia University Press.

Fazioli, K. Patrick. 2013. "The Erasure of the Middle Ages from Anthropology's Intellectual Genealogy." *History and Anthropology*, http://dx.doi.org/10.1080/02757206.2013 .849247.

Ferguson, Adam. 1995. *An Essay on the History of Civil Society*. Cambridge: Cambridge University Press.

Flaherty, Gloria. 1992. *Shamanism and the Eighteenth Century*. Princeton, NJ: Princeton University Press.

Fontenelle, Bernard le Bouvier de. 1818. *Oeuvres*. 3 vols. Paris: A. Belin.

Foucault, Michel. 1971. *The Order of Things: An Archaeology of the Human Sciences*. New York: Pantheon Books.

———. 1976. *The Archaeology of Knowledge and The Discourse of Language*. Translated by A. M. Sheridan-Smith. New York, Hagerstown, San Francisco, and London: Harper Colophon Books.

Frame, Donald. 1965. *Montaigne: A Biography*. New York: Harcourt, Brace, and World.

Franklin, Julian H. 1963. *Jean Bodin and the Sixteenth-Century Revolution in the Methodology of Law and History*. New York and London: Columbia University Press.

Freud, Sigmund. 1989. *Totem and Taboo: Some Points of Agreement between the Mental Life of Savages and Neurotics*. Translated by James Strachey. New York: W. W. Norton.

Frois, Luís. 1994. *Traité de Luís Fróis sur les contradictions de moeurs entre Européens et Japonais*. Revised edition. Translated by Xavier de Castro. Paris: Editions Chandeigne.

Gay, Peter. 1959. *Voltaire's Politics: The Poet as Realist*. Princeton, NJ: Princeton University Press.

Gellner, Ernest. 1994. *Conditions of Liberty*. New York: Allen Lane/Penguin Press.

Gibbon, Edward. 1983. *The Decline and Fall of the Roman Empire*. 3 vols. New York: Modern Library.

———. 1984. *Memoirs of My Life*. Harmondsworth, UK: Penguin Books.

Gillot, Hubert. 1914. *La Querelle des Anciens et des Modernes en France*. Paris: Honoré Champion.

Ginzburg, Carlo. 1982. *The Cheese and the Worms: The Cosmos of a Sixteenth-Century Miller*. Harmondsworth, UK: Penguin Books.

Glacken, Clarence J. 1967. *Traces on the Rhodian Shore: Nature and Culture in Western Thought from Ancient Times to the End of the Eighteenth Century*. Berkeley, Los Angeles, and London: University of California Press.

Goldsmith, Oliver. 1933. *The Citizen of the World*. In *The Miscellaneous Works of Oliver Goldsmith*, 87–279. London: Macmillan.

Grady, Frank. 2005. *Representing Righteous Heathens in Late Medieval England*. New York: Palgrave Macmillan.

Grafigny, Françoise de. 1983. *Lettres d'une Péruvienne*. In *Lettres Portugaises, Lettres d'une Péruvienne, et autres romans d'amour par lettres*. Paris: Garnier-Flammarion.

Greenblatt, Stephen. 1991. *Marvelous Possessions: The Wonder of the New World*. Chicago: University of Chicago Press.

Habermas, Jurgen. 1991. *The Structural Transformation of the Public Sphere*, Cambridge, MA: MIT Press.

Harris, Marvin. 1968. *The Rise of Anthropological Theory*. New York: Thomas Y. Cromwell.

Hartog, François. 1980. *Le Miroir d'Hérodote: Essai sur la représentation de l'autre*. Paris: Gallimard.

Hay, Denys. 1957. *Europe: The Emergence of an Idea*. Edinburgh: Edinburgh University Press.

Hegel, Georg Wilhelm Friedrich. 1956. *The Philosophy of History*. Translated by J. Sibree. New York: Dover Publications.

————. 1975. *Lectures of the Philosophy of World History: Introduction* (written 1831). Translated by H. B. Nisbet. Cambridge: Cambridge University Press.

Helms, Mary. 1988. *Ulysses' Sail: An Ethnographic Odyssey of Power, Knowledge, and Geographical Distance.* Princeton, NJ: Princeton University Press.

Herder, Johann Gottfried. 1966. *Outlines of the Philosophy of the History of Man.* Reprint of the translation by T. O. Churchill (1800). New York: Bergman Publishers.

————. 1992. *Selected Early Works, 1764–1767.* Edited by Ernest Amenze and Karl Menges. Translated by Ernest A. Menze with Michael Palma. University Park, PA: Pennsylvania State University Press.

————. 2004. *Another Philosophy of History and Selected Political Writings.* Translated by Ioannis D. Evrigenis and Daniel Pellerin. Indianapolis: Hackett.

Herodotus. 1954. *The Histories.* Translated by Aubrey de Selincourt. Harmondsworth: Penguin.

Higgins, Iain Macleod. 1997. *Writing East: The "Travels" of Sir John Mandeville.* Philadelphia: University of Pennsylvania Press.

Hobbes, Thomas. 1968. *Leviathan.* Harmonsdworth: Penguin.

Hodgen, Margaret. 1971. *Early Anthropology in the Sixteenth and Seventeenth Centuries.* Philadelphia: University of Pennsylvania Press.

Hume, David. 1888. *A Treatise of Human Nature.* Oxford: Clarendon Press.

————. 1992. *The Natural History of Religion.* In *Writings on Religion,* edited by Anthony Flew, 105–82. La Salle, IL: Open Court.

Huppert, George. 1970. *The Idea of Perfect History: Historical Erudition and Historical Philosophy in Renaissance France.* Urbana, Chicago, and London: University of Illinois Press.

————. 1984. *Public Schools in Renaissance France.* Urbana and Chicago: University of Illinois Press.

————. 1999. *The Style of Paris: Renaissance Origins of the French Enlightenment.* Bloomington and Indianapolis: Indiana University Press.

Ibn Khaldun. 1958. *The Muqaddimah.* 3 vols. Translated by Franz Rosenthal. Bollingen Series XLIII. New York: Pantheon Books.

Kant, Immanuel. 1978. *Anthropology from a Pragmatic Point of View.* Translated by Victor Lyle Dowdell. Carbondale and Edwardsville: Southern Illinois University Press.

————. 1991. *Political Writings.* 2nd Edition. Edited by Hans Reiss; translated by H. B. Nisbet. Cambridge: Cambridge University Press.

Kelley, Donald R. 1970. *Foundations of Modern Historical Scholarship: Language, Law and History in the French Renaissance.* New York: Columbia University Press.

Kettler, David. 1965. *The Social and Political Thought of Adam Ferguson.* Columbus: Ohio State University Press.

Keynes, Geoffrey. 1980. *The Library of Edward Gibbon.* 2nd edition. London: St. Paul's Bibliographies.

Kieckhefer, Richard. 1974. "Radical Tendencies in the Flagellant Movement of the Mid-Fourteenth Century." *Journal of Medieval and Renaissance Studies* 4:157–76.

Khair, Tabish, Martin Leer, Justin D. Edwards, and Hanna Ziadeh, eds. 2005. *Other Routes: 1500 Years of African and Asian Travel Writing.* Bloomington and Indianapolis: Indiana University Press.

Koepping, Klaus-Peter. 1983. *Adolf Bastian and the Psychic Unity of Mankind: The Foundations of Anthropology in Nineteenth-Century Germany.* St. Lucia, London, and New York: University of Queensland Press.

Kuntz, Marion Leathers Daniels. 1975. Introduction to *Jean Bodin 1975,* pp. xv–lxxxi.

Kuper, Adam. 1988. *The Invention of Primitive Society: Transformations of an Illusion.* London and New York: Routledge.

Lach, Donald F. 1965. *Asia in the Making of Europe, Vol. I: The Century of Discovery.* 2 vols. Chicago: University of Chicago Press.

Lach, Donald F., and Edwin J. Van Kley. 1993. *Asia in the Making of Europe, Volume III: A Century of Advance.* 4 vols. Chicago and London: University of Chicago Press.

Lafitau, Joseph-François. 1974. *Customs of the American Indians Compared with the Customs of Primitive Times.* 2 vols. Edited and translated by William N. Fenton and Elizabeth L. Moore. Toronto: The Champlain Society.

Lahontan, Louis-Armand, Baron de. 1931. *Dialogues curieux entre l'auteur et un sauvage de bon sens qui a voyagé et mémoires de l'Amérique septentrionale.* Baltimore: Johns Hopkins University Press.

Lane, Edward. 1908. *The Manners and Customs of the Modern Egyptians.* London: Dent and New York: Dutton.

Langland, William. 1978. *The Vision of Piers Plowman.* Edited by A. V. C. Schmidt. London: J. M. Dent and Sons.

Larner, John.1999. *Marco Polo and the Discovery of the World.* New Haven and London: Yale University Press.

Launay, Robert. 2002. "Writes of Passage: The Cape of Good Hope in Late Seventeenth-Century Narratives of Travel to Asia." *International Studies in Sociology and Social Anthropology* 83 (edited by Maghan Keita): 89–106.

———. 2003. "Tasting the World: Food in Early European Travel Narratives." *Food and Foodways* 11, no. 1 (2003): 27–47.

———. 2010a. *Foundations of Anthropological Theory: From Classical Antiquity to Early Modern Europe.* Malden, MA and Oxford: Wiley-Blackwell,

———. 2010b. "Cardinal Directions: Africa's Shifting Place in Early Modern European Conceptions of the World." *Cahiers d'Etudes Africaines* 5 (2-3-4), 198–199–200, pp. 455–470.

———. 2015. "Echoes of the Class Struggle in France: Exoticism, Religion, and Politics in Fustel de Coulange's *The Ancient City*." In *Corridor Talk to Culture History: Public Anthropology and Its Consequences, Histories of Anthropology Annual, Vol. 9.* Edited by Regna Darnell and Frederic W. Gleach, 81–94. Lincoln, NE, and London: University of Nebraska Press.

Layton, Robert. 1997. *An Introduction to Theory in Anthropology.* Cambridge: Cambridge University Press.

Lecomte, Louis. 1990. *Un Jésuite à Pékin.* Paris: Editions Phébus.

Lehmann, William C. 1960. *John Millar of Glasgow.* Cambridge: Cambridge University Press.

Leibniz, Gottfried Wilhelm. 1994. *Writings on China.* Translater by Daniel J. Cook and Henry Rosemont Jr. Chicago and La Salle, IL: Open Court.

Léry, Jean de. 1994. *Histoire d'un voyage en Terre de Brésil.* Paris: Livre de Poche.

Lestringant, Frank. 1990. *Le Huguenot et le sauvage: L'Amérique et la controverse coloniale en France au temps des Guerres de Religion, 1555–1589.* Paris: Aux Amateurs de Livres.

———. 1993a. *Écrire le monde à la Renaissance: Quinze études sur Rabelais, Postel, Bodin et la littérature géographique.* Caen: Paradigme.

———. 1993b. "The Philosopher's Breviary: Jean de Léry in the Enlightenment." In *New World Encounters*, edited by Stephen Greenblatt, 127–38. Berkeley, Los Angeles, and London: University of California Press.

———. 1994a. "Léry ou le rire de l'Indien," preface to Léry 1994, 5–39.

———. 1994b. *Mapping the Renaissance World: The Geographical Imagination in the Age of Discovery.* Translated by David Fausset. Berkeley and Los Angeles: University of California Press.

———. 1997. *Cannibals: The Discovery and Representation of the Cannibal from Columbus to Jules Verne.* Translated by Rosemary Morris. Berkeley and Los Angeles: University of California Press.

Letts, Malcolm. 1949. *Sir John Mandeville: The Man and His Book.* London: Batchworth Press.

Lévi-Strauss, Claude. 1963. *Totemism.* Boston: Beacon Press.

———. 1985. *The View from Afar.* Translated by Joachim Neugroschel and Phoebe Hoss. New York: Basic Books.

———. 1991. *Histoire de Lynx.* Paris: Plon.

Levine, Joseph. 1991. *The Battle of the Books: History and Literature in the Augustan Age.* Ithaca, NY: Cornell University Press.

Li Shenwen. 2001. *Stratégies Missionnaires des Jésuites Français en Nouvelle-France et en Chine au XVIIè Siècle.* Saint Nicolas, QC: Presses universitaire de l'Université Laval; Paris: L'Harmattan.

Lobo, Jeronimo. 1984. *The Intinerario of Jeronimo Lobo.* Translated by Donald M. Lockhart. London: Hakluyt Society.

Locke, John. 1947. *Two Treatises of Government.* New York: Macmillan.

Lovejoy, Arthur O. 1936. *The Great Chain of Being: The Study of the History of an Idea.* Cambridge, MA: Harvard University Press.

Lovejoy, Arthur O., and George Boas. 1935. *Primitivism and Related Ideas in Antiquity.* Baltimore and London: Johns Hopkins University Press.

Lubbock, John. 1865. *Pre-Historic Times, as Illustrated by Ancient Remains and the Manners and Customs of Modern Savages.* London and Edinburgh: Williams and Norgate.

Machiavelli, Niccolò. 1996. *Discourses on Livy.* Translated by Harvey C. Mansfield and Nathan Tarcov. Chicago: University of Chicago Press.

Mandeville, Bernard. 1924. *The Fable of the Bees.* 2 vols. (First published 1714.) Oxford, UK: Clarendon Press.

Mandeville, Sir John. 1983. *The Travels of Sir John Mandeville.* Translated by C. W. R. D. Moseley. Harmondsworth, UK: Penguin.

Manuel, Frank E. 1959. *The Eighteenth Century Confronts the Gods.* Cambridge, MA: Harvard University Press.

Marburg, Clara. 1932. *Sir William Temple: A Seventeenth-Century "Libertin".* New Haven: Yale University Press.

Marshall, P. J., and Glyndwr Williams. 1982. *The Great Map of Mankind: Perceptions of New Worlds in the Age of Enlightenment.* Cambridge, MA: Harvard University Press.

Mason, Peter. 2015. *The Ways of the World: European Representation of Other Cultures from Homer to Sade.* Canon Pyon, UK: Sean Kingston Publishing.

Meek, Ronald. 1976. *Social Science and the Ignoble Savage.* Cambridge: Cambridge University Press.

Métraux, Alfred. 1963. "Les précurseurs de l'ethnologie en France du XVIe au XVIIIe siècle." *Cahiers d'Histoire Mondiale* 7:721–38.

Millar, John. 1960. *The Origin of the Distinction of Ranks.* Reprinted in Lehman 1960, 173–322.

Mollat, Michel, and Philippe Wolff. 1973. *The Popular Revolutions of the Late Middle Ages.* London: George Allen & Unwin.

Montaigne, Michel de. 1962. *Oeuvres complètes.* Paris: Editions Gallimard.

Montesquieu, Charles-Louis de Secondat, Baron de. 1964. *Lettres Persanes*. Paris: Garnier-Flammarion.

———. 1968. *Considérations sur les causes de la grandeur des Romains et de leur décadence*. Paris: Garnier-Flammarion.

———. 1979. *De l'esprit des lois*. 2 vols. Paris: Garnier-Flammarion.

Morel, J. 1909. "Recherches sur les sources du *Discours de l'inégalité*." *Annales de la Société Jean-Jacques Rousseau* 5:119–98.

Morgan, Lewis Henry. 1985. *Ancient Society*. Tucson: University of Arizona Press.

Moseley, Charles. 2015. "The *Travels of Sir John Mandeville* and the Moral Geography of the Medieval World." *Journal of Multidisciplinary International Studies* 12:1, http://dx/doi.org/10.5130/prtal.v12i1.4381.

Muthu, Sankar. 2003. *Enlightenment against Empire*. Princeton, NJ, and Oxford, UK: Princeton University Press.

Nakame, Géralde. 1982. *Montaigne et son temps: Les Évènements et les essais*. Paris: Librairie G.-Q. Nizet.

Navarrete, Domingo Fernandes. 1962. *The Travels and Controversies of Friar Domingo Navarrete, 1618–1686*. 2 vols. Edited by J .S. Cummins. Cambridge: Hakluyt Society.

Niderst, Alain. 1972. *Fontenelle à la Recherche de Lui-même (1657–1702)*. Paris: Editions A. G. Nizet.

Nisbet, Robert. 1969. *Social Change and History: Aspects of the Western Theory of Development*. London, Oxford, and New York: Oxford University Press.

O'Gorman, Edmundo. 1972. *Quatro historiadores de Indias*. Mexico City: Allianza Editorial Mexicana.

Oz-Salzberger, Fania. 1995. Introduction to Ferguson 1995, vii–xxv.

Pagden, Anthony. 1986. *The Fall of Natural Man: The American Indians and the Origins of Comparative Ethnology*. 2nd edition. Cambridge: Cambridge University Press.

———. 1993. *European Encounters with the New World*. New Haven and London: Yale University Press.

Pagden, Anthony, ed. 2002. *The Idea of Europe: From Antiquity to the European Union*. Cambridge: Woodrow Wilson Center Press and Cambridge University Press, 2002.

Parkman, Francis. 1983. *France and England in North America*. 2 vols. New York: Library of America.

Pascal, Blaise. 1921. *Lettres écrites à un provincial*. Paris: Garnier.

Person, Willard J. 1994. "What to Wear? Observation and Participation by Jesuit Missionaries in Late Ming Society." In *Implicit Understandings*, edited by Stuart B. Schwartz, 403–21. Cambridge: Cambridge University Press.

Phillips, Seymour. 1994. "The Outer World of the European Middle Ages." In *Implicit Understandings*, edited by Stuart B. Schwartz, 23–63. Cambridge: Cambridge University Press.

Pinot, Virgile. 1932. *La Chine et la formation de l'esprit philosophique en France, 1640–1740*. Paris: Libraire orientaliste Paul Geuthner.

Pire, G. 1956. "J.-J. Rousseau el les relations de voyages." *Revue d'histoire littéraire de la France* 61:155–78.

Pocock, J. G. A. 1975. *The Machiavellian Moment: Florentine Political Thought and the Atlantic Republican Tradition*. Princeton, NJ: Princeton University Press.

———. 1981. "Gibbon and the Shepherds: The Stages of Society in the *Decline and Fall*." *History of European Ideas* 2, no. 3: 193–202.

———. 1989. *Politics, Language, and Time*. 2nd edition. Chicago: University of Chicago Press.

———. 1999. *Barbarism and Religion, Volume 2: Narratives of Civil Government.* Cambridge: Cambridge University Press.

———. 2005. *Barbarism and Religion, Volume 4: Barbarians, Savages and Empires.* Cambridge: Cambridge University Press.

Polo, Marco. 1958. *The Travels.* Translated by Ronald Latham. Harmondsworth, UK: Penguin.

Polybius. 1979. *The Rise of the Roman Empire.* Translated by Ian Scott-Kilvert. Harmondsworth, UK: Penguin Books.

Pufendorf, Samuel. 1991. *On the Duty of Man and Citizen according to Natural Law.* Edited by James Tully and translated by Michael Silverthorne. Cambridge: Cambridge University Press.

Quesnay, François. 1888. *Oeuvres economiques et philosophiques.* Paris: Jules Peelman & Cie.

Rigault, Hippolyte. 1856. *Histoire de la querelle des anciens et des modernes.* Paris: Hachette.

Rousseau, Jean-Jacques. 1971. *Discours sur les sciences et les arts: Discours sur l'origine et les fondements de l'inégalité parmi les hommes.* Paris: Garnier-Flammarion.

———. 1987. *Essai sur l'origine des langues: Où il est parlé de mélodie et de l'imitation musicale.* Paris: L'École.

Rubiés, Joan-Pau. 2000a. *Travel and Ethnology in the Renaissance: South India through European Eyes, 1250–1625.* Cambridge: Cambridge University Press.

———. 2000b. "Travel Writing as a Genre: Facts, Fictions and the Invention of a Scientific Discourse in Early Modern Europe." *Journeys: The International Journal of Travel and Travel Writing* 1, no. 1/2: 5–35.

Rule, Paul A. 1986. , *K'ung-tzu or Confucius? The Jesuit Interpretation of Confucianism.* Sydney, London, and Boston: Allen & Unwin.

Sagard, Gabriel. 1990. *Le grand voyage au pays des Hurons.* Quebec, QC: Bibliothèque Québecoise.

Sahagun, Bernardino de. 1950–1982. *General History of the Things of New Spain: Florentine Codex.* 13 vols. Santa Fe: School of American Research ; and Salt Lake City: University of Utah.

Said, Edward. 1978. *Orientalism.* New York: Random House.

Sayre, Gordon M. 1997. *Les Sauvages Américains: Representations of Native Americans in French and English Colonial Literature.* Chapel Hill: University of North Carolina Press.

Shackleton, Robert. 1961. *Montesquieu: A Critical Biography.* London: Oxford University Press.

Sikka, Sonia. 2011. *Herder on Humanity and Cultural Difference: Enlightened Relativism.* Cambridge: Cambridge University Press.

Smith, Adam. 1976. *An Inquiry into the Nature and Causes of the Wealth of Nations.* 2 vols. Edited by A. R. Campbell, A. S. Skinner, and W. B. Todd. Oxford: Clarendon Press.

———. 1978. *Lectures on Jurisprudence.* Edited by R. L. Meek, D. D. Raphael, and P. G. Stein. Oxford: Clarendon Press.

Smith, Roger. 1995. "The Language of Human Nature." In *Inventing Human Science: Eighteenth-Century Domains*, edited by Christopher Fox, Roy Porter, and Robert Wokler, 88–111. Berkeley, Los Angeles, and London: University of California Press.

Sobecki, Sebastian I. 2002. "Mandeville's Thought of the Limit: The Discourse of Similarity and Difference in 'The Travels of Sir John Mandeville.'" *Review of English Studies*, New Series, 53, no. 211: 329–43.

Spence, Jonathan. 1984. *The Memory Palace of Matteo Ricci.* New York: Viking Press.

Spinoza, Benedictus de. 2007. *Theological-Political Treatise.* Translated by Michael Sivlerthorne and Jonathan Israel. Cambridge and New York: Cambridge University Press.

Stocking, George W., Jr. 1987. *Victorian Anthropology*. New York: The Free Press.

———. 1995. *After Tylor: British Social Anthropology 1888–1951*. Madison: University of Wisconsin Press.

Tacitus. 1942. "Germany and its Tribes." In *Complete Works of Tacitus*, translated by Alfred John Church and William Jackson Brodribb. New York: Modern Library.

Temple, William. 1754. *The Works of Sir William Temple*. 4 vols. Edinburgh: G. Hamilton and J. Balfour.

———. 1963. *Five Miscellaneous Essays by William Temple*. Edited with an introduction by Samuel Holt Monk. Ann Arbor: University of Michigan Press.

Thomas, Keith. 1983. *Man and the Natural World: Changing Attitudes in England 1500–1800*. Oxford and New York: Oxford University Press.

Thwaites, Reuben Gold, ed. 1896–1901. *Jesuit Relations and Allied Documents: Travels and Explorations of the Jesuit Missionaries in New France, 1610–1791*. 73 vols. Cleveland: Burrows Brothers.

Todorov, Tzvetan. 1982. *La Conquête de l'Amérique: La question de l'autre*. Paris: Editions du Seuil.

Trautmann, Thomas R. 1987. *Lewis Henry Morgan and the Invention of Kinship*. Berkeley and Los Angeles: University of California Press.

———. 1997. *Aryans and British India*. Berkeley, Los Angeles, and London: University of California Press.

Trautmann, Thomas R., and Karl Sanford Kabelac. 1994. "The Library of Lewis Henry Morgan and Mary Elizabeth Morgan." *Transactions of the American Philosophical Society* 84, nos. 6–7: i–xiv and 1–336.

Trenchard, John. 1723–24. *Cato's Letters*. 4 vols. London: Printed for W. Wilkins, T. Woodward, J. Walthoe, and J. Peele.

Trigault, Nicolas. 1942. *The China That Was: China as Discovered by the Jesuits at the Close of the Sixteenth Century*. Translated by L. J. Gallagher, S.J. Milwaukee: Bruce Publishing.

Trigger, Bruce G. 1985. *Natives and Newcomers: Canada's "Heroic Age" Reconsidered*. Kingston and Montreal: McGill-Queen's University Press.

———. 1989. *A History of Archaeological Thought*. Cambridge: Cambridge University Press.

Tuck, Richard. 1979. *Natural Rights Theories: Their Origins and Development*. Cambridge and New York: Cambridge University Press.

Varisco, Daniel Martin. 2007. *Reading Orientalism: Said and the Unsaid*. Seattle and London: University of Washington Press.

Vasari, Giorgio. 1998. *The Lives of the Artists*. Translated by Julia Condaway Bondanella and Peter Bondanella. Oxford and New York: Oxford University Press.

Vermuelen, Han. 2015. *Before Boas: The Genesis of Ethnography and Ethnology in the German Enlightenment*. Lincoln, NE, and London: University of Nebraska Press.

Vernière, Paul. 1977. *Montesquieu et l'esprit des lois ou la raison impure*. Paris: Société d'edition d'enseignement supérieur.

Vico, Gambattista. 1968. *The New Science of Giambattista Vico*. Revised edition. Translated by Thomas Goddard Bergin and Max Harold Fisch. Ithaca, NY, and London: Cornell University Press.

Voget, Fred. 1975. *A History of Ethnology*. New York: Holt, Rinehart, and Winston.

Voltaire. 1785. *Oeuvres Complètes de Voltaire*. Vol. 35. Kehl: Imprimerie de la Société Littéraire-Typographique.

———. 1922. *Le Siècle de Louis XIV*. 2 vols. Paris: Garnier Frères.

———. 1960. *Romans et Contes*. Paris: Garnier Frères.

———. 1963. *Essai sur les moeurs et l'esprit des nations*. 2 vols. Paris: Garnier Frères.

————. 1966. *Dialogues philosophiques*. Paris: Editions Garnier Frères.

Voragine, Jacobus de. 1969. *The Golden Legend*. Translated by William Granger Ryan and Helmut Ripperger. New York: Arno Press.

Vyverberg, Henry. 1958. *Historical Pessimism in the French Enlightenment*. Cambridge, MA: Harvard University Press.

Weiss, Roberto. 1969. *The Renaissance Discovery of Classical Antiquity*. Oxford: Basil Blackwell.

Whatley, Gordon. 1986. "Heathens and Saints: *St. Erkenwald* in Its Legendary Context," *Speculum* 61/22:330–63.

White, Hayden. 1978. *Tropics of Discourse: Essays in Cultural Criticism*. Baltimore and London: Johns Hopkins University Press.

White, Sophie. 2012. *Wild Frenchmen and Frenchified Indians: Material Culture and Race in Colonial Louisiana*. Philadelphia: University of Pennsylvania Press.

Wood, Frances. 1996. *Did Marco Polo Go to China?* Boulder, CO: Westview Press.

Zacher, Christian K. 1976. *Curiosity and Pilgrimage: The Literature of Discovery in Fourteenth-Century England*. Baltimore and London: Johns Hopkins University Press.

Zammito, John. H. 2002. *Kant, Herder, and the Birth of Anthropology*. Chicago and London: University of Chicago Press.

Zhiri, Oumelbanine. 1995. *Les Sillages de Jean Léon l'Africain du XVIè au XXè siècle*. Casablanca: Wallada.

Zupanov, Ines G. 1999. *Disputed Mission: Jesuit Experiments and Brahmanical Knowledge in Seventeenth-Century India*, New Delhi: Oxford University Press.

INDEX

Printed in Great Britain
by Amazon

59737494R00152